S0-BFD-399

PUFFIN BOOKS

The Priests of Ferris

Nick and Susan return to O a year after they saved the world
from the evil Halfmen of O. A frightened boy called Limpy
is sent to take them back to O and they are bemused by his
talk of priests.

Only when they set off to find the Woodlanders and are
pursued by vicious dogs and men wearing strange leather
suits do they begin to understand that this isn't the O they
have left behind. One hundred years have passed and O is
now in thrall to a tyrannical religion, based on Susan herself,
which demands human sacrifice, and strict obedience to the
priests.

An exciting and wonderfully imaginative book.

Maurice Gee is one of New Zealand's foremost novelists.
As well as his highly successful children's books, he is an
award-winning writer for adults.

Other books by Maurice Gee

The Halfmen of O
Motherstone
Under the Mountain
The Fire-Raiser
The World Around the Corner
The Champion

THE
PRIESTS OF
FERRIS

MAURICE GEE

Puffin Books

PUFFIN BOOKS

Penguin Books (NZ) Ltd, cnr Rosedale and Airborne Roads, Albany,
Auckland 1310, New Zealand
Penguin Books Ltd, 27 Wrights Lane, London W8 5TZ, England
Penguin USA, 375 Hudson Street, New York, NY 10014, United States
Penguin Books Australia Ltd, 487 Maroondah Highway, Ringwood, Australia 3134
Penguin Books Canada Ltd, 10 Alcorn Avenue, Toronto, Ontario, Canada M4V 3B2
Penguin Books Ltd, Registered Offices: Harmondsworth, Middlesex, England

First published by Oxford University Press 1984
Published in Puffin Books 1987
5 7 9 10 8 6 4

Contents

Chapter one: Limpy   7

Chapter two: The Priests of Ferris   18

Chapter three: Seeker   31

Chapter four: Soona's Dream   46

Chapter five: The Blue Bears   61

Chapter six: Nick Whistles a Tune   77

Chapter seven: Stonehaven   92

Chapter eight: Soona   110

Chapter nine: The High Priest   124

Chapter ten: As Humble as the Worm . . .   141

Chapter eleven: On Deven's Leap   155

Chapter twelve: Susan   177

CHAPTER ONE

Limpy

'Shall we go then?' Susan asked.

'Might as well. But there won't be anything. The soil won't be right. Or the climate. Hey,' he said, grabbing at ideas, 'what if it runs wild like gorse or blackberry? The Ministry of Agriculture won't like that too much.'

Susan smiled. A year hadn't made any difference in Nick. He was still a know-all, still believed he knew more than anyone else. It had made a difference in her. She was no longer a child. She'd started growing up on O, and a year of remembering had turned her into a woman. Child/woman, her mother called her. It would be stretching things, she thought, to describe Nick as boy/man.

They walked over the bridge and through the paddock and made their way along the rim of the gorge. 'Remember . . . ' Nick said, but she stopped listening. The presence of Jimmy Jaspers was strong in this place and she didn't need Nick to bring him back. She missed the old man in a way close to grief and wondered if perhaps he had died in the year since she'd seen him. Dying would not bother him too much, as long as it happened in the bush, or by a creek, or on a mountain. But she wanted to believe he was still alive and that somehow they would meet again, on Earth or O. She wanted to hear about the places he had explored, the Yellow Plains, the Hotlands, and about the waterfall he had named after her.

They came down to the shingle flat by the mine shaft

and stood on one of the tailing mounds looking at the opening. It wasn't a place to have nightmares about, even when you knew where it led. Even when you thought of Odo Cling and Otis Claw. They were dead, dead and gone, and O was a happy world. She felt pleased with herself, recalling what she'd done. And she felt a deep longing to see O again and meet her friends. 'I wonder what it's like there. What do you think Breeze and Brand are doing?'

'I'm not going to find out,' Nick said. 'What if something broke down halfway through?'

'We shouldn't ever go unless we have to,' Susan said.

'That'll be never. Hey, if the Shy has grown we can pretend to discover it. A new species. We'll be famous.'

'It's not a game,' Susan said.

They went on up the creek. She had not been so far since the day a year ago when Nick had left with his parents. She had waved as the car drove up the road, and then wandered through the paddock and along the creek, only half admitting to herself she was going to the place where the seed was planted. Two weeks in the ground should be enough for a shoot to come through. But one bend in the creek away, she had stopped. Something told her she was here too soon. It was almost as if she heard Breeze's voice – the seed must not be troubled. She sat on a stone in the creek, enjoying the stillness and the sound of water, knowing that just round the corner a miracle was taking place.

Now she saw the stone again, but stopped and held Nick by the sleeve. 'Do you smell it?'

'What?'

'It's like lemon blossom.'

'I can't smell anything.'

She was sorry she'd brought him; but she had waited

because he'd been on O. 'Let's go quietly,' she said, letting go his sleeve.

She went on several steps, then stopped again. Several times in her life things that should have surprised her had come as no surprise, they had fitted into a place waiting in her mind. She stared at the stone, the footprint marked in water on its top, and knew it was something she had expected. Nick, skimming pebbles, did not notice. She turned and said to him, 'I want you to go back to the house.'

'Hey – '

'No. Listen. Get my pack. The K2 Junior. Put in a jersey each. And our parkas. And sneakers and socks. We'd better have a change of underpants . . . '

'We're not going back to O.'

'And some food. Bread, cheese . . . '

'It's too risky.'

'Raisins and peanuts. Chocolate. Some plums.' She stopped him breaking in. 'At least get my stuff. You needn't come if you don't want to. If anyone sees you, say we're having a picnic.'

'No.'

'Nick, they've sent for me.' She gave him a push. 'Don't argue. There's a sign. You'll see when you come back.'

She watched him out of sight, then turned and looked at the stone again. The footprint could not have been more than five minutes old. As she watched the sun began to dry it. She did not know why she was sure it came from O. But it belonged to that world just as surely as the smell of Shy.

Susan went on up the creek. She walked on moss round the bend and came to the place where she had planted the seed. It was deep in shade. She had chosen it for that and

9

privacy. Here and there a shaft of light sloped down through the tree cover. A fantail flipped about, feasting on insects. She saw the Shy at once, a silver plant growing no higher than a daphne bush, with a dozen blue flowers just visible in its leaves. It was rather stiff, she thought, a bit like a pen and ink bush, a formal drawing at a chapter head, and for a moment she was disappointed. She had hoped for something that climbed down rocks and grew in crevices. Then she saw its symmetry, its silver leaves and magic flower, and it overcame her. She dropped on her knees to worship it, and almost as if she had expected him she saw the boy in the deepest shade, kneeling in the same attitude. The white soles of his feet stared at her – one of them bent in a way so painful it made her wince. But like her he was lost in the Shy, in its magical scent. She stood up and went to him and put her hand on his shoulder. He jumped like a cat, arching and spitting, then lay on his side and stared at her.

'I won't hurt you. Who are you?' she said.

He made no answer. She saw his throat working as he tried to get words out.

'Do you come from O?'

He nodded and made a sound that might be 'yes'. She found him disappointing. Why did he cringe? He had eyes that slid away from hers, and a weasel face. But she wondered if his cheeks were so hollow and his arms so thin because he was starved.

'What's your name?'

He croaked again. Impatiently she said, 'I'm Susan Ferris.'

The effect that had on him was horrifying. He began to whimper. He seemed to want to burrow into the ground and hide himself.

'What is it? Get up.'

10

But the boy kept his forehead pressed on the earth.
'Who sent you?'

His answer was muffled. 'My sister.' He raised himself but would not lift his eyes. 'Her name is Soona.'

'Where are you from? Why did she send you?'

'We live in a village called Stonehaven. We are fishermen.'

'Yes?'

'The priests – they . . . ' His eyes flashed at her and she saw hatred in them. 'They have taken Soona.'

'Why? Who are the priests?'

'They have taken her for the Miracle.'

'What's the Miracle?' She shifted impatiently when he made no answer. 'None of this makes sense. Why did she send you to me?'

'She sent me to the Woodlanders. The legends say they know the way to Earth – to Susan Ferris. But the priests . . . '

'Yes?'

'They say that is heresy. The only way to Susan is through them, and through the Temple. The Woodlanders are . . . '

'Go on.'

'Vermin, they say. They must be exterminated.'

'Your priests sound like Odo Cling and Otis Claw.'

The boy writhed at the names. 'They are the Dark Ones. No one speaks of them.'

She felt sorry for him, but could not understand what he was saying. The world he spoke of did not sound like O.

'So you found the Woodlanders?'

'Yes. They said it was time for you to come.'

'What village did you go to? Shady Home?'

'Yes.'

'Were Brand and Breeze there?'

The boy looked up. He seemed to be able to look at her now, even though his eyes kept sliding away. 'The one who taught me was called Verna.'

'Ah.' Susan smiled. It was her O if Verna was there. 'Was she married? She was going to marry Walt.'

'There was no Walt. Verna's mate was Swift.'

'Swift?' She looked at him sadly. Verna and Walt had been so close a pair. She could not believe the Woodlander girl had taken someone else. She turned away and looked at the Shy. It was all that kept O clear to her. 'Was Jimmy Jaspers there?'

'No.' He was kneeling again, forehead denting the earth.

'Where was Jimmy?'

'They say –' his voice was faint, 'the priests say, he lives on Earth with Susan Ferris and . . .'

'And who?'

'Nicholas Quinn.'

'Why are you frightened of him?'

'He –' The boy was trembling. 'He is the Terrible One. He comes for sinners. He slew Odo Cling.'

'Yes, he did. But he's not terrible. He's a sinner himself. And he's on O, not Earth.' She decided to say no more, and ask no more. Something had gone badly wrong on O, but it was no use getting it in bits. She would have to wait until she got there.

'Get up,' she said to the boy.

Slowly he came to his feet and stood in front of her with his eyes downcast.

'What's your name?'

'Limpy.'

'Because of your leg? How did you do it?'

'An accident on my father's boat. I can't go fishing any more.'

12

She saw how it grieved him, and winced again as she looked at his leg. It was shrunken, bent, and had no flesh on it.

'Does it hurt you still?'

'No. I can move fast in the forest. But they say I'm no good on a boat any more.'

'You must have another name.'

'I like Limpy. It tells the truth.'

She nodded. 'Are you hungry?'

'Yes.'

'Nick will be here with some food in a moment.' She saw how he shrank at the name, but said nothing. 'Why don't you wash in the creek? You smell funny.'

'It's grub-weed. I put it on so the dogs couldn't track me.'

She decided not to ask about that either, and told the boy to wash the smell off. It was like old socks. He went to the creek and she turned her back on him and knelt by the Shy, putting her face in the flowers. The sweetness of the scent made her tremble. If it were not for the Shy she wouldn't trust this Limpy. But he too had seemed to worship it.

Nick arrived and she showed him the plant. The boy in the creek had slunk away and hidden in the ferns. Susan called him out. He came up the bank, moving sideways.

'This is Nicholas Quinn. Nick, this is Limpy. He's from O. Verna says it's time for us to come.'

Nick said nothing. The boy, in his homespun shirt and belt of flax, was proof enough. He stared at him and offered to shake hands, but Limpy jerked away.

'What's the matter with him?'

'He thinks we're special. Jimmy too.'

'Has he seen Jimmy? Have you seen him?'

'He thinks Jimmy's here on Earth with us. We'd better

go and find him, Nick.' She turned to Limpy. 'Did you use Shy to get here?'

'Yes.'

'So it still works.' She knelt beside the plant and made Nick kneel. 'You too, Limpy.'

'We'd better take one for coming back,' Nick said.

'Only what we need. That's the rule.'

'What if we can't find any there? Is there plenty growing?' he asked Limpy.

'I have never seen it. The priests call it Claw's weed. They root it out.'

'So we'd better take two.'

But Susan stopped him. Verna would know where the flower grew. She reached into the plant and picked a blossom close to the stem. It came away easily, bleeding a drop of moisture on her fingers. She spoke her thanks, and waited for the others, pleased to see them reverent too, and started down the creek with the flower in her palm. Nick caught up and walked beside her, and Limpy came behind, carrying his flower and eating a plum Nick had given him.

'Do you think he's lying to us?' Nick whispered.

'He's keeping something back. But we've got to trust him.'

They came to the shaft and stood between the mounds. Nick rapped the timbers at the entrance. 'This is going to cave in soon.'

'Did you get everything?'

'Yeah. Your Mum said be careful.' He grinned sourly. 'It's no fun telling lies.'

'I'm sorry, Nick.'

'At least there won't be any Halfmen.'

They went into the shaft, Nick leading. He had a pocket torch and he checked every beam. Several had

14

rotted almost through and new falls of rock lay on the floor. 'This is the last time,' he breathed.

'Dad says he'll dynamite it soon.'

They came to the end. Nick put his torch in the pack. 'How do we do it? What day are we going to, Limpy?'

'The day I left. Hold my arms. We'll come out together.'

'I hope so.' Susan felt in the dark and put her hand on his shoulder. He flinched but she said quietly, 'It's all right. Nick, are you ready?'

'Yes.'

'Are you ready, Limpy?'

'Yes,' he whispered, 'let us go.'

They raised their Shy flowers to their faces. 'Now,' Susan said.

It was less painful than their first time through, when the agent had been the yellow smoke of Otis Claw, but somehow less easy than the second, when they had been returning home. The dark and the whirling frightened them, and when the motion stopped and they found themselves on hands and knees on the floor of the cave a feeling like car-sickness overcame them. They knelt a while before climbing to their feet.

'Are you there, Nick?'

'Yes. Where's Limpy?'

'I'm here,' the boy said. They heard a sound like sobbing in his voice. 'I didn't think I'd ever come back.'

Susan felt for his arm. 'You're all right. Home on O. Have you got your torch, Nick? Let's get out of here.'

He took it from the pack and led them down the tunnel. There were falls of rock he did not remember. And when they reached the entrance they found it half collapsed, with only a narrow opening to the plateau. But they were so eager to see O they hardly noticed. The sun was

15

shining, the air was fresh. They ran out of the cave and saw the hills and Wildwood spread before them.

'It hasn't changed. It's beautiful. It's better than Earth.'

Far away a rough line marked the rim of Sheercliff. Beyond was the land called Darkland, but no pall of smoke lay over it. The sea gleamed and Susan's island lay on it like a boat at anchor. The sky curved back, pure silver, pure blue, and the mountains, running north and south, shone with ice in the afternoon sun. The trees of Wildwood climbed up to the snowline, and ran into the south, turning misty blue and misty purple. Perhaps, she thought, Jimmy Jaspers had explored the southern lands by now.

The boy, Limpy, ran by her and crouched on the edge of the plateau. She went to his side but he caught her by the shirt and pulled her down. Here on O he was sure of himself. 'There might be priests.'

She knelt in the shade of thorn trees, staring down the slope. Nothing moved. Only, far away, a bird circled lazily and made her think of the Birdfolk, Redwing and Wanderer. She hoped there would be time to visit them. Nick took off his pack and knelt beside her. 'What are these priests?' he said to Limpy.

'We must find grub-weed so the dogs will not find us.'

'I'm not going anywhere till I know. There's something wrong here, Susan. I can't see the path any more. And the entrance of the cave has fallen in. Look, over there, by Sheercliff. Isn't that a building in the sun?'

She looked where he was pointing and saw a glittering light like a piece of mirror.

'It wasn't there a year ago,' Nick said.

'The Temple,' Limpy said. 'That is where the High Priest lives. And where the Miracle will take place.' He looked at Susan as if he hated her.

16

She felt it like a blow. More than anything he had said, more than talk of priests and dogs and Temples, it told her O was changed. 'Why does he hate me?'

Nick picked up his pack. 'Don't worry about him. We can find Shady Home by ourselves.'

'You will die,' Limpy said. 'The priests will get you.'

'What priests? From the Temple?'

'Yes.'

'When was it built? We didn't see it there a year ago.'

'It has been there all my life. All my father's. And his father's. It was built in the seventh turn from the Mending.'

'What's the Mending?'

'If you are Nick, and you Susan, then you know.'

And Susan did know. Everything began making sense to her. She felt the blood draining from her face. 'Nick,' she said, 'I put the Halves together. That was the Mending.'

She saw Limpy nodding, and said to him, 'How long ago?'

His answer came as no surprise to her. 'Ancient times. In thirty days it is a hundred turns.'

She heard Nick arguing, but she did not argue. With the Shy you passed through time and space – five minutes or five years, a hundred years. Limpy had brought them into his own time. It made no difference to their going back, but here, now – she saw what it must mean.

'Nick,' she sobbed, 'oh Nick.' She leaned against him. Tears ran down her face. 'They're dead. Brand and Breeze and Jimmy. Jimmy's dead.'

CHAPTER TWO

The Priests of Ferris

When evening came they reached the edge of the forest.
Exhausted from their scrambling on the hills, they made
beds of fern and slept till dawn. Nick took food from the
pack and handed it round. They drank from a creek, then
Limpy scouted ahead and found the way safe. They
pushed on till midday and reached the forest floor.
Grub-weed might be found there, Limpy said. He went
off with his knife and Nick and Susan sat on the roots of a
tree, listening to the sounds of Wildwood. The wind
made a soughing in the trees, the stream tinkled, birds
chirped and fluttered in the undergrowth or made soft
bell-notes higher up. But for Susan the magic was gone.
Once before O had been grey to her, before Breeze had
given her the Shy, and now it was grey again. She tried to
tell herself death was natural, time had passed, nothing
evil had happened to Jimmy and Brand and Breeze. They
had simply grown old and died. But she could not make
herself believe it.

'He still doesn't like us,' Nick said.

'Who?'

'Limpy. I wonder what this stuff about priests is. He
could be making it up to scare us.' When she made no
answer he patted her knee. 'Cheer up. I'll bet Jimmy had a
ball before he died. I wonder if he named a mountain after
me. Here, have a plum. I'll tell you what, I'll plant the
stone. Then they'll have plums the way we have Shy.'

But he could not lighten her mood. O was no longer
her world and she wanted to be out of it, on Earth. It

seemed dangerous, and the thought of the priests frightened her. Without her friends she was lost and afraid. She would go to Shady Home and talk to Verna – a new Verna, not the one she knew – then go home. There was nothing here she wanted to do any more.

Then, oddly, for a moment, she was happy, something comforted her, she could not tell what. An Earth sound. Then she had it: far off, the barking of dogs. It was a sound that meant home to her – the dogs on the hill with her father, Ben the huntaway turning the sheep.

'Listen,' Nick said.

'Yes.'

But he was on his feet, staring round. And she remembered: dogs on O were the dogs of Otis Claw, the black man-killing hounds he had used for his sport in the underground throne-hall long ago. She remembered the sounds they made as they attacked. Claw was dead, but now, according to Limpy, the dogs had new masters, the priests.

Nick was struggling to get his pack on. 'We've got to get out of here. If those dogs get our scent . . . '

'Maybe they've got Limpy's.'

'That's his bad luck.'

'We can't just leave him.'

'He knows his way round. Hurry, Susan. They're getting close.'

The sound was a hunting cry – hungry, eager – and suddenly it increased, as if the pack had come round a hill. Shouts of men were mixed in it. Yet they could not tell its direction and their running seemed to take them closer to it. Then Limpy came bursting through the fern, running lopsidedly, and he gave a shout of rage when he saw them.

'Where are you going? I was leading them away.'

'Where are they?'

'You're running straight at them.'

'How many?'

'Too many. I couldn't find grub-weed. They've got my scent. Now they'll get yours.'

'Can we get away?'

'No chance.'

'Can we walk in a creek? We've got to do something.'

The baying of the dogs swelled in volume and the harsh cries of men, and women too, took an eager note.

'Take off your pack. Scatter the food. Scatter everything. That will delay them.'

Nick tore off the pack. He threw clothes, cheese, chicken legs, peanuts, in every direction. He hurled the pack away into the ferns. They turned and ran, heading downhill in the direction of a creek they had crossed in the morning. Limpy went along in a kind of scuttle, swinging his bad leg wide, but he kept ahead of Nick and Susan with no trouble, and called them on when they seemed to tire. The slope became steeper and they slid down between worn boulders, braking with their feet. The noise of the dogs faded away, but as they reached the creek a squealing and a yelping came through the trees.

'They've found the pack,' Limpy panted. 'The priests will lose control. But then they'll let the hunters go. They'll be running free. Each priest has a tracker and a hunter.' He set off up the creek, wading thigh-deep. 'Our only chance is to find a place where dogs can't climb.'

'We're going the wrong way,' Nick said. 'Our scent will flow down the creek.'

'The hills are this way.'

'Then let's get out and run. This is slowing us down.'

It made him feel better when Limpy obeyed. They scrambled out on the far side of the creek and ran along the bank. Soon the water ran in noisy rapids, but even so the sound of the dogs came again.

'They've got to the place where we went in.'

'Ten minutes,' Nick said, looking at his watch. 'We've got about a kilometre on them.'

'They'll take a while to pick us up again,' Limpy said.

But they could not keep their pace up. The creek came tumbling out of a gorge. They had to climb through water and haul themselves over slippery stones. Moss broke away in handfuls and slid under their feet. White water pressed on their thighs. Their only comfort was that dogs would find it hard here too.

They climbed for twenty minutes. The gorge levelled out. They stood listening at the head of the rapids but the noise of the water drowned everything. It tumbled out of sight round a bend, and down there somewhere dogs and priests were coming. Ahead, boulders the size of houses choked the gorge. They began to run between them, and climb along their sides. Several times they had to go back and start again. Then the creek turned, and a waterfall blocked the gorge.

It was like being caught in a bottle, Susan thought. But Limpy was scouting about. He ran, half swimming, through the pool at the base of the fall and disappeared in ferns by a shingle bank. 'Here,' he cried. A tiny stream trickled from a side gorge. It was so narrow they had to turn sideways to get in. It widened out a few steps on and gave them room to scramble three abreast. But as they climbed they heard the barking of dogs.

'Why are they chasing us? Why?' Susan cried.

'Everything that moves they hunt. The whole of Wildwood is their enemy.'

The gorge had sides leaning in. It stretched on and on like a road. The afternoon sun shone down the length of it, lighting up the stream, bringing half an hour of warmth to plants growing in the rocks. It seemed wrong to Susan that she and Nick were running for their lives while the sun shone so cheerfully. This was the place for a picnic, not for death. She felt she should turn and wait for the priests, try to talk reasonably with them. Then she remembered the Halfmen of a hundred years ago, just one of her years, and knew this hunt was real, these priests were the inheritors of Otis Claw's world. Breeze had said there was no knowing which way men would go, they had their chance for good or evil – and they had chosen evil a second time.

She ran on, scrambling over rocks. The walls bent over, shutting out the sun. It seemed no time since she had been running from Odo Cling and his Bloodcat. A hundred years, and nothing had been gained. It made her cry out with rage.

'Come on Sue, don't get frightened now.'

'I'm not frightened. I'm just so mad at them. We gave them a chance.'

'We shouldn't have bothered. Come on, Limpy's getting ahead.'

But the boy had stopped and was staring back, and when they turned and looked where he was pointing they saw the first of the dogs loping up the gorge. It had them in sight and was running silently. A second came through the fern, and a third, and each gave a single bark, and set out after their leader in a bounding run. They went from sight, reappeared, in the rock-strewn gorge. Others came, and the whole pack was there, flickering, black against the stone. They seemed to flow like water.

'There,' Limpy said. 'Climb.' He pointed up. Halfway to the sky, a fissure showed in the rock. Narrow handholds angled down from it. Someone had cut them long ago but now they were smooth. Susan started to climb and found her hands and feet sliding out.

'Don't fall,' Nick said. 'If you fall we're done for.'

She kept her body pressed against the rock and climbed like a crab, trying to think only of what she was doing – hand, foot, hand, foot. She watched her fingers and her bright-red sneakers. Two, three body-lengths off the ground – now she was out of reach of the dogs. But Limpy had said some of the priests carried cross-bows. They would shoot them down like wooden dolls in a fair. She kept on steadily, as fast as she dared, trying not to think of the drop below. Then she heard a hideous yelping, a scraping of claws on stone. The dogs were at the base of the rock, leaping frantically. She had an impression of a black sea writhing at her feet, and teeth, eyes, red mouths, flashing in it like fish. Nick was safe behind her, but Limpy, was he all right? She risked looking down, and saw him slash with his knife at a dog that had caught the edge of his cloak. The animal fell back howling, and Limpy pulled himself another step up. He put the knife in his belt. 'Go on,' he yelled.

They edged towards the fissure twenty metres up from the gorge floor. Susan came to it and heaved herself on to a lip of rock at the opening. She reached back and helped Nick. Limpy ignored her hand and pulled himself up beside her. He wiped dog saliva from his cloak. 'How deep is this cave?' They went into it, but it ran back only twenty steps and ended in a rough wall. They felt it with their palms, and felt their way back along the walls to the mouth. There was no way out. Again Susan felt she was caught in a bottle.

'Someone lived here once,' Nick said. He had his foot on stones, football-sized, making a rough fireplace on the floor. Dead ashes lay in it and animal bones were strewn about. 'Men, not Woodlanders.'

'Men hid here from the priests,' Limpy said. He was at the cave mouth, looking down the gorge.

'We can use these stones. Throw them down. We can hold out quite a while.'

'Some will climb. Others will cover them with cross-bows,' Limpy said. 'Here they come.'

They went to his side and looked where he was pointing. Half a dozen figures were running up the gorge, leaping nimbly on the boulders. Each held a dog on a leash, and they ran as silently as dogs, accompanied only by a clicking sound. They seemed like skeletons, all dressed in white.

'Your priests,' Limpy said.

'They are not mine.' They were figures from a dream, they seemed to float along without the use of limbs.

'They're Priests of Ferris.'

'Then,' she said, 'I'll tell them to go away. I'll tell them who I am.'

'They won't believe you.'

'Why?'

'It happens all the time. There's always some crazy girl claiming she's Susan Ferris come again.'

'What happens to them?'

'They are taken to the Temple.' He gave a strange smile. 'They are given a chance to prove it.'

'How?'

Limpy shrugged and turned away. 'Those are girls from the villages. But the ones who run are quarry for the dogs. The priests will not give us the chance to prove anything.' He looked at the animals standing patiently at the foot of the wall. 'They know. They can wait.'

'I'm going to try anyway,' Susan said.

'She can show them her birthmark,' Nick said.

'They all have the Mark. They burn it on themselves,' Limpy said.

The priests saw them standing in the cave mouth. They slowed and walked quietly to the dogs, which sank on their haunches.

'So,' the leader said. He was not even breathing heavily. He was a young man, Susan saw. They were all young, all seven; and two were women. She saw their shapes plainly, under the skin-tight leather of their suits. It was as shiny as vinyl, white and supple, encasing them, covering even their hands and feet. They looked naked standing there. Their faces too were white, the colour of bone.

'At night,' Limpy whispered, 'they turn their suits inside out. Then they are dressed in black.'

'But their faces . . .?'

'White. Always white. They paint themselves. See their eyes. They never blink. It is part of the training.'

The seven pairs of eyes showed no feeling. They had the blankness of eyes in statues.

'You cannot escape the Priests of Ferris,' the leader said. His voice made no rise or fall. That must be part of the training as well, Susan thought. Anger began to rise in her that these machine-like creatures, these walking skeletons, used her name.

'You are not Priests of Ferris,' she said loudly.

'Do you challenge us? Then you challenge the High Priest. You challenge Susan.'

'How can I challenge myself? I'm Susan Ferris.'

The eyes of the priest never blinked. But she could tell he was shocked. There was a shrinking in him, then a swelling of rage. His voice, though, remained the same flat voice. 'Heresy. You speak heresy.'

25

'Heresy,' said his followers. 'She has the evil tongue.' They were like a class of children, speaking by rote.

'What is the penalty?' the leader said.

'Death is the penalty,' they answered flatly.

'You can't kill me for being myself,' Susan cried.

'You're mad,' Nick joined in. 'You're all mad. I'm Nicholas Quinn. I've known her all my life. I'm her cousin.'

'You speak heresy too. You have uttered names only priests may speak. You must die now.'

'They must die.'

'Make the chant,' the leader said.

The priests formed a circle. Each had bones on a leather rope hanging on his chest. They untied them and held them in the circle – bones of every length, some whole, some with broken ends. These had made the clicking as they ran. Now they clicked again as the priests beat them against each other and set up a wailing, like the wailing of cats.

'The chant of death,' Limpy said. 'When it is finished . . .'

'Those things,' Nick said. 'They're human bones.'

'Yes,' Limpy said. 'Ferris bones. No novice is a priest until he has them. The ones that are broken most are the holiest.'

'How do they get broken?'

'They are the bones of heretics. Blasphemers. Unbelievers. Every novice, before he graduates, must sniff one out and take him for trial at the Temple.'

'What sort of trial? What do they do?' Nick was not sure he wanted to know. The hideous wailing, the broken bones – it could only be horrible.

Limpy said, 'In the teaching we learn how Susan flew

from Deven's Leap. The sinners are taken there, to the place of the Miracle.'

'So the trial . . .?'

'Yes.' Limpy spread his arms like wings and gave a bitter smile. 'It happened to my grandfather. A novice came and sniffed him out and rolled on the ground as though he was poisoned. Those could be his bones down there.'

'They throw them off?'

Limpy smiled again. 'If they are innocent they fly, like Susan. So far none have been innocent. And the priests wear their bones.'

Susan had listened, not in any surprise, with a sense that everything she heard she already knew. It was inescapable, a step-by-step unfolding with its start in things she'd done in the hope of saving O. And *this* was the end. She could not escape it, she saw the hideous logic in the story – but she could say no. She could refuse to have any part in it, from this moment on.

'No,' she cried, 'they're not my priests. They can't use my name.'

She ran into the cave and seized a stone from the fireplace. She brought it back to the entrance. The dogs looked up, lolling their tongues. The priests clacked their bones and wailed on a rising note, working to a climax. She lifted the stone over her head and hurled it down at them. They had ignored her cry. They had reached the end of their chant and gone down on their haunches, thrusting their bones together in the circle, where they made a pyramid. The stone smashed into it, crushed it flat, sending chips of bone flying about. They flung themselves away from it, crying as though at something supernatural. Then they stood and turned, facing Susan, seven white skeletons with unblinking eyes.

'You're not mine,' Susan cried. 'I'm Susan Ferris. You can't have my name. Your religion is finished. I'm finishing it now.'

The leader held the haft of a thigh bone in each hand. He raised them slowly and showed their newly-broken ends. For the first time there was feeling in his voice. He seemed to be grieving. 'Blasphemer, you have broken my Ferris bones.'

'They're not Ferris bones. You can't have my name.'

He seemed not to hear. 'These were holy bones. I sniffed out a man who had dreamed of the Terrible One. He had dreamed of Jimmy Jaspers, sleeping by the side of a great white bear. There were no bones more holy than these.'

'They're not holy. You can't kill people like that.'

Again he did not hear. He dropped the broken ends of the bones at his feet. One of the dogs nosed them. He took no notice. 'I must have new ones. All of us must have bones. Until we wear them again we are not priests.'

Nick was at Susan's shoulder. 'Now you've done it.' He had gone pale. 'We'll have to fight. Watch out for the cross-bows.'

The two priests who carried them unstrapped bows from their backs and levered the strings.

'Into the cave,' Limpy said. He took his knife from his belt and crouched at the entrance, shielded from the bowmen by the lip of stone. Nick began to carry the firestones one by one from the back of the cave. Below, the dogs set up a whining. Susan leaned past Limpy and looked down. The leader of the priests was on the steps, already a body-length clear of the ground.

'Down,' Limpy cried. She saw the bowmen aiming and leaped back. Two bolts came humming into the cave and ricocheted off the ceiling. Nick saw his chance. He ran forward while the men were loading and hurled a rock at the climbing priest. A shout of pain came up and a yelping of dogs.

'Got him on the arm,' Nick yelled. 'He fell in the dogs. I bet he won't be climbing any more.'

Limpy jerked him back and a single bolt rattled in the cave. 'They'll shoot in turn. They can pin us down. Another one will climb.'

'And if they don't they can starve us out,' Susan said.

They crouched listening, and soon heard the breathing of a priest. They heard the soft scrape of fingers on stone. Two, perhaps three or four, were climbing. Then softly, even more softly, a voice breathed, 'Follow me.'

'Who was that?' They jumped around. No one was in the cave.

'Follow,' whispered the voice. It had a distant sound, as though it came from a pit.

'Where are you? Who are you?'

'Go to the end of the cave. The door is open.'

'Are you a Stoneman?'

'Yes. Now go to the door. The priests are coming. I hear them climb.'

'Come on, Limpy. Quick.'

'There are no Stonemen. It's a trick.'

'I've met them. They're our friends. Make him come, Nick.'

Nick grabbed Limpy by his cloak and pulled him after Susan into the back of the cave. Where there had been stone an opening showed, waist-high, narrow, leading into darkness. Susan pushed Limpy down on his knees.

'In you go. Quick.'

'No.'

'Do as she tells you,' the voice whispered. It filled the

cave, lapping soft as water. 'All who run from priests are friends of ours.'

'In.' She pushed him and he crawled into the opening. 'Nick, go on.'

'You first.'

She did not argue, but crawled into the hole. It led to a tunnel, running level. A deeper quiet – the sound of emptiness, she thought – told her when she reached the other end. She knelt at the opening, looking back. Nick came along, scuttling like a possum, and beyond him, in a square of light, she saw a part of the cave mouth. A priest sprang into it, and stood there, crouched like a wrestler. Another came up beside him. They were white as foam, shining in the light. They peered into the darkness, and came stepping forward, soft as cats.

'Priests of Ferris, stop,' said the voice.

The priests froze, and crouched, and peered. One of them spoke: 'Stonemen, give us our prey. They have broken our Ferris bones.'

'Your bones are foul. Do not follow into the dark.'

'We know all your exits. We know your holes. They cannot escape.'

'Wait then. But do not follow. The world of Stone is not open to you.'

And slowly, without a sound, the tunnel began to close. The band of light grew narrower, and Nick and Susan and Limpy were locked into the dark.

CHAPTER THREE

Seeker

'Tell me your name,' Susan said.

'First let me get out of this cupboard. The light would have killed me.'

She heard stone sliding again, and padding steps with the rubbery sound of suction. Then the Stoneman's voice came in front of her. 'We know each other already.'

'Are you Seeker? A hundred years have passed.'

'The generations of Stonefolk are longer than those of humans. But I am old. I am ready to die. I have waited only for the fulfilling of the prophecy.' His voice had the asthmatic wheeze, the hedgehog snuffle, she remembered.

'Where are you?' She reached out.

A damp touch came on her arm. 'Here, Susan. It is good to meet again.'

'Where's Finder?'

'Finder was impatient. He wished to know what the great secret was. It is many turns since he passed into Stone.'

'I'm sorry.'

'Do not be. It is release. This boy who limps is frightened of me, Susan.'

She heard Limpy shifting nervously. 'Limpy, he's our friend. Put out your hand. Let him touch you.'

Limpy was breathing quickly. 'The priests say – they say – '

'They say we are vermin,' Seeker said. 'They say that about all of us. Woodlanders. Birdfolk. Seafolk. All the

31

Folk. Ah Susan, joining the Halves together did not bring happiness to O. Is this Nicholas Quinn?'

'Give him your hand, Nick.'

'How do you do?' Nick said. It was strange to be talking to someone you could not see. He felt Seeker touching his hand, exploring his face.

'There are tales about you, Nick. I am pleased we have met. But hear the priests.' It was a sound like mice scratching in a wall. 'They dig with their knives. It will take them many turns to break through here.' He made an angry snuffling. 'Honest stone deserves a better mason. Let us go where we cannot hear.'

He set up a humming for them to follow, and they went along, stepping carefully. The sounds of the priests died away.

'Where are we going, Seeker?'

'Deeper yet. Away from priests and the smell of light.'

'We can't stay long. We don't have any food.'

'I know. We will go under the hills. The priests do not know as much as they think. There are ways out they have never found. You will be safe.'

They kept their hands before them and parted the darkness like drapes, but there was never any change, no blush of light, however distant, nothing to hold on to, except the sound of their guide. Susan had followed him once before, but he seemed smaller now, his snuffling was closer to the ground, and she wondered if age had shrunk him or whether it was just that she had grown. There were sounds of lapping water, rushing water – that was familiar. But this time she did not have to climb walls and hang upside-down over rivers.

'Seeker, I gave the stone-silk gloves to the Woodlanders.'

'They keep them still. It was well done.'

'Seeker?'

'You have not changed. You keep on asking questions.'

'A prophecy? You said you waited for it.'

'Ah. Wait until we rest. Then I will tell you.'

They kept on walking – by an echoing chasm, by a waterfall, down a slippery path where water dripped, through broken stones that jarred their feet. Always Seeker hummed, giving them something to follow, and now and then he warned them of dangers – potholes and wells and stalactites.

'How does he see?'

'He doesn't see.'

'He must have built-in radar, like a bat.'

Limpy kept silent. Susan heard his uneven step. Once, reaching back, she felt his knife in his hand.

'Put it away.'

'The priests say they lure people into caves and eat their flesh.'

'Do you still believe the priests?'

'We eat only things that grow in the lovely dark,' Seeker said. 'We eat mushrooms and lichen, and blind worms. Very sweet. You would taste sour, human boy.'

They climbed into drier, warmer caves. 'There is water here you can drink.' Seeker stopped. 'And over there a warm spring to bathe in. When you have rested I will take you to an opening into Wildwood where there will be no priests.'

'Do they really know the exits?'

'Their dogs sniff them out. But we make new ones so that we may talk with the Woodlanders and give them hiding places in the hunt.'

'Do they hunt you?'

'They come in with torches and so we must retreat. But

33

Stone is endless. They can raid no further than the margins.'

The children crouched in the warm dark and listened while the Stoneman spoke of caves and caverns, chambers, halls, pits and wells, underground rivers, springs and waterfalls, as though they were farms and beaches in the sun. And when he spoke of priests they swarmed like beetles, destroying what they touched. The High Priest sat in his Temple like a spider in a web.

'The Woodlanders tell us of him. A little man, old, but dangerous, and quick as a lizard.'

'Why do they kill?'

'It is their teaching. Susan said O belonged to humans – easy, child – and all other creatures must be wiped out. So they make a holy war against us. Stonefolk, Woodlanders, Seafolk, Birdfolk.'

'I didn't say it.'

'We know that. Woodlanders know. But humans believe a different tale. How Susan flew and brought about the Mending. And gave the rule of O to Humankind and left her staff and her holy book with the priests.'

'It's all lies.'

'Not to humans. O has become an evil place.'

'I've got to see him. I've got to talk to this High Priest. That's why I'm back. To face him the way I faced Otis Claw. Seeker, what's the prophecy?'

'Ah, that. I must tell you. But wash first. Drink. We have as far to go as we have come.'

'How long have we been walking?' Nick asked. He flipped back the leather hood on his watch and peered at the luminous figures. At once Seeker shrieked with agony. They heard him fall and thrash upon the floor.

'Cover it. Cover your watch,' Susan cried. She lunged

34

at the little patch of light, but it jerked away and vanished as Nick snapped the cover shut.

'I'm sorry. I didn't think.'

'Where's Seeker? Where are you, Seeker?'

She felt her way towards the sound of his groaning and knelt by him, putting out her hands. He was shuddering, she seemed to hear a rattle of bones in his chest, but when she felt his skin it was spongy and damp. She traced the shape of a torso, stubby arms, a soft head, with hairs like a coconut.

'Seeker, are you all right?'

He did not answer. Then she felt one of his hands, with its rubbery pads, come up and lie on her arm.

'I am dying, Susan.'

'No . . . oh no. It was only a watch.'

'I'm too old. The light cut through me like a knife. Do not grieve. Nick? Is Nick there?'

Nick knelt beside Susan. 'Can't we help? Can't we do something?'

'I am broken inside. But it was time to die. Listen, Susan. I must tell you the prophecy.'

'Don't talk.'

'The prophecy. I must speak before I die. Hold my hand, child.'

She took his alien hand between her own and held it tightly.

'Do you remember Watcher?'

'He guarded the Half.'

'Yes. He was old. Like me he wished to die. But he waited for the ending of your task. And I came to him. Brand, your friend, came to the Throat and called to us that you had placed the Halves, you had mended the break in Humankind. So I journeyed to Watcher with the news, and I told him, and he said . . .'

'Yes?' Susan asked. She was frightened Seeker had died. She could not hear his breathing any more.

'Watcher had the gift of dreaming. He told me your task was not done yet. You would come again and banish the great Lie. It was in his dream. I asked him what that was, the Lie. He did not know. He said it was the lie about Susan Ferris. He . . .'

'Yes?'

'He said I would save you. And Nick. And a boy who limped. When? I said. Where? Anywhere, he replied. Wherever you happen to be, that is the place. So . . . I waited until he died, I laid him in Stone, and I went back to the Folk, and took a wife, and fathered children. And I lived until I was old – too long. Then I grew tired of babble. I came here. I lived as a hermit, I lived in silence, by the gate. Watcher had said anywhere, so the gate would do. And you came – with Nick and a boy who limped. And I saved you.'

'Yes.'

'And now you must banish the Lie.'

'How?'

'I do not know. But in the dream – in Watcher's dream – you walked with one, a man, very old, who carried an axe. And walking with you both was a white bear of the south.'

'Jimmy. Jimmy Jaspers.'

'Watcher did not say his name.'

'But Jimmy's dead. He died years ago.'

'He was in the dream. That is all I know. Susan.' His voice was faint, no more than a whisper. 'Listen. I am dying. I cannot show you how to find your way out of Stone. There is only one way and you have no guide. Nick. Listen. Put your left hand on the wall above me. Walk ahead. You will climb. Never let your hand leave the wall. Are you listening, boy? You with the limp. Stonefolk do not eat men. Tell them that.'

'Yes,' Limpy whispered.

'Listen to what I am telling Nick. After you have climbed you will come to a river. Walk by the side of it until it vanishes. You will hear it booming. Go down then through a turning passage, deep down, very deep, and you will come to a lake in a cavern. Still keep your left hand on the wall, and pass around it. You will swim. Then climb on a path over the lake – take care, it is slippery. At the top go straight along – there are holes and fissures – and you will reach a place where tunnels meet. One is large and you will smell the air that comes from Wildwood. Avoid it. Priests know that way. Take the tunnel next to it, wide enough only for a child. Nick, you will find it very tight. Climb then, and you will come out soon above the forest. But remember, do not hurry. Feel your way. Do not get lost. Stone goes on forever.' Seeker sighed, and shudders ran through his body. 'I can do no more. Susan, Susan, do you have my hand?'

'Yes.'

'Hold it, child.' His grip grew tighter. She had to lean close to hear his voice. 'I'm glad we met again.'

'I'm glad too.'

'Do not move me. Here is a good place. I shall lie in the heart of Stone.' He gave a sighing breath and loosed his hand.

Susan knelt beside him a moment. She tried to arrange his arms across his chest but they kept sliding off.

'Is he dead?' Nick whispered.

'Yes. Why didn't you leave your watch at home?'

'I'm sorry. I didn't know.' She wondered if he was crying. 'Should we leave him here?'

'He said this was where he wanted to be.'

37

'We must go on,' Limpy said. 'We must find the way outside. If we get lost down here we'll never come out.'

'Wait for me a while,' Susan said. 'I want to say goodbye to him.'

Nick moved off towards the sound of the spring. He found the cold pool and drank, and washed his face and hands in the warm one. He heard Limpy drinking and washing beside him. 'I didn't mean to kill him,' he whispered.

'That is a strange weapon you wear,' said the boy.

They heard Susan talking softly to Seeker. Nick could not make out all of it, but thought she was thanking him and promising something. 'Sleep in Stone,' she whispered. 'I will end the Lie.' Then she said, 'Come here, Nick. Keep your hand on the wall while I have a drink.'

He went towards her voice and touched her hair. She took his hand and put it on the wall.

'Where is he?' Nick said.

'By your feet.'

She went to the spring, and Nick squatted, sliding one hand and feeling for Seeker with the other. He felt the Stoneman's bristling hair and shivered with revulsion. Then he said, 'I'm sorry,' and he took one of Seeker's hands and held it in his. He wondered if he should leave his watch as an offering, a way of apologizing, but thought how dangerous it would be if other Stonemen found it. So he stayed holding the hand of this being he had not seen, and would never see, until Susan and Limpy came from the spring. Then he laid it down by Seeker's side, and they started on their journey.

Nick took the lead, sliding his hand on the wall, Susan came behind, keeping in touch with him by voice, and Limpy in the rear. Nick felt his way with every step. He tried to read the tunnels by whistling softly and listening for the echo. After climbing for a while they heard the rushing of water far away, and it grew louder as they went along, and soon they stood by the side of a river. It made a hissing sound, and far off was a booming like machinery. They shuffled towards it, keeping a wall on their left. The noise increased until they seemed to be inside a drum playing an endless roll. They could not hear each other's voices, even when they shouted. Nick pulled Susan close behind him and made her hold his hand, and Limpy hers. The water rushing by only metres away pulled them like gravity. They heard it being gulped into a hole, and far away exploding against stone.

Nick found the tunnel he was seeking and pulled Susan and Limpy into it. They were deaf and dizzy, battered with sound. But the noise was dulled by intervening rock and it fell to a murmuring as they climbed – deep down, deep, as Seeker had said – and after a while died altogether. Only their panting and the scuffing of their feet broke the silence. Nick began whistling again, trying to find the size of the passage.

'We'll rest when we get to the lake.'

It was a long time, hours it seemed, but a sense of huge space drew them suddenly forward and seemed to drag the breath out of their lungs.

'Nick?'

The word floated off and set up echoes. The lapping of water made a sound like bat wings. They sank down by the wall.

'I'm hungry.'

'Me too.' He looked at his watch. It was almost two hours since they'd left Seeker.

'We can't rest too long,' Limpy said.

'Just a few minutes. We have to keep moving to stay warm. Can we drink this water?'

Limpy tried it and spat it out. 'It tastes of mud.'

'We've got to find clean water.'

'Then let's keep moving.'

'Susan's got to rest.'

She took no notice of their argument but thought of Seeker and the prophecy. It made no sense because of Jimmy. Jimmy was in it – and Jimmy was dead. Yet the priest too had spoken of a dream, of a man and a bear. And she saw it clearly – Jimmy in his bush singlet, with his axe on his shoulder, and at his side a bear, white and sleek, yet shambling and padding in a friendly way. It was like a vision. For a moment they were so real she almost called out to them. Then they faded. They were dead, man and animal. It was only a dream. And she thought of Watcher's prophecy that she would end the Lie, and that became the real part, that was what she must do. Face the High Priest. Face him alone. That was why she was back on O. To end the religion grown up in her name. To stand before this man who sat like a spider in its web, and tell him all his teaching was a lie. It terrified her. She thought of Otis Claw. She had done it once and it seemed unfair that she should have to do it all again. Jimmy and the bear came back into her mind, to comfort her. Surely two dreams so much alike had a meaning.

Nick pulled her up and they started off. Coldness cramped her joints. They waded in shallow water at the edge of the lake. It came over her knees, over her waist, icy cold. Soon they swam one-handed, keeping their touch on the wall.

'I hope nothing lives in this.'

'Seeker would have told us.'

But the water was threatening, it seemed thick and slow, and every lap or splash was the sound of some creature sliding at them. They found the bottom again and pulled themselves along, clutching handholds, and splashed out shivering. The path was there as Seeker had promised and they climbed it, keeping their backs to the wall. They felt they were leaving some place deeply hidden, where even Stonefolk would not stay long. The lapping and fluttering of the water fell to tiny sounds, tiny stirrings.

'It's slippery,' Nick said. 'Make sure of your feet before you move.'

The path took them high, narrowing then widening, and now and then passing an overhang that forced them on their knees. It turned away from the lake and the sounds were gone. A sense of being closed in grew on them.

'Another tunnel.'

'This is where he said to watch for holes.'

'Here's one. There's a way round the side. We'll have to crawl.'

The holes and cracks in the floor seemed endless. Now and then Nick dropped in pieces of stone. Several seemed to fall for hundreds of metres before striking bottom. One splashed in water, far away. And one made no sound at all. It seemed to fall out of existence. They crawled on silently, with knees worn raw.

At last Nick stood up. 'I think we're past. It's widening out.'

'Yes,' Limpy said. 'I smell the forest.'

'I smell trees. Sunshine,' Susan said.

They felt their way along. The scent of the outside grew stronger.

'Stop,' Nick said. He listened to his voice. 'We're in a chamber. The air's coming in from over here. Yes, here it is. It's a pity we can't go this way.'

'No,' Susan said. 'We've done what Seeker told us.

41

Don't stop now.' She felt her way past him along the wall. 'Here's the hole. You can get through.'

Past the narrow entrance the hole widened out. But the ceiling was low, closing down like the roof of a mouth. Twice they had to drag themselves on their stomachs. Nick scraped his head several times, and at last took off his shirt and wore it like a turban for protection. Then he stopped. 'Dead end.'

'It can't be.' They felt all round.

'There's a rock fall over here,' Susan said. 'And some air. It's a funnel.'

Limpy wriggled past her. 'It goes up. We'll have to climb.' They heard him grunting. 'Up here. There's not much room.'

This part, with the air of Wildwood sifting by, was the most difficult of all. The hole went straight up like a chimney, then angled through a fissure, and turned again like a question mark. It went down, and up, and down, and pools of stale water lay in each hollow. It seemed to Susan that Seeker could not have tried this passage.

'Light,' Limpy said. 'I see light.'

It lay ahead like something spilled and forgotten. They crept towards it, only half believing, screwing up their eyes against the pain – but it was light, and when they could endure it, they looked through the broken hole and saw the sky forked like a lightning bolt. A green creeper curled over the rocks.

'Wildwood,' Susan whispered. 'We're safe.'

'Not yet,' Limpy said. 'Stay here. I'll scout.'

'Seeker said the priests don't know this hole.'

'Seeker did not know everything.'

He crept away from them and knelt at the edge of the crack, peering out. Then he turned and beckoned, holding a finger to his lips. 'See,' he said, when they were at his side.

The hole came out in the roots of a tree high on a hill, with a cliff angling across it into the forest. Down there, a hundred metres away, where the trees began, a cave shaped like a church door stood in the cliff. 'That's the way he told us not to take.'

'There aren't any priests.'

'Look again.'

They saw them then, figures crouching in the rain-worn limestone. They were hidden from the cave, half-hidden from the children, and they waited still as cats beside a mouse hole.

'A different band,' Limpy said. 'There will be hundreds hunting us.'

'Where are the dogs?'

'There.' He pointed further off at the trees, and they saw dogs in a pack, in the shade, with priests watching them.

'While the breeze blows from that direction we are safe.'

'How do we get away?'

'When the sun goes down they will feed their dogs. And sing their hymns. There will be noise enough. We must take our chance. Once in the forest I can find grub-weed.'

'Can you eat it?'

'I need water more than food,' Susan said.

'Soon. It is nearly sundown.'

Shadows covered their hiding place and crept along the hill and the priests in the boulders seemed to turn grey.

'Won't they leave someone watching there?'

Limpy shook his head. 'Everything comes second to the ritual. See, they are leaving.'

The priests came out of the boulders and walked in a band down to their camp. The dogs began yelping. Away in the west colours climbed in the sky, pink and lilac, and small clouds slid southwards on the horizon, smooth as pebbles. The hills behind the priests were lit by an afterglow. But the priests themselves were like a cluster of grubs on something dead. There were ten of them. They fed the dogs with meat and bones from a sack and the animals snarled and fought and then lay gnawing. The priests made a circle and as the darkness grew, at the moment the sun sank below the horizon, they stripped off their leather suits and turned them inside out, and dressed again, moving jerkily, in perfect time; and now instead of being white they were black. They held their Ferris bones in the circle and beat them against each other and sang a chant as the forest darkened.

'Now,' Limpy said. They crept out from the tree roots and went down the hillside, keeping low in the boulders.

'The wind's turning,' Nick whispered.

'We have time. And the dogs are feeding.'

A yell from the circle made them freeze, but it was only a solo chant from a priest. Other voices joined in and the chatter of bones grew faster.

'They are finishing,' Limpy said.

'What are they singing?'

'Thanks to Susan for their hunt. They caught a Woodlander today. That is why the dogs have meat.'

'No,' Susan whispered.

'Woodlanders are vermin to them. Dog's meat, that is all. And we are dead as well if they catch us.'

They went down through small trees into the forest, and Susan knelt. She thought she was going to be sick.

'Come on,' Limpy said roughly. He seemed to understand how she felt.

'I'll stop them. I promise,' she whispered.

They struck deep into the bush and came to a creek. Limpy let them drink, then led them on, looking for swampy ground where grub-weed might grow. After a while he told them to rest. He limped off into some rushes and came back presently with two grey roots shaped like sweet potatoes. 'I have put mine on.' He split the tubers with his knife and showed them how to rub juice on their skins. 'It will hurt. But it kills our scent.' He grinned at Nick. 'And you can't eat it.'

The sting was sharp, but moving helped them forget. They travelled for another hour, heading away from the creek, then Limpy found a place where they could rest. They still had not eaten, but all they could think of was sleep. They made beds of fern and lay down.

'I'm filthy with mud,' Nick said.

'You can wash tomorrow, when we have more grub-weed,' Limpy said.

'Can you find us food?'

'Berries. Fish. We will not starve. Shady Home is four days south.'

'Tomorrow you can tell us about your sister,' Susan said.

'Yes,' Limpy promised, 'I'll do that.'

His voice was grim. As she went to sleep Susan wondered sadly why he should still be blaming her for all the things that had gone wrong on O.

CHAPTER FOUR

Soona's Dream

The birds of Wildwood woke them with their song. A pale light was creeping through the trees. They lay a while, listening for other sounds. Then Limpy went hunting for food. Susan and Nick burrowed more deeply into the fern and whispered to each other, warm and hungry. They talked of home.

Limpy brought back fruit and berries. But he would not let them eat until they had rubbed grub-weed on themselves. The burn of it on their skin spoiled their breakfasts. It was mid-morning before they found a creek where they could drink. Then they washed, although Limpy grumbled at the lost time. They washed their muddy clothes and put them on wet, and found the coolness eased the pain of the fresh application of weed he demanded.

Through the rest of the day they pressed on south. Towards evening they climbed over a hump of land at the foot of hills and something about the place made Susan stop. She told Limpy to wait and climbed a short way towards the hills until she had a clearer view of them. 'Nick,' she called. She pointed at the scar running up the mountain wall. It was hollowed out as though by a giant scoop. The face of it was clothed in stunted trees and clinging ferns, although here and there sheets of rock shone in the evening sun.

'It's the Living Hill.'

Limpy had come up with Nick. 'I have heard of it,' he whispered. 'Marna died here.'

'She's somewhere under our feet. This mound is the earth that came sliding down.'

'We're standing on her grave,' Nick said.

They went on thoughtfully, down the side of the mound into the forest, and found a dry cave in the foot of the hills. While Nick and Susan made new beds of fern Limpy went out for food. He came back with more fruit and a trout he had speared with his knife on the end of a stick. He made a fire-drill and soon had branches blazing on the cave floor. 'We'd starve without you, Limpy,' Susan said.

'We must put it out before dark.' He watched anxiously until the wood fell into embers. 'Smoke is dangerous too. Dogs can smell it and priests see it.' He laid the gutted fish in the coals and soon they were picking the cooked flesh out on sticks. It was a sober meal. Crouched in the shadowy cave by the dying fire, they felt unsafe. And the flank of the hill outside troubled them.

'Marna died. And now Seeker's dead. Who'll be next?'

'Jimmy's dead too.'

'What about the dream? Watcher saw him with a bear. He saw me too. And the priest sniffed out a man who dreamed of Jimmy and a bear.'

They shivered, remembering the chase. 'It's no use thinking of Jimmy. He can't help us. Limpy, you'd better tell us what's happened on O.'

'You know most of it. A hundred turns ago, Susan came. It was the Mending. Then she and Nick and – Jimmy Jaspers – ' he still found the name hard to say, 'they went to live on Earth, and all who obey the priests will follow them.'

'No,' Susan said.

'That is what they say. It is in the holy book. Before

47

you – before Susan left, she gave the task of ruling to the priests.'

'This is lies.'

'It is the teaching. Only heretics deny it.'

'It's still lies. You tell him, Nick.'

'I can see how it happened, though,' Nick said. 'Someone had to rule, and whoever it was used you. He saw his chance. Probably there was some sort of real religion – or some superstition. You saved them, after all. Then someone came along and got it organized. Once the Temple was in power that was the end. You'd better tell us about your sister, Limpy.'

Limpy stirred the embers. He seemed to find it hard to look at Nick and Susan. Sadness, not fear, made him keep his face away from them.

'I will tell you about Stonehaven, where I live. It is a village in the south. All down the coast are villages. The men go out to fish. We live from fishing. The land is poor and the coast is rocky. We only have small fields for crops, patches of soil in the sides of the hills.'

'What about Soona?'

'Our houses are built of stone,' the boy went on. 'They climb one above the other up the hill. Forty houses, that is all. Twenty boats inside the breakwater. And a gutting-shed, and a smoke-house. And a temple, where the priest lives with his dogs.' Limpy dropped his stick in the ashes. 'When winter storms come, waves crash over the breakwater and spray beats like hailstones through the town. Then we sit inside by our fires, mending our nets and making crayfish pots. My grandmother tells tales and my mother sings and Soona . . . Soona would play tunes on her flute.' Limpy looked up. His eyes were wet with tears. 'Stonehaven is the best place in the world.'

'What happened, Limpy?'

Again he did not answer. He wiped his eyes and went on at his own pace with his tale. 'When I was eleven I went out with my father on his boat. That is the age when we go. It is hard work. But I love the sea. I do not like this forest. I love boats and wind and storms. One day – one day . . . we were harnessed with my uncle's boat. We were pulling in our nets to share the catch. Our holds were full and my uncle had space in his. The sea was rough, it was dangerous. And I was careless. I slipped, and my leg was crushed between the boats.'

He looked down at the bent limb thrust out awkwardly. 'My uncle knows medicine. He said the leg was too badly hurt to save. But my father would not let him cut it off. I am his only son. Without me he has no one to work on his boat. He hoped my mother would be able to set my leg well enough for me to work again. Besides – he loves me. Soona and I are his children. So we sailed for Stonehaven – and the journey, in the storm . . .' Limpy shivered. 'It was more than three years ago, but I cry out in my sleep even now. When we came home, my mother nursed me. She set my leg, and the priest came and laid his hands on it. But my uncle was right. The leg was too badly broken – and now you see it.' He dragged his leg into the light and they saw again the unnatural bend, the painful twist, the muscles torn and wasted. 'Even so, I could have worked. I am quick. I am strong. My father saw it, and when I was well again he wanted to take me back on his boat. But the priest said no.'

'The priest?' Nick said. 'What's he got to do with it?'

'The priest's word is the law. To disobey the priest is heresy.'

'Why did he say you couldn't go?'

'He said my crooked leg showed my lack of faith. He had laid his hands on it and if I had had faith it would have

49

healed. Susan would have healed it. But she turned her back on me. He said I was lucky he did not send me for the Test. But he said he would be merciful, and he forbade me to go to sea again. So my father had to sell his boat, he sold it to my uncle, and now he works as crewman for my uncle's son. My uncle has two boats and is rich. Every year he makes a gift to the Temple.'

'I see,' Nick said, 'I see.'

'And you,' Susan said, 'what do you work at?'

'I work in the gutting-shed. I hang the fish for smoking. I sew sails and weave ropes. It is honest work. But it is not the sea.' He scooped a handful of dust from the floor and threw it on the embers, putting them out. Nick and Susan waited. Although his story was sad they sensed that he had told it only to put off a sadder tale. They heard him shifting in the dark, lying down on his bed. Quietly they found their own beds too. They stared up at the black roof of the cave. Presently Limpy spoke again.

'Now I will tell you about my sister, Soona.'

'Don't, Limpy. Not if you don't want to.'

'She is why I came to the Woodlanders, to find the way to Earth and Susan.'

They lay still on their beds and listened as he spoke.

'Soona is two years younger than me. When we were small I minded her while my mother and grandmother worked in the sheds. We played around the stone tables where they cleaned the fish, and under the drying racks in the smoke-house. I watched her on the harbour wall, and when we were old enough we sat out in the sun weaving nets, or we climbed the cliffs together after seabirds' eggs. She took me picking berries in the woods. She loved the woods, but I did not like them, I liked the sea. People began to whisper that she talked to Woodlanders. And

50

some took their whispers to the priest. But the priest was angry with them. He would not listen. Soona was his favourite. She was clever. He allowed her to learn reading. She is the only one in our village who can read. He allowed her to learn the flute. She played in the temple while the priest sang the Message. We were very proud of Soona. But we were frightened too. There had been clever children in our village before. My parents remembered what had happened to them.'

His bed rustled as he moved.

'One day it happened. Soona was ten. It was the time when the priest came to heal my leg. He laid his hands on me and sang a chant. When it was over he talked with my parents. He told them he had chosen Soona to train for the priesthood. You must understand, that is a great honour in our land. Families dream of a son or daughter chosen. But my family – we are different. For one thing, we are small. Most parents have many children. But my parents have only Soona and me. And my father had come – he had come not to believe.' Limpy moved convulsively, as though what he had said frightened him. 'In our house we did not practise the rites. No one knew of it. The priest did not know. We did not thank Susan for our food. We did not pray at dawn and at dusk, unless someone was with us. Then we prayed. We went to the Temple, we had to do that. But at home we were unbelievers. We did not speak of it, we kept very quiet. If he had known the priest would have sent us for trial. And my sister Soona, *she* hated Susan most of all. She hated the priests. She knew they hunted Woodlanders with their dogs, and hunted unbelievers, and threw them down Sheercliff from Deven's Leap. So when the priest told us she was chosen, she said no, and my parents said no.' Limpy shivered. 'One does not say no to a priest.' He was quiet for a long time.

'What happened, Limpy?'

'My parents told him they had only two children. They must keep Soona at home to work. But the priest would not listen. He told her to be ready to leave for the Temple in the morning. Then Soona told him she had seen Susan in a dream, and Susan had told her she must stay with her parents, she was not meant for the priesthood, there were other things she must do. The priest was angry. But no one, not even he, can argue with Susan. He tested Soona, of course, but she was clever, he could not shake her. So he punished us in the way I have told you. He kept me from the sea. He ruined my father. But Soona was saved from the priesthood, that was the most important thing.

'After that we pretended to be more pious. We gave the priest no excuse to examine us. And the village looked on Soona as a saint. People told how she had seen Susan in a dream. We thought their talk would make the priest angry. But he encouraged it. Ah, he was clever. One night he sent his dogs to sleep outside our door. And through the days that followed they lay there in the street and would not move.'

'Why did he send them?' Susan said.

'It was a sign. So he said.'

'A sign of what?'

'We were in the time of the hundredth turn. All through the land priests from the Temple were searching for a girl . . .'

'What for?'

'To go to the Temple. To take part in the Miracle. Our village is small, and far away. When we heard of it we never thought they would come so far.'

'What sort of miracle? Please, Limpy. Tell me.'

'It is said – the High Priest has said – that in the hundredth turn Susan may perform the Miracle as a sign of favour to Humankind. But if she is angry the girl will fall.'

'Fall?'

'They will throw the Chosen One from Deven's Leap. Susan will save her – or she will not.'

'That's – terrible.'

'It is terrible. Yes.'

'And Soona? Soona was chosen?'

'Our priest sent a message to the Temple. He told them of the girl who had seen Susan in a dream. So they came. He showed them his dogs at our door, guarding her. He brought Soona out. She was the right age. She was beautiful. And pious. And clever. In all the land there was no girl so perfect for the part. So they took her. They put her in a cart and wheeled her away. My father could do nothing. They would have set their dogs on him. And my mother – she sits by the ashes at the fire and will not speak. But it was a great day for Stonehaven. And our priest. He had found the Chosen One. It is said he will be called soon to a high place at the Temple.'

They lay still in the cave for a long time. There was no rustle of ferns. No one spoke. Nick could think of nothing to say. Susan was too full of wild emotions to trust her tongue. But at last she said, 'When did you think of looking for me?'

'Soona thought of it. We talked while the dogs lay at our door. She knew what was going to happen. She told me it was true what people said, she had talked with the Woodlanders. They had told her all they knew about Susan, all the stories handed down to them. Susan was a human girl, they said. She was not holy. Earth was another world, like O. Soona told me I must go deep into

53

Wildwood. The Woodlanders would come for me, she said. They would tell me how to find Susan and bring her back to O. She told me she had dreamed of Susan truly, not the Susan of the priests, the real one. She would come, it was in her dream. She would face the High Priest and show him the Lie. I could not believe. It was too much. But Soona made me promise to do as she said.'

'How am I going to save her?'

'The dream did not show.'

'And how will I end the religion?'

'She saw you face the High Priest, that is all.'

'Was Jimmy in the dream?'

'Only you and the Priest. So . . . when they had taken her, I ran away to Wildwood. I slipped out in the night. I did not tell my parents, they would stop me. But I know it must grieve them terribly. They have lost their children.'

Nick and Susan thought of their own parents. But they could not turn back now. They could not leave O until Soona was safe. And Susan believed in Soona's dream. She must go to the Temple and face the High Priest. It seemed to her as frightening as facing Otis Claw.

'I travelled for a night and a day,' Limpy said. 'On the second morning when I woke I heard the dogs. The priest of Stonehaven was hunting me. I could not escape him, but I ran. Then I heard a voice telling me to stop, and I found someone running at my side. It was a Woodlander. I had never seen one, except when hunting parties of priests brought a body back and fed it to their dogs. He was small, and beautiful. He had fur on his face, brown and silver. He could run as swiftly as a deer.'

'We know the Woodlanders. We have seen them.'

'He asked me who I was and why they chased me. I told him I was Soona's brother. Then he showed me how to use grub-weed, and we escaped from the dogs. He took me to Shady Home and I met Verna and told my tale. I told her I must go to Earth and bring Susan back. And she said yes, it was time. She said the real Susan must come to O and destroy the false one. So they taught me all the ways of living in the woods – how to travel quickly, how to climb, how to find food and cure my ills. And they told me all the old tales – different from the ones in the holy book. How Susan flew with wings made in Shady Home – '

'I made them,' Nick said.

'Wings Nick made. How Susan joined the Halves and made Humankind whole. And how you went back home to Earth. I tried to believe. I think that I believe Verna now. And I know the priests are evil men who lie. I should have known sooner, like my sister.' He brooded a while in the dark, then shook himself. 'When I had learned her lessons, Verna sent a woman out to pick the Shy. She was gone many days. The Shy is rare. But she came back and Verna gave me the flower and told me how to use it. I set out on my journey. Woodlanders came with me on the way. Then I went on alone, and found the cave, and came to Earth. To Earth!' His voice had a wondering note. Again he shook himself, rustling the ferns. 'I came out by your stream and smelled the Shy. I found the plant and knelt by it, and soon Susan came. The rest you know.'

'But I don't know how I'm going to destroy the Temple. And save Soona.'

'Verna said to bring you to Shady Home. She has something to give you from long ago. Perhaps you will find the answer there.'

'Maybe,' Susan said. She was afraid, but angry too. When she thought of people using her name to terrorize a world, and Soona wheeled away in a cart and her mother grieving by the cold fire, she felt an anger that made her want to rush to the Temple and break it down with her hands. 'How far are we from Shady Home?'

'Three or four days. It's south, that's all I know. When I came I didn't come this way.'

'I think I can find it,' Nick said.

'It is not the Shady Home you knew. The Woodlander villages move about because the priests come hunting with their dogs. We must go south and hope Woodlanders find us. They told me they would wait in the forest.'

They slept, and rose at dawn, and went on south along the foot of the hills. In the afternoon the sun grew red, shining through a haze of smoke far off towards Sheercliff.

'The priests are burning forest where they have found the Shy,' Limpy said.

They found another cave in the evening, and cooked more fish and ate fruit and sat by the fire talking. Limpy was worried that Woodlanders had not found them. Susan told him stories to cheer him up. She told him about the Birdfolk and how she had flown to Mount Morningstar. She told him how Jimmy Jaspers had chopped down the bridge and saved them from the Bloodcat, and how she had met Seeker and Finder and climbed down the Throat of the Underworld. She described the Shady Home she had known, and her friendship with Brand and Breeze. Nick chipped in, telling how he had made the gliders, and how Jimmy had killed Odo Cling, and how they had flown to Darkland. They told the whole tale, until the Halves were joined and Otis Claw dead. Limpy listened without saying a word. They could not tell whether he believed them or not.

'The priests tell these stories, but they tell them differently.'

'Then they tell lies,' said a voice. A Woodlander woman stepped into the light. Susan thought she was Breeze and almost cried out the name, then saw this girl was younger and her fur more golden. She came forward quickly and touched Susan on the shoulder. 'Welcome to Wildwood again. My name is Dawn. Welcome Nick. I have been listening to your stories.' She knelt and looked at Susan, then she smiled. 'Yes, you are the way I thought you would be. My mother's grandmother was your friend.'

'Was she Breeze? You look like her.'

'I am descended from Breeze and Brand. My mother knew them when she was a girl. They never forgot you, Susan. It grieved them terribly to see this evil cult grow up among Humankind.'

'How can I destroy it? What do I do?'

'I don't know. There will be a way. Tomorrow we will start for Shady Home. When you have talked with Verna you will know. But Limpy, you must put this fire out. The glow from the cave shows in the forest. If I can find you, priests can.' They threw dust on the fire and lay down on their beds in the gathering dark. Dawn slept at the mouth of the cave. Her quiet breathing came to Susan as she went to sleep. She seemed to lie between them and the danger outside, and it comforted Susan so that she slept all through the night without dreaming.

For the next three days the Woodlander girl led them south. They travelled in the forest at the foot of the Shining Cliffs, and once saw a band of priests filing along the Lizard Path. They hid in the bush and watched them cross the bridge over Mountain's Grief – a stone bridge now. Had Jimmy built it? He had said he was going to rebuild the bridge. Somewhere near them in the forest the old wooden one must have rotted away. The bones of the Bloodcat must lie near.

They struck away from the cliffs, deeper into Wildwood, passed through the Sink Holes, and then went further south, climbing into uplands where the trees grew smaller and herds of deer grazed on the downs. From the bare top of a hill they saw how the land was narrowing. The mountains stood close by and over beyond the forest the sea stretched out and merged its blue with the blue of the sky.

On the fourth day they reached Shady Home. The mountain range had flattened into hills and the Woodlander village was by a creek that tumbled from a hidden valley filled with giant trees. It was built on levels up the hillside. The Woodlanders crossed on rope walkways from houses in the trees to others on the ground higher up. Nick saw how the site gave them protection. No one could attack from behind, while look-outs had a clear view over the downs and forest. But in one way it was the Shady Home they had known. Children still played by the stream and their shouts rang in the trees.

Dawn led them through the village. They gathered a train of Woodlanders, who touched Nick and Susan and called out their names wonderingly. Verna's house was on the hill, where the creek broke from the valley. She waited by her door: an ancient Woodlander woman in the cloak of age and honour. She touched them with her dry hands, and led them into her house. She gave them food and drink and told them to rest before they talked. But they were too excited for that.

Susan said, 'I knew another Verna once.'

The old Woodlander smiled. 'She was my mother. She told me many tales of you.'

'And your father . . .?'

'He was Walt.'

'Ah,' Susan said. This world was the O she knew at last.

She told Verna how she had planted the seed and how the Shy had grown on Earth, and about their journey, how Limpy had led them down from the cave, and how the Stoneman Seeker had saved them. Then Verna told the lives of Brand and Breeze and Walt and Verna. And she told them how the Temple had begun. It was as Nick had guessed. There was a time of lawlessness after the Halves were in balance. Men seemed lost, they seemed to be waiting for someone to rule them. But some left the lowlands and settled in the forest, and others travelled north and south and set up villages on the coast and lived from fishing. They were the lucky ones. In the cities people starved and preyed on one another, and everywhere cults and superstitions grew up. Then one grew stronger than the others – the cult of Susan. It made a holy book, it set up rites and doctrines and invented enemies, and people flocked to it, and soon it ruled.

'Who were the enemies?'

'The Woodlanders. The Birdfolk. The Seafolk. All who were not human. It was never a religion of love. Hatred and power were its attractions. That way the people were kept in order. The Temple ruled.'

'In my name,' Susan whispered.

'In your name.'

'I must stop it. Soona dreamed I would face the High Priest.'

'Yes. But listen. Once, long ago, Jimmy Jaspers came to Shady Home. I was a child, not five turns old. I remember him. An old man with a strange weapon, an axe. And he travelled with a Varg, the great blue bear that lives in the south.'

'Blue?'

'Sometimes he is blue and sometimes white, as the sun shines on his fur when he moves. Jimmy Jaspers stayed with Brand and Breeze, and the Varg lay sleeping at the door. They stayed one night. When morning came Jimmy Jaspers lifted me up and sat me on the bear's back for a moment. I have never forgotten. Then he said goodbye and went away south, and he was never seen in Wildwood again. But Susan, he left something for you.'

'He knew I would come?'

'He must have known.' She went to a little alcove by her bed and felt in it and came back with a small wooden box. 'I have never opened this. Brand and Breeze left it with my mother and she with me.' She put the box on the table. 'Now it is yours.'

Susan looked at it. There was no ornamentation. It was the size of a lunch box, with a hasp of twig. She shifted it into a patch of sun. Nick came to her side.

'Open it.'

The hinges creaked a little. When the sunlight reached inside they saw a roll of parchment in the box. It was mottled grey and brown and tied with plaited flax. Susan lifted it out. 'Nick, this is nearly a hundred years old.' The flax broke in her fingers and the parchment crackled as she opened it. They held it flat on the table and looked at the pale marks on it.

'A letter, Nick. It's a letter from Jimmy.'

CHAPTER FIVE

The Blue Bears

Deer Susan and deer Nick,

I'm not much good at letters but heer goes. I just cum up from Darkland by the citty theer and sum funny things is hapnin I can tell you. Theers sum geezers cashin in on what you dun yung Susie. They reckin your pritty speshul well you are but not that way. Bad times is cummin thats for sure. Odo Cling was a boy scowt compeered with sum of these blokes.

I dont go much on dreems but I had wun the uther nite. I reckin its becorse Im frends with Ben. We got a way of talkin him and me. Anyway I dreemed that you was cummin back to O. And I seen that youd be needin me and Ben. So wen you get heer cum and get me. It dont matter how much times gone by. Ill be down south at Mount Nickolis. Wen you get theer arsk the Vargs weer to go. Dont let them sceer you theyr not as bad as they look. Tell them who you are. Just sort of make a pickture in your hed.

Thats enuff. This writins bloddy hard werk.

Love. Jimmy.

P.S. Dont go tryin to do nuthin without me. I saw in me dreem that Id be theer. Wissel me fayvrit tune wen you cum.

'He named a mountain after me,' Nick said.

'Ben must be the bear. Was that his name, Verna?'

'That was it.'

'Read the letter out,' Limpy said.

Susan read, and when it was finished he said, 'It was a hundred turns ago. I don't see what good it does us now.'

'We've got to trust Jimmy. He says it doesn't matter how much time's gone by.'

'He's dead,' Limpy said. 'Unless he went to Earth, like you.'

'We've got to go and find out,' Nick said. 'And I want to see Mount Nicholas.'

'My sister will be dead by the time you get back.'

'How many days have we got?'

'Twenty-three.'

'We can do it. If there's a chance of finding Jimmy we've got to take it.'

'What chance is there?'

'Verna . . .?'

'You must trust him. If he dreamed he would be there then he'll be there. He dreamed you would be coming back, remember.'

'Yes. Limpy, will you come? Please. We need you. We'll save your sister, I promise you.'

'You must travel into the land of the Birdfolk,' Verna said. 'If I send a messenger they will be ready to help you. You will be at Mount Nicholas in five days.'

It took them a while to persuade Limpy, but when he had agreed Verna sent out the messenger. She rolled the parchment and tied it with new cord. 'There is something else in the box. You did not take it.'

They looked where she was pointing, in the corner. Nick thought it was a pebble, but Susan knew at once what it was. She picked it up reverently. 'My stone-silk gloves.' She rolled them out and smoothed them on the table. 'I gave them to Brand. He's given them back.'

'He must have thought you would need them,' Verna said.

Susan drew the gloves on. She felt them enclosing her hands, fitting like skin, and she shivered as she remembered her climb across the stone ceiling in Otis Claw's throne-hall. Nick ran outside and brought in a stone. She held it in her hand, then turned the hand over. The stone remained where it was, fixed on the silk. *Let go*, Susan thought; and the stone fell. Quietly she peeled off the gloves and rolled them up. She put them in her pocket.

'Thank you, Verna. I'll look after them.'

'Use them to pull the Temple down.'

'Yes,' Susan said. But the thought of Jimmy gave her more confidence than the gloves. If somehow Jimmy was alive, she would manage. If he was not . . . She would not let herself think about it.

They slept that night in Verna's house. Susan dreamed of great white bears, and climbing, and falling, and a figure that would not come out of the shadows. Was it Jimmy? Or was it a priest, dressed all in black? In the morning they changed their clothes for Woodlander cloaks. They said goodbye to Verna and shouldered their blankets and packs of food and started out. Dawn was their guide. She would travel to Mount Nicholas with them.

They went south and east through the forest and climbed through the hills cutting Wildwood off from the Yellow Plains. At midday on the second day they filed through a pass and saw the plains burning white in the sun. Far north, beyond the dust and haze, lay Morninghall and Mount Morningstar. But they were going south, across the tundra to the frozen tip of the continent where a block of mountains stood against the sky. They saw a white gleaming in the cold air, and turned towards it, travelling along the side of the hills, then breaking down into a plateau above the plain. Rivers tumbled from it but they turned their backs on them and pressed on south. The land rose gradually, covered with spiky grass and trees lying close to the ground, smoothed into cobblestones by the wind. They made their evening camp in a hollow. Nick and Susan lay in their blankets watching the strange constellations and inventing names for them. Then Limpy told their real names, and Dawn pointed out a yellow star Woodlanders said was the sun of Earth. 'Children sometimes call it Susan's star.'

Limpy shivered. 'The priests would say that was heresy.'

'And they would kill these friends who come to help us,' Dawn said. She pointed in the northern sky and they saw a flickering on the field of stars. Limpy cried out, but she said, 'It is Birdfolk coming to our fire.' She threw dry branches on it, making it flare. Soon they heard the beating of wings, and out beyond the light a voice cried sternly, 'You are in our land. Say your names.'

Susan stood in the firelight. 'We are Susan Ferris and Nicholas Quinn. And Dawn the Woodlander. And Limpy from Stonehaven.' She grew aware of shapes wheeling round the hollow, round and round, a giant circle, closing in. Their wind lifted her hair and flapped her cloak. The fire flattened out and sent flames darting at her legs. Then the Birdfolk landed, with a leathery flap and a creaking of bones. They stood beyond the firelight, ten dark figures ranged about the hollow like stone angels. One of them came forward and colour seemed to burst from him – from wings and breast and legs. He was red and gold. A second followed – a Birdwoman, green and blue and silver.

'Your messenger reached us,' the Birdman said. 'But it is past belief Susan should come. A hundred turns have passed.'

'I am Susan. Only a year has gone by for me.'

'Show me the Mark.'

Susan put her arm out and he looked hard at her birthmark. 'It proves nothing,' he said to the Birdwoman. 'Human girls burn this mark on them.'

The Birdwoman came close and looked in Susan's eyes. 'If you are Susan, tell me the gift my ancestor gave you. Tell me her name.'

'Her name was Brightfeather. She was the daughter of Redwing and Wanderer. She gave me a brush for my hair. And I lost it on the Lizard Path, when the Bloodcat chased us.'

'What was the colour of the feather you chose?'

'Red and blue. Brightfeather dried my clothes for me. She nearly lost one of my socks.'

The Birdwoman laughed and said to her mate, 'Only Susan would know that.'

'Yes. You are Susan. Welcome to our land again. Welcome, Nick. And your friends. I am Yellowclaw.'

'And I am Silverwing,' the Birdwoman said. 'We come from Morninghall. And our friends are from other Halls of our land. We fly the borders, on patrol, to keep out priests. But tell us why you have come back.'

'We're looking for Jimmy Jaspers. He left a letter for us saying he'd be at Mount Nicholas.'

'Jimmy Jaspers? The one the priests call the Terrible One? He came to us, many turns ago. A hundred turns. He told us what you had done. And he forged a weapon in our workshops – an axe. He wore your feather at his throat. Red and blue.'

'I gave it to him. It belonged on O.'

'It was well given. But surely he is dead now. No one lives so long.'

Susan told them about the letter. They nodded their

heads wisely. Wonders were not unknown on O. And she told them she meant to destroy the Temple.

'Yes, it is evil. Priests come over the passes and shoot us from the sky with their cross-bows. And we cannot follow when they run back to their land. The Prohibition holds. We cannot fly west or south of the mountains, we tumble from the sky. So the Temple goes on.'

'I'm going to stop the Temple. That's why I'm back. To see this High Priest. But first we've got to get to Mount Nicholas.'

'We'll take you as far as we can. The messenger told us to bring nests. Remember Susan, how Wanderer carried you in a nest?'

She remembered, and warm in her blankets, by the fire, with Birdfolk sleeping like tall statues, she remembered the flight; and half awake, half sleeping, imagined she was making it again, but this time to Mount Nicholas, far away in the south, where Jimmy was waiting.

In the morning they saw the Birdfolk properly. There were ten of them, eight giant warriors, standing three metres tall, and two Birdwomen. In the dawn sunlight their colours gleamed. Silverwing was the most beautiful, Susan thought. She looked as if she had been cast in some shining metal, then studded with sapphires and greenstone and lapis lazuli.

When they had eaten and put their gear in their packs they climbed into the down-lined nests Yellowclaw and the warrior birds had brought. They were used for carrying young before they could fly and were more like shopping bags than anything else, Susan thought. She made herself comfortable, with only her head peering out, and watched while the others climbed into theirs – Nick with a grin, Limpy nervously. The Birdman carrying Nick would need to be strong. He had grown a lot, and looked twice as heavy as Limpy. Dawn, light as an elf, would be no trouble.

The unladen Birdfolk sprang into the air and beat their way up easily, leaving the four with the nests labouring and creaking. But they won height gradually and set their heads at the distant south. Behind, the plains lay in a haze, like a yellow puddle, and the western hills and the tongue of forest beyond made strips of dark brown and dark green, and the sea stretched endlessly, silver and white. The land rose ahead, climbing in easy steps, with creeks wandering down, marked as though in snail-slime, and waterfalls brushed-in, and hollow lakes and black thorn groves. Far ahead the tip of the continent gleamed like a cloud.

The Birdfolk took turns carrying, and for two days they flew south. They beat into a wind off the mountains. At night Nick and Susan slept by the fire, and the Birdfolk came close, fluffing out their feathers. They huddled shoulder to shoulder like love-birds on a perch.

'Tomorrow you will see Mount Nicholas,' Silverwing said.

'But we must stop before we get so far,' Yellowclaw said. 'We will set you down at the pass. Then you must go down, and climb the glacier on the other side. But through the pass it is Varg country.'

'Jimmy said not to be scared of them.'

'No man has ever made friends with a Varg,' Yellowclaw said.

'Don't frighten them,' Silverwing said. 'The Terrible One wasn't an ordinary man.'

Yellowclaw sighed and shook his head. He seemed to enjoy looking on the dark side. 'It is the Prohibition,' Silverwing whispered. 'He is our mightiest flyer. He flies higher even than Wanderer flew, and sees the lands beyond our borders. But he can never fly there. It makes him melancholy.'

They slept, and rose, and went on their way towards the pass. The Birdfolk flew heavily through mist, with feathers damp, but in mid-morning the sky cleared, and the pass lay ahead, a V in hills where snow lay thin on the tops, like frosted glass. Across a valley clogged with bush was Mount Nicholas, a knuckle of ice, a giant fist clenched against the sky. It was squat rather than tall; and ugly, strong. It disappointed Nick at first, and then it pleased him. It was not a shape he would forget. A glacier ran from its eastern flank and curved into the bush, as sharp in its line as a scimitar.

One of the leading Birdfolk stumbled in its flight and managed to turn and glide down to the hillside above the pass. He lay spread like a fallen glider while the others tended him. The carrier Birdfolk landed.

'We have reached the barrier,' Yellowclaw said. 'We can go no further.' He looked through the V at Mount Nicholas. 'How long must our punishment last? If I could see the land beyond, and fly south, south . . .' He gave an angry flap of his wings and turned away.

'The Prohibition is in our minds,' Silverwing said. 'There is no barrier, yet we cannot fly. It is carved in stone on the wall of every Hall – "Unless ye be as Humble as the Worm . . ." It is our pride that locks us in our land.'

'If I knew how then I would do it. I would be humble,' Yellowclaw groaned.

Silverwing laughed at him. 'You,' she said. 'Pride in your strength drips from your feathers. Stop complaining now. Say goodbye to these groundlings who go where we may not.' She turned to Nick and Susan, Dawn and Limpy. 'There is a creek in the pass. Follow it down. Soon it will meet the river where the glacier melts. We cannot see any further than that. But I think the Vargs will find you before you have travelled far.'

'No man – ' Yellowclaw began.

'Hush!' She turned back to Susan. 'Trust your friend, Jimmy Jaspers. I have heard a Woodlander's tale that he walked with a Varg.'

'He did,' Dawn said. 'We're not afraid.'

They ate a last meal with the Birdfolk. Then Susan said to Silverwing, 'I would like to take a feather. That way you can travel with us.' Silverwing plucked one from her wing without a word. Yellowclaw gave Nick a feather, and other Birdfolk gave them to Dawn and Limpy. Then the four shouldered their packs and said goodbye and started down the hillside to the creek. Susan turned before she had gone far and looked at the Birdfolk. They stood without moving, tall and lonely; like Easter Island statues, she thought. And she thought how sad they were, creatures so brave and strong and beautiful, yet trapped inside a wall by ancient crimes. She raised her hand in farewell; then went over the hill and out of sight. Later she saw them far away, floating like eagles in the sky.

Dawn took the lead going down the pass. The snowgrass and thorn trees gave way to bush. As they went lower it grew with a tropical lushness and the air seemed warmer.

'It's like a jungle,' Nick said, twisting through creepers and giant leaves. 'I can't see bears living in this.'

But the river was ice cold. They stopped on a shingle fan where the stream from the pass flowed in and looked across the braided water at the bush, grey and misty, on the other side. Mount Nicholas took up the sky. Nick found himself grinning with pleasure as he looked at it. He felt sorry for Susan. Jimmy had promised to name a waterfall after her, but it could never be as impressive as this.

'We'll go up the river to the glacier,' Dawn said. She led them on the shingle bank at the side of the river. Several times they crossed creeks flowing down from the hills. Nick stopped to listen.

'Plenty of birds. No animals,' he said.

'I can smell Varg,' Dawn said. 'They're not far away.' She gave a curious smile, a little nod, as though she heard something the others could not hear. A moment later she stopped and smiled again. 'One is in the forest. He is keeping pace with us. Two are coming behind. And the fourth is on the other bank. If you look you will see him in the trees.'

They stared across the river and saw a movement in the bush; something white or blue. It vanished as they looked.

'They will kill us,' Limpy said.

'Perhaps. I don't know. I know they are hungry. Their minds are full of thoughts of meat.' She gave a troubled smile. 'There's another one ahead. Something hurts her.'

'Can you see into their minds?' Susan said.

'I catch their thoughts. I don't know whether I see or hear.'

'What do they look like?'

Dawn stopped again. 'There,' she said. 'See.'

One of the Varg trailing them had come out of the bush and was ambling up the shallows, with water splashing about its legs. It stopped when it saw them and returned their look indifferently, then lowered its head and drank from the river. Sunlight sent blue ripples up its neck, along its back.

'Huge,' Nick whispered. It was as large as a rhinoceros, but there was no mistaking its bear shape. It seemed a

70

forest and an ice creature both, with its sleek fur and grizzly head. 'Will it attack?'

'No,' Dawn said. 'They're herding us.' She pointed at the Varg across the river, standing on boulders, and the blue/white gleam of the one in the bush.

'Where to?'

'I think towards the leader up ahead.'

'Jimmy said not to be scared of them,' Susan said.

'Jimmy's not here,' Nick said.

They started off again, on pebble beds, and when they rounded the next bend saw the wall of the glacier. It rose as high as a ten-storey building, with a broad melt-lake at its foot. The river escaped in channels through the valley. Along both sides trees stood in black lines.

'There,' Dawn said.

A Varg was outlined against the trees. Dawn led them towards the creature. It had blue unblinking eyes, and they saw a wound on its shoulder with blood leaking into the fur. Something, a force, seemed to come from the animal, buffeting them like a wind. It made them shrink and cringe and walk more slowly.

'She is angry,' Dawn whispered.

Susan remembered Jimmy's letter and tried to make a picture of herself in her mind, but she found she was simply saying her name over and over. Yet the Varg swung its head, fixed her for a moment with its eyes. There was no friendliness, no interest there, she felt she was looking into empty holes, and knew that she, and all of them, were in deadly danger.

Dawn stopped. 'Wait here. Be still. It's me she wants to talk with.' She approached the Varg and stood several paces off, staring in its eyes. She was no taller than one of the creature's legs, yet watching, Susan felt she was its equal, and the Varg knew it. She struggled to see,

71

struggled to hear, what was passing between them, and glimpsed a jumble of pictures: sea, forest, priests, dogs. The Varg turned its head at her and gave a growl. 'Don't, Susan,' Dawn said. 'You will make her angry.' After a moment she walked to the animal's side and looked at the wound. Blood was dribbling from it, making a track through the fur on the Varg's leg.

Dawn turned to the others. 'Wait here. Don't move. I won't be long.' She turned and ran down the river bank, past the Varg standing there, and vanished in the trees.

'They'll kill us now,' Limpy whispered.

'I don't think so. Not yet. I'm hungry, anyway. I'm going to eat.' Nick opened his pack and took out the dried goat's meat the Birdfolk had given them. He was trying to keep their courage up. 'I wonder if she'd like some.' He walked up to the Varg and held out meat, but the animal only growled. Then it lay down and closed its eyes.

'It's losing a lot of blood, I think it's dying.' He bent and looked at the wound, but a growl, a bark of anger, came from one of the Varg down the river.

'Come away, Nick.'

He came back and sat with them. They ate, and drank water from the river. Shadows from the trees crept on the shingle and the face of Mount Nicholas turned pink. Nick looked at the Varg behind them. There were four, only twenty metres away, in a quarter circle, lying with their heads on their paws, like sheep dogs holding sheep. 'You couldn't get away from these things.'

The river was in shadow when Dawn came back. She ran over the shingle and the Varg lifted their heads. 'Susan,' she said, panting, 'come and help me.' They went to the Varg and knelt beside her. 'She's very sick.' The wound was bleeding steadily.

'What happened?'

'She was catching salmon at the river bar. Priests of Ferris came in a boat. They're frightened of the Varg and hunt from the sea. They shot at her with cross-bows. One of the bolts struck her in the shoulder. She swam to the forest and escaped. Another Varg tore the bolt out with its teeth. But unless we stop the bleeding she will die.'

She opened her pouch and took out some yellow fruit and a bundle of leaves.

'I know these,' Susan said. 'Breeze used them for my rope burns when Odo Cling tied me up.'

'I hope I have enough. There are not many growing this far south.' Dawn split the fruit and laid the leaves inside. She left them for a moment, then opened them and took leaf skeletons out. 'Give me the halves one by one.' She squeezed juice in the wound.

The Varg opened her eyes and lifted her head. She gave a grunt of pain as Dawn smeared juice on her fingers and worked it in the cut. 'If I go deep enough the artery will heal.'

'Have you told her?'

'She knows.'

The other Varg came close, herding Nick and Limpy. Dawn finished working on the wound. She went to the river and washed her hands. 'Now,' she said, coming back, 'you must talk to her, Susan. They know you are human, that is all. They don't like humans.'

Susan looked at the wounded bear. Even lying down the creature came up to her shoulder. She said, 'I am Susan Ferris,' but the Varg watched her with its eyes unblinking and showed no sign of understanding.

'Speak in pictures,' Dawn said.

'And you'd better be quick,' Nick said. 'I think they're going to eat us.' The Varg behind him was making a low continuous hungry grumble.

Susan wondered where to start. She thought the best thing to do was show she was an enemy of the priests, so she imagined one, dressed in white, holding dogs on a leash. She meant to put herself in the picture, running away, but had no time. The wounded Varg gave a roar of anger and rose to her feet. Those behind towered on their hind legs, with claws extended and lips drawn back from their teeth. Dawn ran in front of them, holding up her arms. Susan had an impression of images flashing from the Woodlander's mind, but the Varg towered higher. 'I can't stop them. Show them Jimmy Jaspers,' Dawn cried.

Susan did not know what picture to think of. The four great beasts seemed to blot out the sky. 'Jimmy,' she cried; and at once a picture came – Jimmy standing by the bridge, with his axe in his hands, taunting Odo Cling, daring him to cross. And a second picture fitted in beside it: Jimmy saying goodbye, accepting the feather. 'Keep it, Jimmy. Wear it for me.' 'I will. I will, Susie.' Nick was there too, and Brand and Breeze, standing on the plateau in the midday sun. She concentrated on keeping the picture clear, then added to it. She saw the old man placing the feather carefully round his neck, and her affection for him, her grief at losing him, made tears trickle on her cheeks.

'Susan,' Dawn's voice said, 'open your eyes. You're safe now.'

She opened them and blinked the tears away. The Varg had dropped back on all fours and were looking at her in a thoughtful way, although a rumble of uncertainty came from one. She turned to the leader and found she had sunk to the ground. Dawn slipped by and looked at the wound. It was bleeding again. She busied herself, squeezing more juice in. 'Now,' she said, 'start again, Susan. Go very slowly. And be careful.'

So Susan told her story. Soon it seemed natural to speak in pictures not words. She slipped them into her mind like slides into a viewer. And slowly she told their adventures. She showed the struggle against the Halfmen – and how Jimmy Jaspers had saved them twice. She placed the Halves on the Motherstone. Otis Claw died. And she said goodbye to Jimmy. The bears 'listened', nodding now and then. They gave an impression of sagaciousness.

Then Susan told about her return to O. Carefully she showed priests hunting with their dogs, and though the bears rumbled they made no move. She showed their flight, and their rescue by Seeker. Then she brought them to Shady Home. She did not think the bears would understand writing, but she imagined Jimmy writing his letter while the great blue bear lay at the door. She showed the opening of the box, and herself reading, and then the journey south, the flight with the Birdfolk. The bears stirred at the image, and Dawn made pictures, showing it was true.

It was dark when they finished. Only the blunt crest of Mount Nicholas stood in the light. Susan was exhausted. She sat down in front of the wounded Varg and rested her head in her arms. Then she found an image slowly forming in her mind. It was a picture of herself and Jimmy. She wondered where it came from, she had not thought of it. They stood facing each other in a place she could not recognize. There was ice all around, shining blue. The picture grew sharper and made her head ache.

'Answer,' Dawn whispered.

'What?'

'She wants to know why you want Jimmy Jaspers.'

'To destroy the Temple.'

'Tell her then.'

All Susan could do was make a picture of the old man in

her head. Then, with great effort, she placed herself beside him. She imagined Deven's Leap, with a temple of white marble built on it – a temple she had never seen. Priests swarmed in it like wasps, and the High Priest sat on his throne, with painted face, with yellow eyes, and Ferris bones hanging on his chest. Jimmy raised his axe and banged on the gates, and they swung open. She walked in, Jimmy at her side, and faced the Priest. And hen somehow, in a way she could not reverse, Jimmy faded, he was gone, and only she was there, standing alone, as in Soona's dream.

She could make no more pictures after that.

CHAPTER SIX

Nick Whistles a Tune

They walked on Varg trails in the bush, with the glacier on their right hand, gleaming through the trees. The bear in front flickered in the shadows, white and blue. He rippled like flowing water, and the pad pad of his feet was the only sound. Nick and Susan, Dawn and Limpy, followed silently.

They had set out in the dawn, leaving the wounded Varg by the river. The bear who led them was an old creature with a shaggy head and bad-tempered eyes. They felt he would just as soon kill them as help them. But two others, younger, came behind and sent reassuring images to Dawn and Susan. They made pictures of the glacier, a cave and a creek, and the sun at its high point in the sky. Jimmy was in the cave, Susan thought, and the sun meant they would get there at midday.

The bear led them out of the bush and climbed among the weathered ice towers of the glacier. They crossed it at an angle, heading for a valley gouged in the side of Mount Nicholas. The glacier made a groaning, as though huge forces pulled in it. The ice towers leaned with a gravitational weight. Susan looked down the length of its curve through the bush to the wide shingle river. She could not understand why all that ice did not simply tumble down in an avalanche.

They scrambled over boulders on the other side and stood on Mount Nicholas. A stream from the tops dived under the glacier and boomed away with a sound too loud for it. They went up the valley by its side and wound up a path over a bluff, and there, at the snow-line, found the cave. A giant boulder beetled over it, with a forward thrust that seemed to push them away. The bear led them to it, and faced them, rolling its head as though denying them entry. But the young bears came up and butted him aside in a friendly way. Susan found a picture of Jimmy forming in her mind.

'Is he in there?'

'We'll need torches,' Nick said, peering into the cave. 'How far in do we have to go?'

The bears made no answer, and Susan guessed they did not know. The cave was probably a forbidden place. She looked at it uncertainly. There was only one way Jimmy might be alive, but now she was so close to him it seemed impossible.

Dawn and Limpy ran back to the glacier and gathered broken branches from its edge. They managed to get four alight, and holding them high, went into the cave. It was cold inside – as cold as a freezing chamber in a meat works, Nick thought – and the walls and floor were filmed with ice. They climbed, curving left, then right, walking by globes of ice bulging on the walls. The light of their torches struck into them, making them glow with the purity of sapphires, emeralds. Columns of ice stood up from the floor and seemed to play like fountains. They came to a chamber so wide their torches were lost in it, gleaming in a corner, like glow-worms. Boulders lay on the floor, side by side, row after row. They walked among them, lost in wonder, not daring to speak. Hundreds, hundreds, white boulders – white bears.

'This is where they come to die,' Susan whispered.

'Like the elephants' graveyard,' Nick said. His voice came back in an echo. 'Do you think Jimmy's here?'

'Somewhere.'

'If they're all dead then he's dead too.' He laid his hand on one of the bears. Its fur was ridged like knife blades. 'Frozen stiff.'

Although there was no hope now, they searched among the bodies, their voices growing hollower. It was Dawn, scouting ahead, who found Jimmy Jaspers. They heard her shout of surprise, or shout of fear, and ran towards her torch, far down the hall. She stood before two columns of ice running from the ceiling to the floor. The light shone into them, rainbow-coloured, magnified, and there in the smaller Jimmy stood, with his eyes closed, and his arms folded, and a smile, or grimace of pain, on his lips. They saw his whiskers, his sparse hair, his stained teeth, and his throat – a turkey throat; his chest-hair, grey and tangled, above the rags of a bushman's singlet. It seemed he might open his eyes and step out and speak to them.

'Jimmy, Jimmy,' Susan whispered. She put out her hand, but it met only the smooth ice of the column.

'This must be the bear,' Limpy said. He was at the thicker column, and the bear glittered inside, blue as bird shells. He stood three metres tall, with yellow claws unsheathed, and snout lifted as though testing the wind.

'Ben,' Dawn said softly. 'The Vargs told me about him. He roamed further than any bear before him. And came home with a human friend. They entered the cave, but not to die.'

'They're dead,' Limpy said. 'A hundred turns in ice. They must be dead.'

'I thought we'd find them hibernating, not set in ice,' Susan said.

'You can't hibernate for a hundred years,' Nick said. 'Not even bears.'

'So it was all for nothing. Poor Jimmy.' She laid her

79

forehead on the ice column. That was as close as she could come to him.

'We're not giving up yet,' Nick said. 'We've got to get him out.'

'Let him be at peace.'

'Don't be wet.' He pushed her away from the column. 'Jimmy said come, and here we are. He doesn't look dead to me. This could be some sort of suspended animation. Deep freeze. They're experimenting with it on Earth. So maybe the bears know how to do it.'

Susan looked into the column again. There was no doubt Jimmy seemed unchanged. He looked as cunning and greedy as ever; and his colour was healthy. There was no feeling of death about him. If it weren't for the ice encasing him he looked as if he might stretch and yawn. And suddenly she wanted to get him out. She thought of him suffocating in there. She wanted to get him into the air, into sunlight.

'His axe,' she said. 'Where is it?'

They found it lying at his feet, as though he had placed it there. But it was set in ice and Nick could not get it free. He sent Dawn and Limpy outside for stones and chipped at the ice with them until he had freed a sheet with the axe in it. They carried it outside and broke it free and thawed it in the stream and in the sun. Then they made new torches. The bears watched, and Dawn told them what they meant to do.

'They say we can bring Jimmy Jaspers out but not Ben.'

'We'll leave Ben to Jimmy – if he wakes up.'

Back in the cave Nick stood on a pile of stones and attacked the column above Jimmy's head. He chopped it like a tree. The ice was almost as hard as iron, jarring his hands, making him frightened the axe would break. But

Jimmy had made the handle from a thorn branch and tempered the blade, and slowly the ice was eaten through. Then Nick hacked a circle round Jimmy's feet and drove wedges of stone under the ice. The column leaned and fell and the others caught it and lowered it to the ground. Jimmy lay there on his back as though it was all no business of his. There was only one way to get him outside. Nick trimmed the ragged base and they rolled the ice column like a tree trunk. When they came to the downward slope they let it slide, but it got away from them, running like a sled. It burst from the cave, scattering bears, and charged down the hill, throwing up a bow wave of earth. It came to a halt standing upright, with Jimmy on his head.

'It's his sense of humour,' Nick said. They dug the column out and rolled it to the stream. Then Nick and Susan worked on it through the evening and into the night. Nick chipped with the axe and Susan with a stone and the water of the stream also made inroads on the ice, melting it slowly. Limpy and Dawn built a fire on the bank and made Nick and Susan sit by it from time to time and warm themselves. But always they crept back to where the column lay beached like a driftwood log. Susan chipped round Jimmy's face and throat, striking delicately. Tiny splinters broke away. Nick hacked with short blows down the length of his body, sending little hail storms of crushed ice into the stream. The bears watched. The wounded female had struggled up from the river and she lay by the fire, with Dawn close by her side, and kept her pale unblinking eyes on Jimmy. Once she limped to the stream and licked the ice on his face with a sand-papery tongue. It seemed to Susan an act of homage.

At last they were done. Jimmy's back was still encased in ice but only a paper-thin sheet covered his front.

Already the toes of his boots were free, and the knot of his belt. Susan washed handfuls of water over his face, smoothing the ice, and she watched as Nick struck gently, at knee and hip, with the heel of the axe, and lifted sheets of ice away like a mould. Then she tapped around Jimmy's skull and along his jaw. Cracks showed in the ice. She chipped, and got her fingers in, and lifted the glassy mask away. She knelt looking at Jimmy in the light of a torch Dawn held close. Plugs of ice filled his mouth and nose. She felt his hair. It was as sharp as needles. And his cheeks and throat were iron-hard.

'What do we do? He's still not alive.'

'And he's not dead,' Nick said.

'The Vargs say bring him to the fire,' Dawn said.

So they freed Jimmy from his bed of ice and dragged him to the fire and laid him close. Light danced on his face, making him wink and leer.

'They say sleep now,' Dawn said. 'They will do the rest.'

'What are they going to do?'

As if in answer the female limped to Jimmy and began licking his face. The others gathered about and fell to licking and the rasp of their tongues filled the air.

'They look as if they're eating him,' Nick whispered.

'I trust them. I'm so tired. I've got to sleep.'

They warmed and dried themselves at the fire and wrapped themselves in their Woodlander blankets, warm as mohair, and lay down on beds Limpy had made. The last sounds they heard as they went to sleep were the tongues of the bears.

Dawn woke them in the morning with herb tea and jungle fruit. The bears were gone – hunting, Dawn said sadly – and Jimmy lay as though sleeping on the other side of the embers. They went around and knelt by him. Susan touched him softly on the forehead.

'Nick, he's warm.'

Nick lifted one of the old man's arms and let it drop. He put his ear to his chest. 'His heart's beating. Only just. Is he breathing?'

'It's hard to tell.'

'Wait a minute.' He fetched his Woodlander knife and held it in the stream to make it cold. Then he put the blade by Jimmy's lips. After a moment a faint misting showed.

'The bears are worried,' Dawn said. 'They have made his heart beat and his blood flow, but it must be stronger. He breathes, but not enough. They think he's waiting for something. Some message that will make him want to live.'

Nick put his mouth by Jimmy's ear. 'Jimmy,' he yelled, 'it's us. Nick and Susan. Wake up.'

'No,' Susan said. 'That's no good.'

'Well, how do we wake him?'

'I don't know. He'll die if we do the wrong thing.' She looked at his wicked old face. Wicked or kindly? There was no telling whether Jimmy was bad or good. All she knew was that she could not go on without him. She would never be able to fight the priests by herself. And more than that – she loved him. He was dirty, bad-tempered, dishonest – but she loved him. 'Jimmy, why didn't you say how to wake you up?' Then the old man seemed to wink at her, he seemed to grin. It was only a trick of her mind, but something told her she must trust him. Trust Jimmy. He was cunning. He would never let them get this far and fail.

'Nick,' she said, 'it must be in the letter.' She went over it in her mind, sentence by sentence. And then she came to the end, and she had it. How like Jimmy to put the most important thing in a P.S. She laughed. 'Dawn's right, he's waiting. He told us what to do to wake him up.'

'How . . . ?' Nick began. He was looking blank.

' "Wissel me fayvrit tune wen you cum." '

'That was just a joke.'

'He was telling us what to do. What could be clearer? The only trouble is I'm no good at whistling.'

'I am. And I know the tune. "Barnacle Bill the Sailor".'

'Whistle it. He's been asleep long enough.'

Nick tried a couple of practice notes. Then he knelt by Jimmy and bent close to his ear. The jaunty little tune rang out in notes sharp and clear. For a moment it had no effect. Then a tremble ran through Jimmy, and grew into a shuddering, a quaking. He sucked in a breath that made his ribs creak. He opened his eyes and stared at the sky. Then he screwed them up like a newborn baby. His mouth opened, trembling, and a bellow of pain came out and made the mountain and the glacier ring.

'Jimmy, Jimmy,' Susan cried. She tried to hold him, but he threw her off. He stood up, rocking on his feet, raised his blind face to the sky, and howled in agony.

'Jimmy.'

The bears came over the glacier and galloped up to them. Even the wounded one came as fast as a charging rhino. And Jimmy stopped his noise, perhaps because the ground shook as though in an earthquake. He saw the bears – the firs thing he had seen – and blinked at them without understanding. Then he turned his eyes to Susan and she saw him struggle to know not who she was, but who *he* was. He seemed like a baby standing there, with his arms hanging. Then his legs gave way and he sat down on the ground and started crying.

She went to him and put her arms around him.

'Susie?'

'I'm here, Jimmy.'

'I'm gettin' born again.'

'I know.'

'It hurts.'

'I know. You're all right now. Go to sleep, Jimmy.'

'Yes. I will. I gotter sleep. I gotter learn again.'

She helped him to lie down.

'Is Nick here?'

'Here I am, Jimmy.' He knelt on the other side of the old man.

'It's good to see you both. I waited a long time.' He sighed and closed his eyes and went to sleep. Susan wiped the tears from his face.

Jimmy slept all through the day and through the night, while Nick and Susan took turns watching him. The bears came and went, and sniffed at him, making growls of approval. Dawn brought leaves that burned on the fire with the smell of billy tea. The smoke curled round Jimmy's face and made him smile. Only Limpy was unhappy, thinking of Soona at the Temple. Time was going by. Now there were only thirteen days left.

'Don't worry, Limpy. We'll get there.'

'Why can't we carry him on a stretcher?'

'Because he's got to wake Ben up. Ben was in his dream.'

So Limpy searched for stones at the side of the glacier and kept himself busy grinding a new edge on Jimmy's axe.

Susan and Nick sat up late by the old man. The fire sank until only a few red embers were left. The stars were very bright, lighting the sky over Mount Nicholas. Dawn was sleeping by the side of the bear she nursed. A friendship had grown up like the one between Jimmy and Ben.

85

'Do you think Ben will be jealous of us?' Susan asked.

They slept, and when they woke the sun was in the sky over the mountain. Jimmy sat between them, gnawing a bone. He wiped his mouth.

'You're a dozy pair. I thought you'd never wake up.'

'Jimmy! You're all right.'

'Course I'm all right. I had too much shut-eye, that's all. Me head feels like I been on a binge.'

'You've been asleep for a hundred years.'

'Yer don't say so. I reckon that must be a bloddy record.'

'Jimmy, do you know what's happened on O?'

'Yeah, I know. I been talkin' to yer mate.' He nodded at Limpy. 'He's put a new edge on me axe.' He spat on the blade and wiped it with his sleeve. 'That's a good job, youngker.'

'Did he tell you about Soona?'

'Yeah. We gotter save her. And put a bomb under them bloddy priests. But first I gotter get Ben out of that cave. He ain't gunner like bein' woke up.'

'You didn't like it.'

'It weren't no picnic.'

'Jimmy, do you know what they call you? The Terrible One.'

'No kiddin'? I don't feel terrible. I feel bloddy horrible, that's for sure. Me head's like a pressure cooker.'

'Jimmy, stop complaining. Have you still got the feather I gave you?'

'Sure I have.' He felt inside his singlet and pulled out the feather on its string. It flashed red and blue in the morning sun. He turned it round, looking at it. 'I guess they're all dead, eh? Wanderer and Redwing?'

'A long time ago.'

'And Brand and Breeze?'

'Yes.'

'It makes yer feel funny.' He put the feather away. 'I'll miss them Woodlanders. An' them Birdfolk.'

'We miss them too.'

'Yeah.' He smiled for the first time and patted their knees. 'It's good to see you. Thanks for wakin' me up. Now I gotter wake ole Ben.'

'How did you meet him, Jimmy?'

'I told yer I was gunner do some explorin', didn' I? Well, I come down here. Come over the pass, an' I saw this mountain, an' I thought, that'll do fer young Nick. Do yer like it, youngker?'

'It's great.'

'I named something after you too, Susie. But I'll show yer that another day. Anyway, I còme down to the river, an' I went out spearin' salmon by the mouth, big ones, big as yer leg. An' when I looked round, there was this bloddy great bear standin' there lookin' at me, lickin' 'is chops just like I was breakfast. Well, I thinks, this is it, the end of the road fer Jimmy. There was nowhere to run. And me axe wouldn't be no good, not against him. You wait till yer see 'im, then yer'll know.'

'We've seen him in the cave.'

'Yeah, that's right. Ole Ben.'

'What did you do?'

'Nothin' to do. I sat down. I'll show 'im I'm not scared, I thinks. Me hands was shakin' so bad I stuck 'em in me armpits to hold 'em still. An' then I thinks, I'll stare 'im out. I'll hypnotize the bogger. Show 'im who's boss. If I blinks first he can have me. I thought I stood a pretty good chance, yer see. I'm good at starin' out. It's a trick I learned to keep me out of fights. But these bears . . . ' He laughed. 'Have yer seen their eyes? They never blink. They can go all day. Course, I didn't know that. Well, I sat there lookin', an' he sits back on his haunches an' looks at me, steady like, but kind of grinnin', like he's not too hungry yet, he doesn't mind wastin' a bit of time. An' we go on all the mornin', an' I ain't had no breakfast, see, I'm starvin', an' there's these three or four bloddy great salmon lyin' right at me feet an' I can't eat 'em. By this time I can tell he's startin' to have a bit of respec' fer me. He's not lookin' so sure of himself, an' I think, maybe he's gettin' tired of the game, but we've got a kind of agreement see, an' he can't eat me till it's over. So I think, I might as well die with me belly full, an' I say to 'im, "How about time out fer lunch?" No answer. He just growls. That's not a nice sound. But still, I can't help thinkin' about them salmon. I think of them baked and I think of them grilled. There's pictures of salmon floatin' in me mind. An' then something funny happens. It's like he sees them, and he shows me one of his. It's there, in me mind, clear as daylight, a picture of this bear eatin' salmon. An' he gets up and walks over to me, never blinkin', and he nudges one of them fish closer to me, an' the greedy so an' so, he keeps three for himself. "Well, thanks," I says, an' then real slow, so's he knows what I'm doing, I closes me eyes. An' yer know what he does? He laughs. They do, yer know. It's somethin' yer don't hear often. An' he closes his eye, just one of them. He winks at me.

'So we had a picnic. I got some driftwood and made a fire and baked me fish, and he swallers his in a couple of gulps, and we moves further up the sand, cause the tide's comin' in, an' yer know what happens then, just when I think everything's hunky dory an' me an' this bear is mates? He sits down, an' he starts starin' at me. An' we're off again. Yeah. The starin' match. We just been havin' a rest, that's all. He starts it up again, an' I know

I'm right back where I started – if I blinks he's goin' to eat me.'

'Oh, Jimmy.'

'It's no laughin' matter. After lunch I likes to have a sleep. But here I am fightin' fer me life. And after a while I figures the only chance I got is to give 'im a fright. Make 'im blink that way. So I start tellin' stories. Like, I think of a bomb, I make this picture, see, and suddenly it goes off. Boom! Or I think of a track in the bush an' I show the bear walkin' down it, an' suddenly he falls in a bloddy great bear trap. That sort of thing. But it's no use. He just sits there grinnin'. So I tell 'im the story of my life. 'E's interested. There's something about the Earth that surprises 'im, specially when I show 'im polar bears and grizzlies. Then I gets on to O. An' I show 'im the fight with Odo Cling, all that stuff, an' 'e knows about Cling, 'e don't like 'im. I can tell 'e's impressed, specially when I chucks Cling orf that cliff. I think that maybe he's startin' to like me a bit. But does 'e blink? No 'e don't. An' my eyes is achin'. They feel like hard-boiled eggs. An' I know that any minute now I'm goin' ter keel over. It's nearly night time, see? We been goin' all through the afternoon. An' I says to meself, this is it. Goodnight Jimmy. I'm past carin' any more. An' then, you know what 'e does, ole Ben? Just as me eyes starts to close?'

'No.'

'No.'

'He closes his. Easy as you like. Closes 'em up.'

'He let you win?'

'He let me.'

'What did you do?'

'Me? I stands up. I goes to 'im, barin' me teeth, real fierce. I makes it like I'm havin' 'im fer dinner. I'm the winner, after all. An' then I lie down on the sand an' I go

89

to sleep. An' the last thing I hear as I pass out is ole Ben laughin'.'

'And you've been friends ever since?'

'Sure. Me and Ben. We went explorin'. Way up north, but that was too hot for Ben, so we came south. When the straits iced up in winter we crossed over an' had a look down there. An' we went out east, past Mount Morningstar. We had five years explorin', me and Ben. Then I had me dream and we went to sleep. Now I better get in there and wake 'im up. 'E's a lazy ole coot.'

'I'll help you,' Nick said.

They went into the cave and Nick and Limpy held torches while Jimmy chopped Ben free. It took all morning, and rolling Ben out and levering him into the creek the rest of the day. The firelight played on the ice, making blue gleams slide across it. Ben lay on his back, with his paws upraised and his yellow claws pointing like flames.

The next day Jimmy chopped the ice away. Ben was too heavy to lift from the stream, so the other bears stood in the water licking him. It was another day before he was warm. Then Jimmy sent everyone away.

'It ain't gunner be pretty. Ole Ben's likely to bust a few things up. An' he'll be hungry. So you youngkers keep out of sight.'

'How will you wake him?'

Jimmy grinned. 'I'll whistle a tune.'

They crossed the glacier and climbed into the bush on the other side. Soon they heard the bear bellowing. The sound made the valley boom and tumbled boulders on Mount Nicholas. The glacier seemed to groan and shift. The sound went on and on, making them ache with pain. Dawn stood leaning on the wounded bear, comforting her. The others knelt on the ground with their heads down, trying to blot the noise out with their arms. When silence came at last they had no strength to stand up again.

Later in the day they saw the bears hauling the carcass of a boar over the glacier for Ben to eat. In the dusk Jimmy and Ben made their way back, moving side by side in the towers of ice. The whole party went down to the river, where Nick and Limpy built a fire. Ben walked as though drunk, and Jimmy was exhausted. Both sank down in the warmth and were asleep in minutes. The other bears slept further off in the trees. The children heard them sighing and coughing. The events of the last few days had overwhelmed them. Everyone, bears and humans, seemed dazed by the miracle of Jimmy's and Ben's return.

The fire died down and they slept. The last faint sunset glow faded quietly from Mount Nicholas.

CHAPTER SEVEN

Stonehaven

Jimmy drew a map on the ground. 'This is us. Mount Nicholas. The river. And Sheercliff is up here. There's two ways we can go. Over the pass, the way you came, or out to the coast and up through Wildwood. That's the way I'd go, I reckon it's shorter.'

Limpy made a cross on the coast. 'That is Stonehaven. I'd like to stop and tell my parents I'm safe.'

'No reason why not,' Jimmy said. 'So let's get started.'

Dawn said goodbye to the wounded bear. She stood conversing silently, and had a smile on her mouth as they started off. 'I've promised to come back. We are like Jimmy and Ben,' she told Susan.

Five Varg escorted them to the coast. They walked down the river bank for an hour, then turned north-west through the bush, climbing on trails that led over hills and down a creek to the sea. Towards nightfall a young bear scouting ahead came loping back. He and Ben and Jimmy and the Varg talked for a moment and Susan had an impression of images flashing back and forth, too quick for her to see. But she glimpsed, or thought she glimpsed, figures in white.

'Dawn?'

'Yes. Priests.'

'Where are they?'

'Down on the beach. It is the party that tried to kill my friend.'

Jimmy came to them. 'There's a dozen of 'em. They've anchored for the night.'

'Have they got dogs?'

'No, not on boats.'

'What are we going to do?'

'Kill 'em.'

'No . . .'

'Come with me, Susie. I'll show you something.'

They went down the trail, moving quietly, and came to the edge of a bluff overlooking the beach. They lay in the trees and ferns looking at the priests. Some were cooking meat at a fire. Others sat cross-legged on the sand, meditating over their Ferris bones. And a third group was pegging something out between the trees and the high-water line. They gleamed white in their leather suits. The sea, bush, sand – it was peaceful, beautiful, Susan thought. She could not believe killing was going to start. There was no reason for it.

'Jimmy . . . ?' she whispered.

'It's gotter be. Don't yer see what they got down there?' He pointed at the priests beyond the fire. She thought for a moment they were pegging out mats, blue/white mats. Then she saw.

'Varg skins?'

'Three of them,' Nick said.

'They're trophies,' Jimmy said. 'They come down here hunting. They kill the Varg and hang their skins in their temples. So when they gets the chance the Varg kill them. That's the way it is.'

'The priests kill everything that lives,' Limpy said. 'Now it's their turn.'

'I couldn't stop these bears if I wanted to,' Jimmy said. 'Look at ole Ben.'

The other bears were used to priests, they stood waiting, patient, but the old bear was rolling his head in grief and rage. His body was swaying from side to side.

'I never seen 'im like this. He's going to charge,' Jimmy said.

'Don't you go, Jimmy.'

'Where he goes, I go. Wish me luck.'

'They've got cross-bows.'

Jimmy gripped his axe. 'An' I got this.' He went into the bush, moving along the edge of the bluff, and a moment later Susan saw him in the trees at the edge of the sand. The five Varg spread out on either side. Then they waited. Waited for old Ben.

Up on the bluff Dawn drew the others back into the bush. 'Hide yourselves. When his rage bursts out he will kill whatever he sees.'

They lay and watched Ben. And at last something broke in the old bear. The shock of it lifted him, propelled him forward over the bluff, roaring. The children ran to the edge and saw him ploughing down, braced on his legs, spraying stones and dust out on both sides. Jimmy and the Varg were charging across the beach, and the priests were scattering, some for the bush, others for the water. Two or three managed to load their cross-bows as they ran.

Dawn and Susan did not stay to watch. They went back into the bush, and Nick joined them a moment later, his face pale. They stood in the trees listening to the fight – a roaring of bears, a shrieking of men, and now and then the twanging of a bow string – until at last it fell to isolated shouts and cries of pain. Limpy came running through the trees. He too was pale but his eyes were gleaming. 'It's over. They're all dead.'

'All of them?'

'Every one. They never had a chance.'

'Is Jimmy all right?'

'Yes. One of the bears is dead.'

'Not Ben?'

'No. We'll wait here a while. The bears are feasting.'

They waited until they heard Jimmy calling, then followed Ben's path, sliding down the bluff. The bears had dragged the remains of the priests into the bush. They were digging in the sand above the tide line, making a grave for their dead companion. He had taken a cross-bow bolt in his throat. When the grave was ready they rolled him in and laid the bear skins on him for burial too. The children picked up broken Ferris bones and took them to the grave.

'They're human bones, Jimmy. Can we put them in?'

They filled the grave and stood by it for a moment, not knowing what to do. But Susan saw how peaceful the bay would be when they had gone – a good place for the final resting. She wished the priests could have been buried too.

'I wouldn't mind havin' me own grave here,' Jimmy said.

They sat on the sand while the bears swam, washing blood from their fur.

'Where do we go tomorrow, Jimmy?'

'Up the coast.'

'We've lost half a day coming here,' Limpy said.

'Not if you're as good a sailor as you say.' He nodded at the priests' boat, anchored off the beach. 'Do you reckon you could take 'er out?'

Limpy looked at the boat, rising and falling on the gentle waves. 'She's got a triple hull. She's built for speed.'

'Well?'

'I can sail her.'

'Will she take all of us?'

'She took twelve priests.'

'O.K. You're the captain. You'd better go and have a look at your ship.'

Limpy and Nick and Susan swam out to the boat. Limpy checked the rigging and ropes and Nick and Susan the supplies. They dropped most of the priests' belongings overboard. Susan found an image of her, with eagle wings outspread and a look of foolish holiness on her face. It made her shiver and she threw it overboard with the rest. But she kept a little book of her 'sayings'. 'Listen, Nick. "Those who believe in me shall fly in Earth, but the unbeliever shall fall and a breaking of bones shall be his punishment." '

'When are you supposed to have said that?'

She turned back to the beginning and read quickly.

'Let me guess,' Nick said. 'You appeared in a vision to the first High Priest and he wrote it all down.'

'That's it. That's it exactly.'

'He must have been a pretty smart operator.'

They slept on the beach, all except Limpy, who could not be persuaded off the boat. He brought it in close in the dawn and the others climbed aboard. Ben settled himself by the deck-house and would not be moved, but Limpy gave the others a lesson on sailing. He showed them how to set sails and keep them trimmed and what to do when the boat jibed. But the wind was a southerly, he said. They would run before it all the way to Stonehaven.

They set out from the bay into open water. The four blue bears stood on the beach watching them go. Later they filed up the bluff and went from sight. The stretch of sand shrank until it was no more than a yellow bite in the long blue coast. Then Limpy turned north and the trimaran sped on the southerly, over the choppy sea, through the morning and afternoon and into the night. They saw no other boats but passed a village, set in a cleft in a headland. Limpy pointed out the temple, a white stone building taller than the others, with outspread stone wings fixed on its dome.

When he had to sleep he put out a sea anchor. They showed no lights. The next day they went north again, with the breeze still behind them. The coast grew wilder. Towards dusk Limpy pointed out a craggy headland.

'Stonehaven is on the northern side. I know a place on the south where we can anchor. No one will find us. If I go in the night we will lose no time.'

He brought the trimaran into a cove behind a reef and they ate and talked until the sun was down. Then Limpy lowered himself over the side and swam ashore. They saw him scurry over the beach into the rocks. 'I'll be back by morning,' he called.

'I hope he is.'

'What we haven't worked out,' Jimmy said, 'is how we're going to rescue this girl. We can't just knock on the door and say we want her.'

'And we've got to destroy the religion too,' Susan said. 'I've got to tell them it's all wrong.'

'They won't believe you,' Nick said.

'We got to show 'em, not tell 'em,' Jimmy said. 'And we got to nobble this High Priest. Maybe I could chuck 'im orf Sheercliff like Odo Cling.' He stopped for a moment and talked with Ben.

'Yeah,' Jimmy said. 'Ben reckons them Birdfolk would be a help. If we had a half a dozen we could fly in an' grab the High Priest. An' rescue Soona too.'

'They can't fly outside their land,' Nick said.

'Sure they can. They just don't know how. Ben knows, don't you old feller?'

The bear nodded.

'But it's no good telling 'em. They gotter see for

themselves. Mind you, we could give 'em a nudge.' He talked to Ben again. The old bear seemed troubled.

'He's not too sure he wants Birdfolk flying outside. They used to be a pretty blood-thirsty lot. That's why they got the spell put on 'em. But I reckon only the good ones would get out. The rest are too full of 'emselves. They'd never do it.'

'Do what?'

Jimmy grinned. 'You've heard about the Prohibition. They got it carved up in all the Halls. "Unless ye be as Humble as the Worm . . . " What could be plainer? It tells 'em exactly what to do. But they're so bloddy pleased with themselves they can't see it. They can't see past flying. The Birdfolk mind don't work in no other way.'

'You mean . . . ?' Nick said. He was so excited he flashed an image at Ben. It was the first time he had 'talked'. The bear grinned at him and sent back an answer.

'I could go to them,' Nick cried. 'I could go to Morninghall and tell them.'

'No,' Jimmy said. 'They gotter see fer themselves, like I told yer. But what you can do is drop a hint. One or two of 'em would prob'ly catch on.'

'Silverwing would. Yellowclaw would,' Susan said.

'I'll go,' Nick said. 'I'll start now. We'll get to the Temple almost as soon as you.'

'You'll need Dawn to guide you,' Susan said.

'Yes,' the Woodlander said. 'We'll go to Shady Home and over the pass. The Birds will find us there and take us to Morninghall.'

They gathered up their belongings and swam ashore. Nick called goodbye from the beach. In his eagerness to go he had hardly noticed Susan. She watched while he and Dawn crossed the sand and merged into the rocks. He was her link with home. Jimmy was a man of O now and had a strangeness about him that sometimes frightened her. And Ben, she felt, associated her with the Priests of Ferris. She felt lonely on the boat and wished Limpy would come. He belonged on O too, but his worries were ones she might share.

Jimmy sensed her mood and tried to entertain her with stories. And soon she was laughing and her depression passed. They lay under their blankets on the gently rocking boat and went to sleep. But Susan had troubled dreams. She dreamed of the Temple, a white building gleaming in the sun, but filled inside with gloomy labyrinths. She ran through corridors, and someone chased her. She could not see if it was the High Priest, but saw a white face flashing in the dark, and something running like a spider. She heard the rattle of bones and fled with arms outstretched – and knew she should not run, but turn and face him. The barking of dogs and cries of men came mingled with the noise of the bones. Then she woke, sweating, calling out, and saw Jimmy and Ben in the stern, facing the land. The sounds came from there. The barking and cries were real. She looked where Jimmy pointed and saw pricking lights on the headland.

Jimmy gave Ben a quick touch and the bear slid into the sea, making no splash. He did not surface for a long time, then Susan heard a noise of water on the reef. 'He'll work his way round to the track,' Jimmy said.

'Are they chasing Limpy?'

'Looks like it'.

The sky lightened quickly and the torches faded. Halfway down the slope she saw men running. One was a priest, holding two dogs. Men with spears and axes came behind. 'Fishermen from the village,' Jimmy said. 'They'll be no trouble. It's that priest we gotter watch.'

'Where's Limpy?'

Jimmy pointed lower down the headland. She saw Limpy scuttling there, in and out of bushes and rocks, sliding and jumping down. Every few metres he stopped to wait for a man behind.

'That must be his father.'

Ben waited hidden at the edge of the sand. In a moment a yell of rage came from up the hill.

'They've seen the boat,' Jimmy said. 'He's letting his dogs go.' The two animals flashed away from the men, darting like weasels down the hillside.

'They'll catch them,' Susan cried.

'They ain't seen ole Ben yet.'

Limpy and his father reached the beach. They ran over it towards the boat. The dogs were close behind and would have taken them before they reached the water. But as they came leaping down the last few metres of path, Ben rose from his hiding place and stood at his full height and gave a roar. The dogs braked frantically, yelping in terror, but their momentum rolled them against his legs. He could have killed them then, with two blows, but he kicked them away and roared again, and they fled yelping, up the hill, past the priest, ignoring his cries, through the fishermen, and along the hilltop towards the forest.

'He'll never see them again,' Jimmy laughed.

Then Ben started up the path, climbing slowly, letting the priest and his followers see him. They broke and ran, with yelps like those of the dogs. The priest ran fastest of all, a skinny frantic sprinter in his night-black clothes. Ben helped them on their way with another roar.

Meanwhile Limpy and his father had swum to the boat. Susan pulled the exhausted man aboard. He lay panting on the deck. Limpy ran to get the anchor up. He raised the sails and the boat started out of the bay.

'Wait for Ben,' Susan cried.

'He's all right,' Jimmy said. The old bear was coming down the path. He ambled across the sand, slid into the water, and surfaced a moment later by the boat. He pulled himself aboard, gouging the deck with his claws.

'Nice goin', Ben,' Jimmy said.

Susan helped Limpy's father sit up. She brought a drink for him and in a moment he was able to help Limpy take the boat through the broken water at the end of the reef. Limpy offered him the tiller.

'No, boy. This is your boat. I'll be crew.'

They reached the open water and the boat bucked as it made its way along the southern shore of the headland. Susan stood by Limpy at the tiller.

'What happened, Limpy?'

'I spent the night talking with my father. But someone must have seen our lamp. It is against the law to stay up late.'

'Is everything against the law?'

'People who talk at night might be plotting against the Temple. We heard the priest coming. So we ran. If Ben hadn't been there we'd be dead.'

'What will happen to your mother and grandmother?'

'They pretended to be sleeping. They are safe. But my mother – when I came she spoke again. For the first time. She will be well.' He looked away, pretending to be occupied with steering. Susan saw tears on his cheeks. His father came to stand at his side. He put his hand on Limpy's shoulder.

'Look to your boat, boy. Bring her into the wind.'

Limpy obeyed. He wiped his face.

'You are a sailor,' his father said. 'No priest will keep you from the sea.' He turned to Susan. 'Are you truly Susan Ferris?'

101

'Yes.'

'A human girl? No more than that?'

'Yes.'

'Then the priests are liars. I have always known it.' He looked from Susan to Jimmy and back again. 'My name is Kenno. I am a fisherman of Stonehaven. And I pledge myself to destroy the Priests of Ferris and the Temple. Will you help me?'

'We'll try,' Susan said.

'And save my daughter?'

'Yes. We'll save her.' It was easy to say at that moment. Later she began once more to wonder how.

After an hour's sailing Limpy turned the boat north and the headland slid behind them. Stonehaven village straggled down the cliffside to the sea. The morning sun lit buildings here and there, and threw long shadows in the streets. The tiny fields of grain made yellow splashes, and the white temple, with its spreading wings, gleamed like a pearl. It was peaceful, Susan thought, picturesque, like a tourist photo of a Mediterranean village. But as she watched, fishing boats nosed out from the harbour wall. Wind swelled their sails and seemed to lift them at the trimaran. A figure in white stood in the stern of the leading boat.

'The priest,' Kenno said.

'They won't catch us,' Limpy said. 'We're too fast.'

'What they will do is sail up the coast to Castle Rock. There are warboats there. Warboats can outsail us.'

'Our best chance is to get well ahead.'

He ordered more sail and Kenno broke out a spinnaker that bellied up and almost lifted the trimaran out of the water. The only thing Susan did not like was the black outstretched wings painted on it. She was starting to hate that emblem. But as the morning went

102

on the fishing boats dropped further and further behind.

They kept well out to sea and sailed through the night, with Limpy and Kenno taking turns at the tiller. In the morning they stopped for an hour on the seaward side of an island and filled their water tanks from a spring. Jimmy fished and Ben, diving off the rocks, caught fish in the kelp and swallowed them whole. Kenno cut a sapling and began making a bow. For a while Susan collected sharp stones for arrowheads, then she went to the southern tip of the island and searched the horizon. There was no sign of pursuing boats. She looked at the sea, heaving among the reefs, and wondered if Seafolk lived in these waters. It would be a good place. Plenty of fish, plenty of edible weed. But before she could make up her mind to call them Limpy signalled from the boat and she had to go back.

They put out to sea and continued their voyage north. Late in the afternoon the sun flashed on some buildings, far away on the shore.

'Castle Rock,' Kenno said. 'The priest will arrive tonight. There will be warboats after us in the morning.'

Behind Castle Rock plains stretched inland to a low ridge where Sheercliff began. It grew in height, bending away north. The land rose gradually beyond, and the dusty blue and green of it was Wildwood. Here and there Susan saw smoke, and it heartened her to see the mountains rising like a wall in the distance. No matter how busy they became, the priests would never manage to destroy those. And she thought of Nick and Dawn somewhere in Wildwood, on their way to Morninghall, over the mountains. She knew she must face the High Priest, and face him alone, but after that she had no idea what would happen. The Birdfolk might be the ones who saved Soona. Saving her was just as important as ending the Temple. She was curious about Soona, and felt an affection growing for the girl who had dreamed of her, dreamed her back to O – even though coming back had brought her into danger.

In the dawn of the following day they passed the mouth of the river Susan had travelled up on her way to place the Halves. The city rose on the plain beyond, with its towers dark over the morning mist. Susan strained to see, but could not make out Otis Claw's palace.

'They say it has fallen,' Kenno said. 'The city was evil and men abandoned it. Now it is a ruin where no one lives.'

'What about the Motherstone? What about the Halves?'

Kenno did not know. But Susan thought if the palace had fallen they would be buried under thousands of tons of rock – lost forever. Safe forever. Men would never interfere with the Halves again.

They sailed on and passed Susan's island. She saw the beach where she had landed on her glider and where she had been rescued by the Seafolk. She would have liked to go ashore, and she turned to ask Limpy if there was time. But the fierce look on his face stopped her.

'What is it, Limpy?'

'Look behind.'

She looked but could see nothing. Kenno came to her side and pointed. She saw two scraps of sail, like tiny pointed hats, far away south.

'Warboats,' he said.

To her they looked like yachts out for a sail. She found it hard to believe they were dangerous. It was only when she realized she could not see their hulls that she understood how large they were. But that also meant they were far away.

'They're too far back to catch us.'

'In two hours they will be in bow shot. And see how one is heading off. They will trap us before we round the cape.'

One of the warboats was heading out to sea. Ahead the coast curved north-east and disappeared in a haze.

'Part of it is an island,' Kenno said. 'There's a way between.'

'Deadman's Channel.' Limpy had gone pale. 'There is draft enough for us and not for them. But what about the other side? The Gut?'

Kenno smiled. 'I have always wanted to see it.'

Jimmy had come close. 'I've heard about this Gut. If it's as bad as they say I don't like our chances.'

'Would you rather face the warboats?'

Jimmy looked at them. Their hulls were starting to show over the horizon. 'I reckon not.' He 'spoke' with Ben, and Susan had an image of a tunnel in the sea, spinning and bottomless. The bear raised his head and seemed to shrug.

'It don't bother him. But what about Susie, here? She gets a vote.'

'It's simple,' Kenno said. 'If we stay to fight, we die. If we risk the Gut, we have a chance of living.'

'Is the Gut a whirlpool?' Susan asked.

'Yes,' Limpy said. 'But sometimes it is worse than others. Fishermen have risked it and got through.'

'Then we'll risk it.'

'We haven't got away from them warboats yet. They're comin' fast,' Jimmy said.

One of the boats was heading towards the far curve of the cape, but the second was making straight for them and seemed to grow larger every minute. When she strained her eyes she made out the spread-wing emblem on the sail. And soon she saw oars along the sides, working evenly and fast, like a centipede's legs.

Limpy kept their boat pointed at a hump in the coastline. The wind stayed southerly and they ran before it. Details on the land became clearer: thorn trees, isolated goats. And on the warboat a towering foredeck, a bow-wave like a sneering white moustache.

Kenno and Jimmy made a shelter for Limpy with hatch-covers. Then they sheltered in the deck-house. Kenno strung his bow. Looking out the front window, Susan saw the channel between the mainland and the island. It ran straight as a suburban street. She saw that Limpy would have only a metre or two on each side. If he got through his father would know he was a real sailor. She decided not to watch. She would sooner watch the warboat.

It was close enough for her to see priest bowmen leaning on the forward rail. She saw their Ferris bones like necklaces. The white close-fitting leather of their suits, their chalky faces, turned them into walking skeletons.

'See,' Kenno said, pointing out a tall priest on the point of the bow. 'It is our priest, from Stonehaven.' Even at that distance Susan saw the burning in his eye. A cry of command rang out from the warboat. The priests raised their cross-bows.

'Down,' Kenno said. 'Limpy, take care.' The boy was crouching in his shelter, with the tiller grasped through the opening of the hatch-covers. Susan heard a second shout from the warboat. She made herself small at the base of a wall. A second later a rapid thudding sounded as bolts struck the deck-house and the shelter. Several came through the window and smashed into the wall across the room.

'Pray that none take our rigging,' Kenno said. He

looked out the door. The first row of bowmen stepped back and a second took its place. Again the commands were shouted, and another volley of bolts struck the boat. They seemed stronger. The warboat was closing every minute.

Susan risked looking out the door. She hoped Ben was all right, forward of the deck-house. Limpy was crouched in his shelter and he gave a pale grin. But his eyes were focussed beyond her, on the channel entrance. She saw rocks flashing by on either side. Kenno jerked her back and a bolt whistled by her face. 'They have snipers in the rigging. But we are in the channel. They will have to haul to or run aground.'

He strung an arrow in his bow. Then he ran from the door and joined Limpy in the shelter. Susan risked another look. She saw him kiss the arrowhead, and offer it to Limpy. The boy kissed it. Then Kenno stood suddenly, drew back the string, released the arrow, all in one motion. Susan did not see it fly, but she watched the Stonehaven priest, and saw the shaft stand in his chest like a branch. He looked at it as if it were unbelievable. Then he toppled slowly into the sea. A shout of rage went up from the cross-bowmen. They released another volley, and it struck the boat. Kenno ran back to the deck-house.

'That was for Soona. And my wife.'

Limpy shouted, 'They're stopping.' The warboat threw about.

'They will put men ashore in boats,' Kenno said. 'We must go through quickly.'

The rocky walls of the channel were speeding by. Susan went on deck. Cross-bow bolts bristled everywhere. She saw holes in the sails where they had gone through. Kenno and Jimmy threw the hatch-covers overboard. Behind, the warboat closed the end of Deadman's

Channel like a door. Priests swarmed down rope ladders into boats. But the trimaran raced on, with its outside hulls almost clipping the rocks. The wind rushed down the channel and lifted it through, and they burst into the open, into a widening lake, with cliffs towering round it. On the other side was a shorter channel to the open sea.

'We go through there,' Kenno said. 'But the Gut is outside. We must go round the edge and hope it doesn't suck us down.'

The boat raced over the lake. Kenno broke out another sail. The greater their speed the better chance they had of passing the whirlpool. But the strange colour of the rocks caught Susan's eye, and she saw they were thickly overgrown with the yellow weed used as food by the Seafolk. She watched closely and saw movements in the rocks. Then Limpy shouted, and she had no more time. They were at the exit, and a hissing, a hollow booming from outside, told them what they must face now.

They sped under cliffs and saw the Gut. And Susan knew at once they had no chance. The whirlpool was worse than anything she could have imagined. The speed of it, the smoothness, horrified her as much as the size. It was as wide as a football field, and sloped in steeply. Cliffs of water raced down and out of sight. It looked as if it should roar, but it only hissed and boomed. And over beyond a black reef, a kilometre away, a mountainous yellow bubbling in the sea showed where the stolen water burst up again from the sea floor.

Kenno shook his head. She had trusted him. He was square, grizzled, sure. But he seemed to shrink. And Limpy, at the tiller, seemed a dwarf. Even Ben was no more than a toy, and Jimmy a ragged old man who should be somewhere else, digging a garden.

Limpy pointed the boat at the cliffs where a road of

water led along the edge of the whirlpool. The hull scraped the rocks, he kept her as far clear of the Gut as he could, and they sped along in a storm of wind. But already a steady tugging had begun, a gravitational pull, and the boat began to lean and curve away from the face of the cliff.

Jimmy came back to Susan. 'We're not going to make it.'

'No.'

'I'm sorry, Susie. It don't matter so much fer me and Ben. We're old, we've had our fun. But you young ones is startin' out.' He gave a laugh. 'What we need now is Nick and them Birdfolk.'

The boat passed the side of the Gut and reached the place where it must break free and head out into the open sea. The wind roared and tugged, Limpy leaned on the tiller. But nothing helped, the pull was too great, and the boat curved round, crossed the front edge of the funnel, and leaned in towards the yellow rocks at the foot of the opposing cliffs. And Susan stared. The yellow rocks! The movement! She saw it again. The rearing up of an inquisitive head. She had a wild hope.

She ran to the rail of the boat, she grasped it with her hands, and leaned over the green racing sea.

'Seafolk,' she screamed. 'Help us! I am Susan Ferris. Help us again.'

CHAPTER EIGHT

Soona

Susan's cry was no stronger than a seabird's call. Yet the rocks were suddenly alive with seals. They slithered down and slid into the water and a moment later, as the boat sped on, their heads appeared along the waterline, and the rippling iridescence of their bodies made a shining carpet deeper down. They kept pace easily, and one, with head raised higher than the rest, called in a voice at once melodious and painful, 'It does not matter who you are. We help all those hunted by the priests.'

'Can you save our boat?' Kenno cried.

'No. You must jump when I say. Do not swim, we will swim for you. But the Varg can save himself.'

The boat curved back to its starting point, and Susan glimpsed priests scrambling along the sides of the channel on the other side of the lake. Then the boat was racing on the water road along the side of the whirlpool, but leaning further in, sliding deeper into the funnel. The seals kept pace, on its outer side. They went across the seaward edge and the yellow rocks came in sight, over a lip of water.

'Now,' cried the seal. 'Jump!'

'Off you go, Susie,' Jimmy said. He and Kenno took her arms and legs and flung her far out over the side. As she turned in the air she saw Ben diving, and Limpy rushing from his tiller. Then she struck the water and it jerked her like a hand, tumbling her along in a flurry of spray. But she felt something under her, lifting, checking her rush, and she grabbed at it and felt her hands sliding on the slick skin of a seal. She felt others, two, three, buoying her up, running her across the pull of the whirlpool. She was on a raft of seals angling out towards the yellow rocks. She could not see Jimmy or Kenno or Limpy, but Ben surfaced ahead, and swam powerfully, and she knew he would not be saving himself unless Jimmy was safe.

The force of the water fell away and soon they were in the rocks. The seals slid out from under her, letting her scramble up by herself. Ben went ahead, and Limpy was at her side. She heard Kenno grunting and Jimmy cursing, and knew they were safe.

'Further up. Hide in the rocks. Priests are coming,' a seal voice said. They scrambled up out of the sodden weed and crouched out of sight among dry boulders. The seals hid themselves, they slid into crevices, became as still as the rocks. From her hiding place Susan looked across the Gut. The boat was deep in it. Only the top half of the sails showed, flapping wildly, making it seem the wings were struggling to fly. One more turn and it was gone. She saw priests appear at the exit from the lake. They stood high on rocks, hauled themselves up the cliff, for a better view down the slope of the whirlpool. A crunching, a snapping of timber, came from deep in the Gut. The priests made no sign.

'Wait,' whispered a seal close to Susan. She saw he was looking at the mound of water beyond the reef and she watched too. A long time passed. Then pieces of timber, fractured planks, reared up in the mound and bubbled there. She heard a faint shout from the priests and saw them rattling their Ferris bones. Then they turned and ran back towards the lake.

'They think we're dead,' Limpy whispered.

'We should be dead,' Kenno said. 'I'll never try the Gut again.'

111

'It's like goin' down a plughole,' Jimmy said. 'You got some pretty handy mates, young Susie.'

Susan turned to the seal. 'Island Lover saved me a hundred turns ago. Now you have saved me and my friends.'

'Are you really Susan Ferris?'

'Yes. I've come to end the Temple.'

'If you can do that you will have our thanks. The priests hunt us. The clothes they wear are made from our skins. There are not many of us left now, Susan.'

Susan felt she could not bear the gaze of those sad brown eyes. 'And they call themselves my priests,' she said.

'How will you destroy them?'

'I don't know.'

'It must be done. Soon there will be no Seafolk. No Woodlanders. Only the Temple. Only the High Priest and his humans. And most of them will be slaves.'

Kenno stepped forward. 'We will not be slaves. The time of the Temple is ending. Everywhere people know the teaching is a lie.'

'Yet the priests are strong. You will not overthrow them easily.' The seal looked at them sadly, letting his eyes go from each to each. 'We cannot help you. But if you return to the sea, call on us.'

They filed along through the rocks and left the booming of the Gut behind. The Seafolk came with them round the headland and showed them the way to go. Ahead, the cliffs flattened out and a wide sea-marsh ran back towards the wall of Sheercliff. A pale mist lay on it, a salty exhalation that seemed to stir thinly in a breeze from the sea.

'You must go into the swamp,' the seal said. 'We do not know what lies beyond.'

112

'The Temple,' Kenno said. 'We will go there.'

They left the Seafolk in the rocks and walked along a beach that slowly changed from sand to mud. Kenno believed Sheercliff was only a day's travelling away. They would have to spend a night in the swamp, but the next morning would bring them to the Temple. The swamp would be dangerous, he said. There were bogs and poisonous insects. But at least they would not be hunted by priests.

'Ole Ben will get us round the bogs,' Jimmy said. 'Bears 'ave got a nose for that sort of thing.'

And Limpy told them grub-weed rubbed on their skins would stop insects biting. The only problem was food. So they went back to the rocks and collected shellfish and a supply of weed. Then they struck out east into the swamp, crossing flats where the rising water bubbled in crab holes and washed into the roots of salty rushes. But soon they got ahead of the water and padded along on dry ground that sank and rose elastically, as though hollow worlds lay underneath. This gave way in mid-afternoon to real swamp – boggy holes, rush pools, stretches of marsh-weed swimming in peaty water. They moved in a small circular world where the boundaries faded away in mist. Limpy had found grub-weed and its juice kept insects off. Ben, leading carefully, testing the ground, twice killed snakes with a blow of his paw. At dusk he found higher ground, an island rising from the swamp, and they made camp there. Limpy made a small fire in a hollow and they baked shellfish and ate them with raw weed.

'What about Ben?'

'He can live orf 'is fat,' Jimmy said. 'He'll be havin' priests for dinner tomorrer night.'

They slept uncomfortably in the humid night,

disturbed by shrieks of creatures in the swamp, and started in the dawn, eager to reach the forest at the foot of Sheercliff. But it took them the whole of that day to come out of the swamp. They came up on dry ground as the sun went down and saw Sheercliff ahead, climbing into the sky, with its stone face glowing yellow. Another half day's travel in thick bush lay ahead. And there, Limpy said, they were likely to meet patrols.

'Where's the Temple?'

'South. There's Deven's Leap. You can see the Temple on the cliff beyond.'

It gleamed as pink as candy in the evening sun, a magic colour. But the building itself was brutal, Susan thought; a marble block, a giant slab, set down on the cliff-top, over-jutting it. Here and there a tower rose, a window glittered. A wall ran from its base along to the swollen dome of Deven's Leap. She stared at that giant outcrop. A year ago – a hundred years – she had launched herself from its brow on her glider and sailed over bush and swamp and sea, south-west to the island. Now she was creeping up on it, slithering up, like a thing from the swamp. She wished she could go boldly to the Temple, bang on the door, and demand to talk to the High Priest. The time was close when something of that sort had to be done.

That night they risked no fire but ate fruit from the bush. They huddled close together and spoke in low voices.

'We can't take 'em all on, that's fer sure,' Jimmy said. 'What we got on our side is surprise. We gotter get close to the big wheel – this High Priest geezer – and grab 'im when we see our chance. Then we got bargainin' power, see? Susie can say 'er piece. If that don't work we'll knock some 'eads together.'

'We've got to save Soona,' Limpy said.

'Where will they keep her?' Kenno said. 'And how do we get into the Temple?'

'If Nick comes with them Birdfolk they can lift us in. We're meetin' them in Wildwood, north of Deven's Leap, so we better get up there toot sweet. There's places we can climb the cliff. I know one not much more'n a day's walk north.'

'They can lift us in at night,' Limpy said. 'We can land on a tower.'

'They can't lift Ben.'

'He can come in through the main gate. Once he starts chargin' they'll never stop 'im. Eh, old feller?'

The bear nodded. He seemed very old to Susan. She did not doubt his strength and ferocity, but even he could not overcome an army of priests. She could not get away from the feeling that he would have some other importance, and Jimmy too, and Kenno and Limpy. If it came to a fight, they had no chance.

'The priests will shoot the Birdfolk down with their crossbows.'

'Not at the Temple,' Kenno said. 'The High Priest is afraid of assassination. More than one has been murdered. Only his bodyguard carry weapons. And they are spears and swords. The priest army stays down on the plains.'

'How big is the bodyguard?'

'More than a hundred men.'

'Chicken feed,' Jimmy said.

But his boasting worried Susan. She wondered if his long sleep had damaged him in some way. He did not seem to bother with thinking any more. He seemed too ready to fight and die. She did not want to die. She wanted to destroy the religion of Ferris, and save Soona, and go back to Earth. Jimmy's sleep had been a kind of death and it seemed he did not mind going back to it.

She lay awake long after the others were asleep. It might be that Jimmy's plan was best – if it was a plan – but it did not seem to need her. It relied on force and threat. She had always thought there was a better way. She would stand alone in front of the High Priest. She would tell him who she was and tell him his religion was a lie. Someone had to say it. She did not believe the Temple would crumble away after that. But something would happen – the words would be out, and she saw them flying like birds, over Wildwood, all through O, carrying the truth and giving it the strength to defeat the Lie. It was her way. Fighting and killing were not. Jimmy and Kenno would do that, if it had to be done. But before they started she would face the High Priest, she would trust Soona's dream. As for Soona, there was a simple way to save her.

Susan slept a while and woke before the others in the dawn. They were curled up in the cold. She smiled at them, Jimmy and Ben, Limpy and Kenno, and said a silent goodbye. But when she rose to her feet the old bear opened his eyes and looked at her. She raised her hand to keep him silent and crept to him and looked into his eyes. She made a series of pictures of what she meant to do. It seemed less easy now, and parts of it made her shiver, but the bear did not object. She asked him to tell Jimmy and make Jimmy carry on with his own plan. She touched his head and he seemed to smile, and closed his eyes and slept again.

Susan went out of the camp and down through the bush to the edge of the swamp. She travelled fast in case the others woke and tried to catch her. At the place where a creek emptied into the swamp she found a patch of grub-weed. She dug several tubers with a stick and broke

116

them and rubbed juice on her skin. Then she travelled south, keeping in the bush at the edge of the swamp. The priest patrols would be further in towards Sheercliff. She ate whenever she found fruit and berries.

By midday she was opposite Deven's Leap. It thrust out from the cliff-top like a giant cumulus cloud, brown and grey. She climbed through the bush towards the base of the cliff, shivering a little at her memories of the place: of standing on the edge strapped in her glider; and of Odo Cling falling, with a seabird shriek, and his legs working like insect legs. She did not want to go too near the place where he had struck. And how many hundreds had fallen since, thrown in the name of Susan off the Leap?

She heard the rumble of a cart and crouched low in the underbrush until it died away. Then she crept on again and came to a road surfaced with gravel. It wound along a valley to the cliff below Deven's Leap, and she saw men working there, and priests and dogs patrolling. The ground was levelled out and strewn with marble chips. Men were raking it smooth, while others shovelled chips from laden carts. On either side, workmen were building stands and draping them with cloths decorated with the wing emblem. It was almost like the preparations for a show. But people would gather here, and sit in these stands, to watch a girl tumble from the sky and strike the ground.

Another cart rolled by, escorted by a priest. His dogs stopped and raised their noses, sniffed the air. The priest waited. Susan felt his pale eyes looking through her. She heard the clicking of his Ferris bones as he turned and looked down the road. He spoke sharply to his dogs and they trotted after the cart. She let her breath out slowly. Carefully she crept back through the bush. Then she made her way towards the swamp, putting a hill between

117

herself and the arena. She found the road again and ran across. From the top of another hill she saw the Temple, blinding white in the midday sun, with black marble wings set in its face. It towered over the cliff almost to a third of its height again. The weight of it crushed her into the ground. But she wondered at its name – the Temple. There seemed to be nothing religious about it. It was like a prison, or a block of offices where the work of some tyrannical government was done. She found the likeness oddly comforting. And she wondered if Nick had been right – the priests were political as much as religious, the High Priest a dictator taking his power from a superstition.

She crept through tangled bush and heaped-up boulders until she came to the foot of the cliff. There she found a corner and tried to sleep. She wasn't going to get any sleep in the night. She tried not to think of the cliff, and the Temple stretching to the sky. But whenever she opened her eyes there it was – the cliff globed and swelling, and the geometrical line of the Temple's underside. In spite of it, she slept; and woke in the dusk, and ate some berries she had kept for her evening meal. The cliff was pink in the sunset, and darkening by the moment. She studied it, trying to choose her line, but no way seemed better than any other, and she decided the best thing was simply to go straight up.

When it was dark she drew the stone silk gloves out of her pocket. She smoothed them on the ground and pulled them over her hands and feet. Again she felt the comfort of their enclosing movement. They seemed to be alive, and seemed to become part of her. She climbed over the boulders, and put her hands carefully on the living rock of Sheercliff, and tried the gloves several times, releasing her hands, fixing them; and when she was satisfied she started to climb. She did not look up or down, remembering the lesson Seeker and Finder had taught her in the Throat: 'You are where you are, no other place exists, while you are *here* you cannot be *there*, you cannot fall.' She told herself it did not matter if she was one metre or a thousand off the ground. Time did not matter either. She had all night.

Slowly she went up, trying to duplicate a lizard's motion. She moved right hand, left foot, then left and right, with everything slowed down so she should make no mistake in ordering the silk to release its grip. She kept her movements short to lessen the strain on her body, but even so the muscles of her arms and legs began to ache and a pressure grew on her spine, as if a cord had tightened there and was on the point of snapping. She tried resting on the upper slope of a bulge in the cliff. That was no good, the pull against her hands and feet was too great, so she laboured on, and after what seemed hours found a ledge no wider than her body and rested there. It seemed as comfortable as a bed and she closed her eyes and dozed a while: 'You are where you are, no other place exists.' Then she prepared herself, cleared her mind of every thought so nothing would get in the way of the order. She would not let herself wonder how far she had climbed. But a cluster of lights showed far below, and without thinking about it, without allowing herself any emotion, she knew they came from the workmen's camp beside the arena.

Later in the night the sky grew lighter. Over the mountains, far beyond her sight, the moon was up. It would shine on the west face of the Temple before dawn, but by that time she hoped to be hidden somewhere. She found another resting place, a dusty little crevice, and dozed again, hearing the feathery stirring of birds. Then she ate the last of her berries, working them to a paste in her mouth and swallowing it like drink. She climbed again – left and right, right and left – with the rock scraping her forehead. Then she sensed something over her and seemed to be caught in a glow. She looked up and saw the base of the Temple angling out. Its white marble seemed to generate light. She hugged the cliff, panting. She did not want to leave it for cold stone. It would be too smooth, she would fall. And if she did not, she would be plain as a beetle crawling on it. Frantically she looked for somewhere to hide, some hole to crawl into. She saw the black swamp far below, and the sea, huge and distant, shining white in the moonlight, and realized where she was.

Her panic lasted moment after moment. She hung on the cliff and cried and whimpered and moaned. But all that time there was something in her untouched – a hard resolve, a recognition of something she must do, that was *necessary*, or else she would never be Susan Ferris again. Someone was using her name, for evil, and had to be stopped. The knowledge of that was indestructible. So she hung on the cliff-face and let panic beat on her like a storm, and in the end, like a storm, it passed. Then she gathered up her strength and climbed again.

She climbed out on the slope of the Temple's base, clinging like a fly, and up another twenty metres of weather-pitted marble, and came to a narrow walkway. It had been made for sentries, she thought, but none walked it now. The ledge was caked with bird droppings. What need was there for sentries on the wall over Sheercliff?

Susan rested a while, trying to decide which way to go. If she went along the walkway she would find herself still outside the Temple. And almost certainly she would meet guards. It seemed best to keep on climbing, find a window. She remembered seeing windows. But she knew she was getting weaker and wondered how long she could go on. As long as I need to, she told herself. And saying that, she stood up and began climbing again. But she did not like the marble. She had a feeling the stone-silk gloves were less sure in their knowledge of it. Once or twice she felt them slip, and she started to command them: 'Grip, hold.' She felt it was her own strength keeping her on the wall.

The moon appeared over the top of the Temple and she seemed to be held in light as bright as day. And day was close. Already the sky was lightening over the sea. She knew there must be sentries on the wall. But they would have no reason to look over. A greater danger was that a patrol down in the forest would see her. She climbed as fast as she dared, climbed on black marble, smoother than white, and almost laughed. Here she was in the centre of the emblem of her religion, climbing on the wings. What a pity it was she could not use them to fly.

Higher up, she passed a window, and heard men snoring inside. It was a barracks or dormitory. Quickly she went higher. Then she began to hear another sound. It came and went, rose and fell, almost beyond her hearing. It was faint and furry, soft as breathing, then it was sharp as a skylark singing. It played and danced, and it was old, old, it seemed to go deep back into time. She strained to hear. She thought of breath, and moving fingers, holes in wood, and then she knew, the sound was familiar, though more skilled than anything she had heard. Someone, high in the Temple, was playing a flute.

Susan knew who it was. Limpy had said she played to them at night, by the fire. Eagerly she climbed towards the sound. The music kept on as though leading her. It seemed to hang down for her like a rope, and while it played she had no fear of falling.

She passed two more windows and realized she was climbing one of the towers over the main block of the Temple. She went sideways and looked around the corner and saw dark courtyards and roof gardens and lamps glowing in corners. Close by, no more than ten metres away, a sentry stood dozing against a wall – or perhaps he too was listening to the music and its beauty made him dream of other places – hillsides, waterfalls, beaches, sea. He sighed and scratched his back on an angle of the wall. She heard his leather suit scraping on stone. Quietly she slid away, crossing the wall to the other side. There she saw more courtyards, and the wall running along the top of Sheercliff to Deven's Leap. The huge stone bulged over the drop. A platform was built on it, and seats stood all about in tiers, draped with cloths starting to glow red and green and yellow in the dawnlight. The cruelty of it made her tremble. But the music kept on and drew her higher up the wall towards the single window at the top of the tower.

She came to it, an opening in the stone, and wriggled in and crouched there getting her breath. The window was a slit, widening as it cut through the wall. The music, slow and sad, wound its way up from a room she could not see. She crept into the slit and peered down. It was deep and dark and she had an impression of rich hangings, of crimson and purple and blue, and a bed full of shadows, under a velvet canopy. A lamp was burning in the middle of the room, making a pool of light, and a girl dressed in white and silver sat by it on a low carved stool and played her flute – a wooden flute. Susan saw black hair tumbling down her back.

She waited until the tune was finished. She heard the

girl sigh and saw her lay her flute on the table and turn down the wick in the lamp so the flame went out. Then she sat in the gloom with her head lowered and her hair tenting her face. Susan wondered if she was crying. But no. Suddenly she stood up. She laughed. She spread her arms and her white and silver robes took the shape of wings. She walked about the room, seeming to fly. It was more than a game. This was Soona's way of being unafraid.

Susan watched until she had finished and was standing by the stool with her arms lowered. Then she said softly, 'Soona. Don't be frightened.'

The girl looked up. She was startled but her look was unafraid. She came two steps towards the window. 'Who are you?'

Susan climbed quickly down the wall. She stood facing Soona. They were the same height, she saw – and probably the same age. She felt a great affection and pity for the girl, and she reached out and touched her.

Soona did not flinch. 'Are you Susan Ferris?'

'Yes.'

Soona smiled. Tears started in her eyes. 'I've been waiting for you. I knew you would come.'

CHAPTER NINE

The High Priest

Breakfast, a bath, a sleep in a bed with silken sheets: all these Susan had enjoyed, while guards stood unsuspecting in the corridor outside. Now, in clean robes, she sat on the bed with Soona, talking quietly of what they must do. In a little while, Soona said, the guards would come with lunch. Then she would be taken for a walk in one of the gardens. And in the evening she would visit the High Priest, who liked to listen while she played her flute. A strange man, Soona said. Sometimes she forgot how evil he was, he seemed so lonely.

'Is tomorrow the day?' Susan asked.

'Yes. At midday. Out on Deven's Leap. I try not to think about it. Tell me how you came here.'

Susan told the story, and Soona smiled at Limpy's part in it. She wept to hear of her mother's grief, but the knowledge that her father and brother were close, somewhere in Wildwood north of the Leap, comforted her. She did not think Jimmy's plan of seizing the High Priest would work. He was too well guarded. Even if Nick arrived with Birdfolk it would not work.

'What we must do is use the gloves to climb to the roof of the tower. Then if the Birdfolk come they will see us. They can rescue us from there and when we are in Wildwood we can all escape.'

'No,' Susan said.

'It's the only way.'

'I came to rescue you. But I came to finish this religion too.'

124

'It was in my dream you would try,' Soona said sadly.

'Then trust your dream.'

'It had no end. I did not see the Temple fall. And now I have been a prisoner here. I've met the High Priest. He is too strong.'

Susan shook her head. 'Your dream is all that's kept me going. I must keep trusting it. Help me, Soona.'

'What will you do?'

'I'll talk with the High Priest. I'll tell him who I am. I'll make him understand how wrong he is.' She saw Soona looking at her with disbelief. 'I can do it. I know I can.'

'Oh no, no,' Soona said. 'You don't know what he's like. He won't listen. He has power. He's not worried about whether something's true or not.' Earnestness and fear shone in her eyes. And yet Susan had to believe she might be wrong. Otherwise her coming back to O was all for nothing. And she could not think of any other way that she might try. She could not creep silently away.

'Tonight,' she said, 'I want to take your place. I'll wear a hood so they won't know it isn't you. Then, when I'm with the High Priest I'll tell him who I am.'

'No –'

'Listen. As soon as I'm gone, put on the stone-silk gloves and climb down the wall. I'll show you how. Hide in the bush. Or in the swamp. When it's all over we'll come and get you.'

'And if you fail?'

'Go to Shady Home. You'll be safe there.'

'No.'

'Are you brave enough to climb the wall?'

'I can climb it. But I'm not going.'

'Soona, listen. This fight is between me and the High Priest. They used me to make their religion. So I'm the only one who can end it. Anyone else will be in the way.'

Somewhere in the Temple a gong was booming. Soona sat cross-legged on the bed listening to it. Her face was pale. She shook her head sadly. 'You don't understand. It really has nothing to do with you. This isn't a religion, it's a government. The High Priest is a king. He's not interested in Ferris bones and religious rites. He's interested in staying on his throne, staying in power. He does it through the Temple, that's all, through superstition and cruelty. Susan, that was the midday gong. I didn't want to show you, but I'll have to. Come with me.'

She climbed off the bed and went to a window of yellow glass in the north wall of the tower. She opened it and looked towards Deven's Leap. Susan went to her side, keeping back a little so no one would see her. The sun was burning in the bright blue sky, shining on Wildwood and the swamp. The marble wall snaked away from the Temple along the top of Sheercliff to the Leap. It was a road, and a party of priests was drawing a cart along it with a dozen people locked inside.

'Heretics,' Soona said.

'What's happening?'

'Every day at midday they bring them here.'

'But they're not going to – they won't throw them off?'

'I told you Susan, they are heretics. That's another name for people who ask questions and break rules.'

'But they won't . . . '

Soona put her arm round Susan's shoulder. 'Come back from the window. There is no way we can help.'

'No. No. I want to watch. I'm to blame for this.'

'You're not to blame. If they hadn't used you they would have used someone else. People would still be thrown off the cliff, or burned or drowned or hung. It makes no difference. A king or priest, whatever his name,

126

would be on the throne.' She pressed Susan away from the window. 'Come back. Now you know how they rule.'

'No.'

But Susan did not watch it all. She saw the cart arrive at the Leap, and the prisoners, men and women, stumble down. The priests arranged them in a row, and led the first to the edge of a scalloped platform built over the drop. He was a big man, with bushy hair and ragged clothes. He pushed his captors away and stood alone on the platform, shaking his fist at the Temple, shouting something. Then he jumped, and fell, turning over slowly in the air, falling down and down, shrinking to a tiny ragged doll. He went from sight behind the bulge of the cliff. There were fifty or so priests on the seats, and twice that many people from the town beyond the Temple. She heard their distant cheering; and their shouting as the second prisoner fought. She did not watch. She turned away and Soona closed the window.

'That is how they rule,' Soona said. 'I have seen it every day. I think of it as I play my flute for the High Priest.'

'Was he there?' Susan whispered.

'No. They were only farmers and fishermen. Perhaps they did not kneel quickly enough. Or pay their taxes. He will watch tomorrow.' She took Susan to the bed and made her sit down. 'Now do you understand? You cannot change things by talking. It is not an argument about what is true or false.'

'I will talk to him. I am here. I won't run away.'

'Then you will die. They will throw you off the cliff.'

'Jimmy and Ben are there. And Nick. And the Birdfolk.'

'They won't be enough. We must escape and fight another way.' The sound of a key turning in the door

127

made her leap to her feet. 'Quickly. Under the bed. They are bringing lunch.'

Susan wriggled under the bed and lay breathing softly. She saw the hem of a skirt, old woman's ankles bulging over shoes, and heard a tray being put on the table.

'Have you been watching, dearie?' came a voice that oozed delight and a false concern.

'Yes,' Soona said. 'I watched.'

'It does my old heart good to see them heretics tumble. But just think little fishergirl, tomorrow it will be your turn. What an honour for you, eh lovey?'

'Out, woman,' said a voice from the door. 'Leave the Chosen One to her lunch.'

The feet shuffled out. 'I'll be watching to see you fly, little one. You won't disappoint an old woman, will you?'

When the door was closed, Susan came out from under the bed. She found Soona shivering. 'It is an evil place. I cannot eat the food she brings.'

Susan could not eat either. She could not forget the tumbling man. Later the woman took the tray away, and priests came to escort Soona on her walk. Susan lay on the bed and tried to sleep. Her arms and legs still ached from her climb. But she could not make her mind be still. She turned over arguments she would make to the High Priest; and protests, denunciations. None of them seemed any more than noise, they seemed unreal alongside the image of the man falling from the cliff. She understood the lesson Soona had tried to teach her. But she could not climb down the wall and run away. She could not do it.

Soona spoke loudly at the door when she came back, giving Susan time to hide. The woman brought an evening meal, and goaded Soona again, but they managed to eat something when she had gone.

'They keep me well,' Soona said. 'Food and clothes and perfumes. This bed is like a queen's bed. I would like to sleep on ferns in Wildwood and drink water from a stream.'

'Go tonight,' Susan said. 'While I'm with the High Priest. Climb down the wall. If I fail, and Jimmy fails, we'll need you free to fight against the Temple.'

She would not listen to Soona's arguments, but when she had eaten took clothes from the wardrobe and dressed herself. She tied back her hair and pulled a hood forward about her face. 'Nobody can tell I'm not you.' She gave the stone-silk gloves to Soona and showed her how to use them. 'Promise me you'll start as soon as I'm gone.'

'Yes, I promise. They'll use you in my place, Susan. That is how it will be.'

'Please, don't argue any more. Play me a tune on your flute.'

Soona played while the room grew dark. She played tunes from Stonehaven, jigs and dances, work songs, market songs, and lullabies and love songs and sad airs she had composed herself. She played the melody Susan had heard as she climbed the wall. Then they heard footsteps in the corridor. They embraced quickly, and Soona hid. Susan pulled her hood well forward and faced the door. It opened and two priests stood there, in black leather, with Ferris bones on their chests.

'Come,' said one. 'The High Priest is waiting.'

Susan stepped forward, with her face lowered.

'Bring your flute,' the other said.

Susan went back and took it from the table, apologizing silently to Soona. The old woman shuffled in and took the tray. 'You've eaten well, dearie. I hope you sleep well too.'

'Get back to your kitchen,' said a priest. He pushed

her out of the room, waited for Susan, and closed the
door. Susan fell in between the priests and they went
along the corridor and started down stairs. They went
down three floors and down a ramp into a garden. She
concentrated on moving as though she knew her way.
They passed fountains and statues – one of herself with
the silly saintly expression she had grown to hate, one of
Nick looking pleased with himself – and crossed a wide
courtyard and went in another door. Then they walked
for a long time in marble corridors so white, so
uncluttered, they made her think of skeletons, and came
at last to huge black doors with the wing emblem
lacquered on them. A priest sentry stood on either side –
different priests, somehow deadlier. Her escort moved
away as though eager to be gone. The doors opened
slowly from inside. A room widened out – a long room,
barely furnished, simpler than Susan had expected. A
throne stood on a dais at the far end, with black and
silver curtains folded behind it. No one sat there,
although a priest with a naked sword stood guard on
either side. At the foot of the dais were two wooden
stools on a Varg-skin mat.

'Come in, child. Don't stand on ceremony.'

She looked in the direction of the voice, and saw a man
sitting behind a desk signing papers. He looked like a
headmaster, except that he was dressed as a priest. Ferris
bones dangled down his chest and snagged his pen and he
pushed them aside irritably. 'Take your stool,' he said,
without looking up. 'I won't be a moment.'

Susan went into the room, with her eyes lowered. She
chose one of the stools and shifted it off the mat. The
priest's pen scratched on paper busily. She glanced at him
– he looked so tired, so mousy. So ridiculous, rubbing his
nose, picking at his chin. She could not believe he was the

High Priest. Surely he was only a secretary. The real Priest would come in soon from behind the curtains.

While she waited she studied the room, but it told her little. It was more an office than a throne-room, for the throne and dais were ceremonial while the desk had an array of pens and inks, and piles of documents in in-trays and out-trays, and books that looked like law books and statutes. Beside it was a frame hung with maps and a second hung with diagrams and tables, and an abacus more complicated than any she had seen. She supposed the Temple, and the land, were run from this room. It all seemed dry as dust. For that reason the guards about the wall, with naked swords, seemed out of place.

The man at the desk finished his papers and pushed them aside. He sighed and took off his glasses and rubbed his eyes. Then he stood up and came towards her. She felt like laughing, he was so short: a little man with a roly-poly stomach and skinny legs and watery eyes and a nose dented from his spectacles. He had old yellow brittle-looking bones about his neck. He looked like a retired judge being taken, against his will, to a fancy dress party.

Yet he was the High Priest. He sat down on the stool facing Susan and said in an old man's voice, 'So Soona of Stonehaven, you have come to play your flute one last time.'

'Yes,' Susan whispered, trying to make her voice like Soona's. She would tell him who she was, but she wanted to give Soona time to get well away.

'Ah child,' said the Priest, 'I cannot tell you how much your playing has meant to me. It soothes me after the cares of state. No one can understand the burdens I carry.'

She risked a glance from under her hood and saw his eyes filled with tears of pity for himself.

'I sometimes think no one loves me,' he said. 'You do not love me. The people do not love me. And yet I work from dawn till dusk for them. And nobody thanks me. They plot to kill me, Soona. But they cannot. I have my guards and they would die for me. So I am safe.' He wiped his eyes and gave a little smile. 'Have you thought of what I said?'

She did not know what that might be, but nodded her head.

'It would be easy, Soona. There are girls in the villages, girls in the dungeons, who look like you. It would be so easy to put one in your place. No one would know the difference when she fell. And you could live here and play your flute. Play it for me now child, and think while you play. You need not die.'

'I will not play,' Susan said.

'What?'

'I will not play for a man who murders people.'

She discovered then that she had under-estimated him. She expected rage, a tantrum like a child's, but his eyes simply widened and grew still. Then his hand shot out, quick as a striking snake, and threw back her hood. 'So,' he said, and flicked his fingers, and a guard ran to the desk and brought his glasses. He put them on and studied Susan's face. 'Unless I am mistaken, you are Susan Ferris.'

'Yes. I am.'

'And you have come from Earth.'

'Yes.'

'Fascinating. We must talk about it. But first we must get the other girl.' He made rapid finger signs to a guard and the man ran from the room. The guards were deaf and mute, Soona had said, so they might hear and tell no secrets, and all their speaking was in finger language. The High Priest made another sign and a second guard searched Susan for weapons.

'Now, tell me how you came here,' said the High Priest, but he stopped, and smiled, and said, 'No, let me guess,' and his eyes sharpened. 'Yes, yes.' His fingers played a message and another guard ran out. 'Unless I am mistaken we shall find Soona on the Temple wall. Do the stone-silk gloves still work, after so many turns?'

His quickness terrified Susan. She had never met anyone so sharp and deadly.

'I've come to end your religion. It's all lies,' she managed to say.

'Of course it is. Of course it is. You don't have to tell me that.' He smiled at her. 'All this mumbo-jumbo. Bones and things.' He rattled the bones on his chest. 'Do you know who these belonged to? Odo Cling. Horrible things! The first High Priest had the idea. A wretched fellow! But clever. Oh yes, clever. Superstition, you see. Ritual. Magic. He saw what was needed. He got things in control. Made a religion, and made the state from that. But he left us all this rubbish there's no getting rid of. Ferris bones. Sniffing out. Well, the priests believe. It keeps them happy. The priests are really my police, you see.'

'But all the cruelty, all the killing. Throwing people off cliffs,' Susan cried.

'Oh, that's necessary,' the Priest said. 'It keeps order. I've got to have order. There's no other way to run the state. And the people like it. They've developed a taste for it. It's fun for them. And it takes their minds off the Temple taxes. Tomorrow will do a lot of good. We'll be able to keep them nice and quiet for a long time after that.'

'But Soona will be dead.'

'Yes. Unfortunate for her. And for you. I can't have you running around. You understand? I can see you're a clever girl.'

Susan could think of nothing to say. None of her arguments were of any use. He agreed with them. But the worst thing, she thought, was his sympathy. He meant to have her and Soona thrown off the cliff – and he sympathized. She almost believed he would weep for them; and for himself, for the hard decision he was forced to make. She began to understand that he was insane. He was clever, and logical, and mad.

Soona came in between two guards. She had dressed in a simple shift for her climb. Her face was streaked with tears. A guard brought another stool, and the three of them, Susan, Soona, and the High Priest, sat cosily together like three children at a fire. The High Priest patted Soona's hand. 'There, there,' he said. A guard handed him the stone-silk gloves and he studied them, sniffed them, tried them on his hands. Then he went to his desk and wrote something.

'They caught me on the walkway. I'm sorry,' Soona said softly.

'It doesn't matter. Don't say anything about Nick and Jimmy and the others.'

The High Priest came back. 'I shall send them to my chemists,' he said. 'I shall have an army that can climb up walls. Now Soona, you must play for me. I find music soothes me after the cares of the day.'

Susan gave Soona the flute. The fishergirl handled it lovingly, and held it for a moment against her cheek. Then she said to the High Priest, 'I shall not play for you, or play again until the land is free.' She took the flute like a stick and broke it in half. One of the guards made a movement, but the High Priest stopped him with a twist of his finger.

'A pity,' he sighed. 'What a great pity. But there are plenty of flute-players – though none as skilled as you. It grieves me Soona that you would not let me care for you. I would have been a father to you.'

'I have a father.'

'What, a poor fisherman? I am the High Priest.'

'You're a foolish lonely little man. And your religion and your empire will come to an end. I'm sorry for you, even though you're evil and you're mad – '

The Priest made a sign and the guard behind Soona struck her with the flat of his hand, knocking her off her stool.

'You must not talk to me like that. It is not proper,' the Priest said. He looked at her sadly. 'You have disappointed me, Soona. I would have saved you. We could have used this girl, Susan, in the ceremony. Now you must both die.'

'She's right,' Susan said. 'Your empire and your religion are coming to an end. There are too many lies and too much cruelty. The people are starting to realize.'

'Dear me,' the Priest said, 'how foolish you are. You children simply don't understand. Lies are part of the system, and cruelty means fear and fear means control. Everything has been thought of. The Temple will last forever. Perhaps you would like to see something. I will show you how well organized we are.' He signalled and a guard ran out, and a moment later five priests filed into the room, with a shuffle of leather-clad feet and a rattling of bones. They kept their eyes lowered, yet one or two sent darting glances at the High Priest, and one hummed a little tune to himself and scratched his nose with a Ferris

135

bone. At the back of each came a guard with a drawn sword.

'These,' said the Priest, 'are the Candidates. Five of them. There must always be five. Each one hopes to be the High Priest when I am gone.' He laughed and said to them, 'Is that not so?' Watching cunningly, anxiously, they nodded, but never spoke. Even the one who played with his Ferris bones nodded his head.

'They don't speak,' the Priest said, 'or make any sound, to each other, or anyone, or even look at each other, or anyone but me, because a guard with a sword stands behind, at every moment of their lives, day and night, and if they make one wrong move, or move their lips, the guard will kill them. Now tell me, with that arrangement, how can there be any plot against me?'

The Candidates nodded wisely, with lowered eyes.

'I was a Candidate for twenty turns,' the High Priest said. 'I lived with a naked sword at my back, and never spoke, and never raised my eyes. But I thought. As these are thinking. And I feared. And I hoped. The strain is great. See, one of these is mad. He was a bad choice. I shall have to replace him. Or perhaps it would be better if they were all mad. I've never thought of that.'

It seemed to Susan she was in a nightmare, the sort where everyday things take on a terrible threat. The reasonable ordinary voice of the High Priest droned on, his ordinary little face puckered with concern and decency, and his fingers toyed with the yellow bones on his chest, and the Candidates stood with lowered eyes and naked swords at their backs.

'When I am dying,' the High Priest said, 'I shall choose one of these to be my successor. His first order will be for the death of his fellows.'

'You're mad,' Susan whispered. 'You're all mad.'

'No,' smiled the High Priest, 'we are sane. We are the State. We are truth and life and order.'

'I am Susan Ferris,' Susan cried to the Candidates. 'Everything you believe is a lie.'

They made no move, nor any sign of interest. The High Priest laughed.

'Child, you are helpless. All power for action rests in me. For life and death. For beginning and ending. Shall I show you?'

His fingers made a movement too rapid to follow, one of the guards lowered his sword and thrust, and a Candidate lay dead upon the floor.

'There,' said the High Priest, 'that is power, and that is truth. It could as easily have been you, Susan Ferris. Understand that who you are does not interest me. Tomorrow you will have a small moment in history, and then it is done. But I will go on. The Temple goes on.' He gave a fastidious shudder – 'The sight of blood upsets me' – and signalled again and guards carried out the Candidate's body and others mopped the pool of blood from the floor. Then, in what seemed the final madness to Susan, a new Candidate was led in and took his place with the others. It seemed to Susan his eyes glowed with satisfaction.

The High Priest took no notice of him, but signalled again, and the guards prodded the Candidates out of the room.

'So you see, Susan, there is no point in struggle. Resign yourself. It will be much easier that way.'

'It will end,' Susan whispered. 'The Temple will end. A lie cannot go on.'

'Oh dear,' said the Priest, 'you are hard to convince. Perhaps it would be better if I had you killed right now.'

'Even without me the Temple will fall.'

The High Priest looked at her thoughtfully. 'I wonder what it is you've been plotting. It strikes me there is some danger in you. I think perhaps I'll put a different sort of guard on you. Better to be on the safe side, I think.' He flicked his fingers, a guard went behind the curtains and a priest came in, leading a Bloodcat on a silver chain. The animal slunk in a cowed way, with ears flattened and belly close to the ground, as if it was hunting. Its yellow eyes fastened on the High Priest and flashed with hatred. But fear was even deeper, and though she was terrified, appalled by the creature, Susan cried out in pity, for it was broken, reduced by some dreadful cruelty. It was a larger animal, better grown, than the one that had hunted her on the Lizard Path. Yet the sinuousness and coiled strength were there, increased and made more terrible by the twisting that had been worked in the cat, its bending to the will of a human master. It was held in some mental vice turned tight by the Priest, and its malevolence and blood lust were increased.

The High Priest reached out and cuffed it on the nose. 'Nice pussy.' The Bloodcat sank down and hooded its eyes. Soona had slipped off her stool on to her knees and buried her face in her hands. She could not look at the cat. Susan put her arm around her. Until this moment she had believed Nick and Jimmy might save them. She did not believe it any more.

'You have seen a Bloodcat?' said the Priest.

'Yes,' Susan said.

'But not like this. He is the largest ever captured. And the only one we have managed to train. And he is mine, Susan. I have him,' he tapped his head, 'up here. I am his master. And now I am going to set him to watch you.' He made a sign to a guard and the man stepped up to Susan and laid the point of his sword on her throat.

'He's not going to hurt you,' said the High Priest. The guard made a small movement of his wrist and she felt a pricking on her throat, a stinging like a sandfly's bite. He withdrew the sword and she saw a drop of blood held on its point. The guard went to the High Priest and gave him the sword.

'Now pussy, a little treat for you,' the High Priest said.

The Bloodcat came to his feet, and the Priest held out the sword as though offering something on a spoon. The cat's tongue flicked, red as blood, delicate as a snake's tongue, and took the drop from the point of the sword. He trembled, all his muscles quivered, and a soft growling sounded in his throat. His head swung slowly round and his eyes fixed on Susan. A change seemed to take place in their colour, a deepening of their yellow, as though a new burning had started in their depths. She felt herself being drunk down into them, and felt that she would never breathe again, think again, without this creature having knowledge of it.

The High Priest laughed. 'Now,' he said, 'if I release his chain there is nowhere you can run, nowhere on O. It is me he hates, oh he hates me deeply, but it is you he will kill. You can never escape him. So whatever plan you have for tomorrow, do not try it. Falling from the cliff is the only way you can ever escape.' He motioned at the priest. 'Take him away now'. The man led the Bloodcat out, but the creature stopped at the curtains and sent one last look at Susan. It burned on her skin and seemed to shrivel her.

'Now, I think we are all tired,' the Priest said. 'Let's get some sleep. You girls have a big day coming up. Ah Soona, how I wish I had been able to hear your flute one last time. Go away now, go away you ungrateful girl, and don't blame me for what happens tomorrow.'

They left him sitting on his stool, a little man, absurdly dressed, with tears of self-pity in his eyes, and followed their guards through the corridors and gardens back to their room.

They sank down exhausted on the bed.

'He's mad,' Susan whispered.

'Yes, he's mad. But he rules O. And tomorrow he will kill us,' Soona said.

They slept uncomfortably, with the High Priest and the Bloodcat in their dreams. In the morning women came with food and clothes and perfumes and cosmetics. They woke the girls and dressed their hair and put silver caps on their heads and slippers on their feet. They dressed them in robes of jet black silk embroidered with silver thread, and painted their faces white and eyes green and lips bright red. Last of all they fastened tiny silver wings on their shoulders.

Late in the morning, guards came and led them out.

CHAPTER TEN

As Humble as the Worm . . .

Starting at first light, travelling until dark, Nick and Dawn reached the mountains in two days. They crossed the pass on the morning of the third day and turned north towards the Yellow Plains. Late in the morning Birdfolk came swooping out of the sky. Nick recognized one of those who had carried them south. Although he did not tell all his mission he made its importance clear, and the Birdfolk fetched nests from a nearby Hall and lifted Nick and Dawn and carried them along the plains to Morninghall.

It was dark when they flew in. The cooking fires in the hollow made a beacon. The Birdfolk landed on the rim and Nick and Dawn wriggled out of their nests and went down through the fires, through a throng of curious Birdfolk, to the entrance of the Hall, where the elders were waiting. A hundred turns before, Wise One had been a female. Now a male had that name. He seemed older to Nick: grey in his feathers, stringy in his neck, beakier, and beadier in his eye – and somehow less wise-looking.

Nick stopped before him and bowed. 'I am Nicholas Quinn,' he said. 'I visited Morninghall a hundred turns ago with Susan Ferris. Today I bring Dawn the Woodlander. We have a message from Jimmy Jaspers and the Varg.'

A murmur of surprise, displeasure too, sounded in the Council. Wise One said, 'In the old days the Varg were enemies.'

'I don't know about the old days,' Nick said. 'It's now that interests me. I've come to help you, and ask for help.'

'A messenger flew ahead of you,' Wise One said. 'We know you claim to have important news for all our kind. Because you are who you are, we will listen. But this must be done in full Council. We have sent for the leaders of the other Halls. They are coming now. In the morning we will listen to your message.'

'I can't wait that long,' Nick said, but Dawn put her hand on his arm.

'We thank you for your welcome,' she said. 'We have travelled far and have little time. But we can wait until the Council meets. Then I pray that you will act quickly.'

'We will act or not, as the Council decides,' Wise One said. 'Nothing more can be said tonight. Now you must eat our food and hear our song. The debt we owe to Susan Ferris and Nicholas Quinn, and to Brand and Breeze and the Woodlanders, is not forgotten.'

So they sat by the fires, and ate and listened. The songs were about heroic deeds, and Nick remembered how once by another fire in this Hall, he had hoped songs would be made about Susan and him. He heard them now and they were unreal. The present, and his task, troubled him. From time to time Birdfolk flew in from other Halls and he felt he did badly in the formal business of greeting and was glad that Dawn was there to say the right things.

Late in the night they were shown their beds. Nick could not sleep. In three days Soona would be thrown off the cliff. And Susan and Jimmy would face the High Priest, and probably die if he did not get there with an army of Birdfolk. But how was he to persuade the Council? If they were all as difficult as Wise One it could take days.

He felt better in the morning when he woke and found

Yellowclaw and Silverwing by his bed. They had flown back from a patrol in the north and had spoken with Dawn already and learned something of the mission.

'You must be careful,' Silverwing warned. 'The Prohibition is a subject painful to Birds. There are some who believe it must not be tested, we must accept. Others will resent outsiders speaking of it. But we will support you.'

'Wise One didn't seem very friendly.'

'He's a cranky old Bird. But he is wise. If you convince him he will help you.'

The Council was held in the Great Hall underneath the Prohibition carved into the rock. Nick read it as he stood beside Dawn waiting for the visiting Birdfolk to assemble. *Folk of the Yellow Plains, For your great sins of Pride and Cruelty, Know that ye are locked into your Land. Unless ye be as Humble as the Worm, never shall ye fly outside the Mountains . . .* Yes, he thought, it's clear enough, but I can see why they don't understand it.

Wise One and the ten leaders of the other Halls arranged themselves in a semi-circle in front of Nick and Dawn. The Birdfolk of Morninghall gathered behind in a throng. Nick heard the rustle and scrape of feathers and the sound of clawed feet on the stone. Wise One called for silence. He introduced Nick and Dawn and reminded his listeners of the debt all Birdfolk owed Susan.

'This human boy is Nicholas Quinn. Of that we are certain, even though a hundred turns have passed since he stood in our Hall. He comes to ask a favour – and bestow one. So he claims. We will grant the first, if it lies in our power. The second – it touches on things we prefer not to speak of with outsiders. Yet because he is who he is we shall listen!' He introduced the leaders – old Birdfolk, male and female, most looking tired from their flight.

Nick had no confidence that he would be able to convince them. But he took the floor and in a clear voice told the story of Susan's return to O. He told of her determination to destroy the Temple, of the waking of Jimmy Jaspers, and the journey to Stonehaven.

'I don't know where Susan is now, but she must be close to the Temple. In three more days Soona, Limpy's sister, will be thrown off Deven's Leap. Susan will try to stop that. She will face the High Priest and tell him who she is.'

The Birdfolk stirred and rumbled and one of the leaders cried, 'It will do no good. One girl, whoever she is, cannot bring down the Temple.'

'There's also Jimmy and Ben. And Dawn and I are going back too.'

'It is not enough. The plan will fail.'

'That's why I've come to you for help.'

'We would help if we could. I speak for all Birdfolk. The Temple is evil. But there is nothing we can do.'

Nick wet his lips. He looked at these towering feathered creatures. He must make their minds work in ways they had not before. He looked at Dawn for help. But she too seemed overwhelmed by the strangeness of the Birdfolk. Then he saw Silverwing and Yellowclaw in the crowd behind the Council. These at least he knew; and he spoke quietly, to them alone.

'Susan asks for an army of Birdfolk to fly to Deven's Leap and help against the Temple.'

The Hall seemed to explode. Birdfolk jumped into the air, beating their wings in fury or disbelief. One old Councillor tottered and had to be held up by his retinue. Another cried, 'This human boy mocks us. He insults the race of Birdfolk.'

Nick kept his eyes on Silverwing. She looked back at

144

him evenly, trying to understand, and he smiled at her. Then he remembered what she had said about Wise One. He found the Birdman's eyes fixed on him, but could not tell whether their glitter was malicious or amused.

'I've got some more to say,' Nick shouted.

Wise One nodded. He raised his wings and cried, 'Silence!' in a voice that was huge for a frail old Birdman. At once the Hall was still.

'This boy is an honoured guest,' Wise One said. 'So we will listen. He does not mock us, however it may seem. He may be foolish, and presumptuous. But we are in his debt, and we will listen. Now boy, explain yourself, and you'd better do it well.'

'Yes,' Nick said. He looked at Wise One now, not Silverwing. 'That is the favour I ask, an army of Birdfolk. The other favour – the one I bring, is to tell you how to fly outside your land.'

Again the Hall exploded, and again Wise One cried, 'Silence!'

'Our thinkers, our leaders, have studied the Prohibition for hundreds of turns,' he said to Nick.

'I know.'

'And none have found an answer.'

'Yes, I know.'

'We have practised humility in every form. There have been Birdfolk who have given their lives to it.'

'I can't tell you what the answer is,' Nick said. 'It's Ben the Varg who knows.'

'A bear!' cried the old Councillor who had tottered.

'The Varg have always known. They read the Prohibition differently from you.'

'A bear!' His followers held him up. 'This boy brings a message from a bear! To us, who are Birdfolk! A bear

145

knows the secret! Why, in the old days our fathers hunted them for sport.'

'They remember it,' Nick said. 'And I think you should read the Prohibition. It says you are locked in for two things, and cruelty is one.' For a moment he thought the old Birdman would attack him, but Wise One spread his wings again, and the Hall quietened down.

'The Varg have no reason to trust us. Why should they tell us how to be free?'

'Because the Temple is a greater evil. And because any who learn to fly outside will have conquered pride and cruelty. There will not be many. Some –' he looked at the old Councillor – 'will never be free.'

'Then tell us the bear's message.'

Nick wet his lips again. This was the hard part. 'The message is,' he said, 'read the Prohibition. Read and *understand*.'

Wise One's feathers stood up on his head – a sign of anger. 'You think we do not understand it?'

'That's what Ben says. He says you must stop reading as Birdfolk. He says . . .'

'What?'

'You have the minds of creatures of the sky, not of the ground. You must turn your thoughts inside out. You must bring them down, forget your wings. Then perhaps you will understand.'

'Our wings are our lives.'

'I know. I know. But look up there, on the wall. Look what it says. "Unless ye be as Humble as the Worm . . ." '

Wise One turned and looked, then swung back. 'Nick, this is too hard. Tell us, tell us.'

'I can't,' Nick cried. He was almost bursting out with it. 'If I do, you haven't worked it out on your

146

own. You'll be trapped in your land till the end of time. But . . .'

'Yes?'

'Ben said I could tell you this. You have been thinking of humility. Think instead of the worm.'

'Riddles. Riddles,' the old Councillor cried. 'I've had enough of this. I'm going home.' He stormed out of the Hall with his followers behind him. But Wise One never moved. He kept his eyes on Nick. 'Is that all?'

'I can't say any more.' And he could not bear the eyes of the Birdfolk on him. He broke through the throng into the open and climbed to the rim of the hollow. Dawn ran after him and stood by his side.

'You did your best.'

'They'll never understand. They're up themselves too much.'

'I think they will. But not in time. It's hard for them. If you can fly you only think of flying.'

'I know. Let's find our things and get out of here. Maybe they can take us to the pass. I want to get to the Temple.'

Before they could move two Birdfolk launched themselves from a window in the Hall and glided down to them. They were Silverwing and Yellowclaw.

'We have been talking,' Silverwing said.

'Everyone's been talking. But nobody's going to do anything.'

'Nick, wings are all we know. Would you expect a Stoneman to come out in the light?'

'I suppose not.'

'Then don't be too hard on us. All the same, we have talked. We see the difference between Birdfolk and worms.'

'What you ask is hard. Crawling in the ground,' Yellowclaw said.

'I don't ask. The Prohibition tells you what to do.'

'Yes.'

'Will you come?'

'We'll try. That's all we can say. But two of us will not be enough. We will see if any others understand. Wait here. It is a matter for Birdfolk now.' He drew one claw-tipped hand out of the feathers on his breast – an action that always made Nick jump – and laid it on his shoulder. 'You have done more for Birdfolk than you know.'

He and Silverwing went down to the mouth of the Hall and talked with Wise One and the Councillors. Nick and Dawn saw an angry movement amongst the Birdfolk, heard shouts of rage. Wise One took a long time calming everyone down. Then there was a discussion, sometimes voices raised, and Birdfolk flapping away, or standing sulkily and coming back.

'It's as bad as parliament,' Nick said.

At the end, Silverwing and Yellowclaw walked apart and waited on the rim. And Birdfolk began to join them – first one, then groups of four and five, until there were forty. They were male and female both, and mostly young, but two or three were giant warriors like Yellowclaw.

Wise One came slowly up the slope to Nick and Dawn. 'There is your army. I hope it will be enough. Others will come, but they need more time. As for me, I am old. I will never fly outside the mountains. But my son is there, and his son. They will tell me what the world is like.' He smiled at Nick and said, 'You know that we must ask for help from the Stonefolk? Never have two races been further apart – in the sky and under the stone.'

'They will help.'

'I hope so. Now, we must prepare. Time is short.'

The Birdfolk armed themselves and gathered supplies. Nests were brought for Nick and Dawn. Late in the morning the 'army' – more than fifty Birdfolk now – left Morninghall and flew south. Wise One and several Councillors, and warriors who had not decided, flew with them. Two of these carried Nick and Dawn. Late in the day they stopped at a place high in the mountains where caves angled into eroded cliffs. Nick and Wise One entered one of them and stopped at the margin of the light. 'This is where Birdfolk and Stonefolk talk. There has been no need for many turns,' Wise One said. He raised his voice and called into the dark, 'Stonefolk. Hear me. I am the Wise One of Morninghall. I come to ask your help.'

No answer came and after several minutes Nick began to move impatiently. Wise One placed his hand on his shoulder. 'They cannot be hurried. They will come.'

It seemed hours later that a voice whispered far away in the dark, 'I am here. Ask your question.'

Wise One spoke with care, sending his voice softly down the cave. 'There has been a Council in our Hall. We have heard a messenger from the Varg and have looked at our Prohibition differently.'

'With what result?' said the voice.

'We have understood it.'

'It has taken you a long time, Birdman. Why do you come to us?'

'So that you may guide us. We would be as humble as the worm.'

Silence filled the cave. It seemed there would be no answer.

'They are deciding,' Wise One said. 'Perhaps they will help, perhaps they won't.'

A new voice came out of the dark – older, furrier, yet somehow more sure of itself. 'How do we know that Birdfolk will not kill and plunder again when they fly outside the mountains?'

'You do not know,' Wise One said. 'I do not know. Yet I believe any who pass this test will have greed and cruelty burned out of them.'

Silence again. Then the voice said, 'It is possible. Who is the one with you?'

'Tell them, Nick.'

'I am Nicholas Quinn,' Nick said. 'I'm Susan's friend. She is at the Temple with Jimmy Jaspers and Ben, the Varg. They sent me with a message to the Birdfolk. We're going to destroy the Temple. At least, Susan is. If she can. But we need the Birdfolk to help. So please, show them the way. If you don't, we've got no chance.'

'What will you put in place of the Temple?'

'Nothing. That's not our job. We'll leave it for the people of O to decide.'

'You think they will choose something better?'

'I don't know,' Nick said. 'I don't know anything. All I know is that the Temple's bad. They're going to kill Limpy's sister the day after tomorrow.'

'And so we must save her. Yes. An innocent child. The reason is good enough, and the risk justified.'

'So you'll help?'

'We will show the way. But know, Birdman' – he spoke to Wise One – 'it is hard. The worm lives in mud, not in stone.'

'We know,' Wise One said.

'Some will die. Others will go mad.'

Wise One made no answer.

'Well?'

'I will tell them,' the old Birdman said. 'Where will Nick go to wait?'

'Down the mountain on the other side there is a gorge, and a river bursting from the stone. Beneath the fall, a cave. There is the place.'

'Dawn will find it,' Nick said. 'How long will it take?'

'All this day and one of your nights.'

They went out of the cave and Wise One told the Birdfolk what the Stoneman had said. None dropped out, and several of those who had been undecided joined the band.

'They see the sky on the other side,' Wise One said.

Yellowclaw and Silverwing came to talk with Nick and Dawn. It was hard to tell what they were thinking. Only in their eyes was there any fear, but they spoke of practical things – food and weapons and place of meeting – and made a formal goodbye when Wise One called them. Then the Birdfolk went into the cave, tall and proud, their feathers flashing in the sun. To Nick it was as if they were being drunk into darkness. Colour became grey. Red and green, blue and silver, purple, yellow, orange; a rainbow, an iridescence, streamed into the cave, and light went out. He could not bear to watch it, but turned away and went down the hill and joined the Birdfolk who would fly the nests and weapons and food higher into the mountains. When he looked again only Wise One was left, standing by the cave.

Through the rest of the day, as he and Dawn climbed higher, as they crossed the pass, and waved goodbye to shrinking specks in the sky, and climbed down to the bush-line on the other side, he thought of the Birdfolk deep in the mountain under them, turning in caves, shuffling in passages, with their great wings useless by

151

their sides. He thought he felt some of the pain they must feel.

Dawn led the way down through the bush, almost as quick in the dark as she was in daylight. At midnight she found a place to sleep. They unstrapped their nests from their backs and ate some food. Nick went to sleep with the distant roar of a waterfall in his ears.

That was the sound they followed in the morning. They worked their way along the foot of hills and entered a gorge, and found the place where the creek broke from its underground passage and leaped fifty metres down a cliff.

'We'll make a fire,' Dawn said. 'They'll be wet and cold.'

'Won't the priest patrols see the smoke?'

'They've all gone to the Temple for the Miracle.'

They hunted for dry wood and hauled it into the gorge and built a mound on a shingle spit down from the fall. Then Nick crept in behind the water, through spray as wetting as rain, and waited by the cave mouth. It was only a narrow split in the rock. The larger Birdfolk would struggle to get through. He went into the dark a little way and listened for some noise, but the sound of the waterfall was too great. 'If you can hear,' he said, 'tell me when they're coming.' Then he waited hours in the dark, crouched and shivering. At last, from far away, a whisper came, drifting like a filament of web. 'The Birdfolk come.' Nick ran outside. 'Light the fire,' he cried to Dawn.

The flames were roaring in the logs when the first Birdfolk stumbled from the spray. Nick ran to them. It took him a little while to recognize Silverwing and Yellowclaw. They looked like two crumpled old vultures, filthy, tattered. Grey mud was caked on their bodies and broken feathers poked out at all angles. They had their eyes closed against the light, and they stood in the gorge side by side, Birdfolk no longer it seemed, but beaten feeble creatures, robbed of strength.

'Yellowclaw?' Nick whispered.

'Take us where we may wash,' the Birdman said hoarsely.

He led them down past the fire to the shallow edge of a pool and watched them wade in up to their thighs and spread themselves like grey bats on the surface. Dawn led other Birdfolk down, and Nick ran back, and they were busy then for the rest of the morning, leading Birdfolk to the pool, finding space for them, helping those who had cleansed themselves to the fire, and feeding them; and closing the eyes of a warrior who came out of the cave and lay down and died.

'Others are dead in there,' Silverwing whispered. 'And some tried to turn back. They will die.'

'There are thirty-four of you,' Nick said.

'Nearly half are lost. And now – I feel as if I will never fly again.'

Yellowclaw was standing with his wings outspread in the sun slanting into the gorge. 'You will fly,' he said. 'We will all fly. I am ready now. We have wriggled and twisted like worms and we will not forget the worm in us. Those who have walked in Stone will fly in Wildwood. That is the lesson. Come with me, Silverwing.'

'Where?'

'To the top of the waterfall. Another walk.'

'And if we are wrong? If our wings are not free?'

'Then we will fall.' He started away from the fire in his stiff walk. Silverwing followed him. They came to the foot of the water, and began climbing up through boulders at its side, flapping and twisting, bats again; and once more Nick felt they had lost their power, so unnatural they seemed. But when they stood at the top of the fall and spread their wings and leaned over the drop, he believed. Their breasts shone with colour again, light played and shifted on their wings.

The Birdfolk at the fire, and those still washing at the pool, all spread their wings in fellowship. If Yellowclaw and Silverwing failed, all would die. Nick and Dawn felt it. It seemed to them the nation of Birdfolk would die.

'Go,' Nick whispered. 'You won't fall.'

And Yellowclaw and Silverwing launched themselves. Just for a moment they seemed to drop. Then their wings found purchase on the air and slid them forward as though on a long chute down the gorge. They swept over the fire, scattering flame, and turned on an upward curve, and beat their wings for the first time, and climbed, climbed, out of the grip of the walls. They climbed. And the Birdfolk in the gorge clapped their wings as Yellowclaw and Silverwing flew in forbidden air, took it for their own, and beat and beat, circling up, high over Wildwood.

CHAPTER ELEVEN

On Deven's Leap

The stronger Birdfolk flew back over the mountains and brought weapons and supplies to the 'army'.

'Others are coming to the cave. The news is spreading. Soon there will be hundreds coming through.'

'We can't wait for them,' Nick said. 'You'll have to fly all night as it is.'

'We'll fly forever if you need us.'

They set off after dark, twenty-seven Birdfolk – seven were too weak to fly after their underground journey – with Nick and Dawn in the nests. Far away, deep down in the night, pin-pricks of light showed the location of the Temple. Later, when the moon was up, nothing could be seen but silver tree-tops, and the sea, with the line of Sheercliff marked on it. Twice the Birdfolk rested, once on a hillside, and once by a river Nick recognized as Sweetwater. They saw human villages, with their temples lit up and the wing emblem gleaming like mother-of-pearl. Yellowclaw led them on wide half-circles round them.

An hour before dawn they reached Sheercliff several kilometres north of the Temple. They landed on a slope above the cliff and waited there, and soon Yellowclaw said, 'A Varg is coming. I feel him in my mind.'

'That'll be Ben. Can you feel him, Dawn?'

'Yes. I've been calling. He's coming with Jimmy.'

'What about Susan?'

'I don't know.'

Soon Jimmy and Ben came down the slope. 'Good on yer, boy, yer a bloody bottler.'

'Where's Susan?'

'Tell yer later. We gotter get under cover. She's gettin' light.'

He led them up the slope, with the Birdfolk circling overhead. They broke through heavy underbrush, deep under giant trees, and came to a rocky hollow, a natural amphitheatre, with growth on all sides round the rim. Limpy and his father waited there. The Birdfolk dropped from the sky and gathered round the humans and the Varg.

'Is this all yer got? They're a scruffy lookin' bunch,' Jimmy said.

'More are coming. This is Silverwing and Yellowclaw from Morninghall.'

'Howdy,' Jimmy said. 'Meet ole Ben.'

The Birdfolk and the Varg faced each other in the thin morning light. Yellowclaw stepped forward slowly. He spread his wings a little, held them forward, a movement that seemed to enclose Ben. The bear rose on his hind legs. They were equal in height; and equal in every way, in strength, in authority, even, though each was different, in colour. They stood together without making a sound.

'They are speaking,' Dawn whispered. 'Yellowclaw is thanking him. Now they are making a pact – for all Birds and all Varg. In olden times they were enemies. Now they are friends.'

'I hope it lasts,' Nick said.

'They have promised. They do not lie like humans.'

Yellowclaw folded his wings and Ben dropped back on all fours. Then Kenno, Limpy's father, stepped forward. 'Now Birdman, will you make a pact with me?'

'What will you promise?'

'I can't speak for all humans. I'm only a fisherman. But

156

I will fight to destroy the Temple. And others will fight. If you help, then I promise friendship. That is all.'

'It will be enough.'

Nick moved impatiently. 'We can do this talking later. Will someone tell me where Susan is?'

'Yeah, well,' Jimmy said. 'Fact is, Nick, they got 'er.'

'Who's got her?'

'Them geezers in the Temple. She done a bunk, yer see. Climbed the cliff with them gloves. She wanted to have a go at this High Priest by 'erself.'

'And you let her?'

'She done it once before, Nick. And it didn't turn out too bad.'

'How do you know they've got her?'

'Ben knows. He can sort of feel her. She's up there in the Temple, locked inside.'

'How is she? Have they done anything?'

'She's scared, son. Real frightened.'

'My daughter is with her,' Kenno said. 'They will throw them off together.'

'How can we save them? What are we going to do?'

'Things ain't exactly equal,' Jimmy said. 'But their army's down below, they only got the guards up here. If more Birdfolk is comin' we got a chance. And Kenno can get 'is revolution goin'.'

'What about now? Today?'

'I'm gettin' to it. There's mebbe a hundred an' fifty guards. That right, Kenno?'

'Armed with swords, not cross-bows. And there are no dogs in the Temple. But the guards are fanatical. They'll die for the High Priest.'

'They might have to do just that,' Jimmy said. 'What we got on our side is surprise. Now, Limpy's been into the town and pinched some clothes. So what I reckon is,

Nick and me and Kenno and Limpy goes in with the crowd, in disguise. We get some good seats, right up front – leave that part ter me. When the time comes, the Birdfolk attack. And we grab the girls.'

'What about Ben? Won't we need him?'

''e's our secret weapon. I thought 'e could go in the gate, but now there's a better way. But we gotter work fast.' He paused. 'There's one other thing. Yer gotter know it.'

'What?' Nick looked at Jimmy and felt his mouth go dry.

'I told yer Ben could sort of feel what's in there. They got a Bloodcat.'

'Can Ben – can he fight it?'

'I don't know. Maybe. Maybe not. Once he could. But he's gettin' old. Slowin' down. You know what a Bloodcat's like.'

'I know,' Nick said. Even with his size and strength, Ben would have no chance. The cat would be too savage and too fast. Yet the bear did not seem worried. All morning he slept in the sun, while Yellowclaw and the Birdfolk strung and polished and tested their bows and filed their arrowheads, and Kenno and Limpy and Dawn wove a sling of vines and Jimmy sharpened his axe.

Towards midday, when everyone was ready, Ben rose and yawned and shook himself, and seemed to smile.

The road was paved with marble and the cart rolled on it with a friendly sound. It was almost as if she were having a ride at a fair, Susan thought. Instead of ponies though, priests pulled the cart, and ahead of them the Candidates walked in single file, each with his attendant at his back. The road shone in the sun, snaking on the cliff edge, and down on her left, far down, the swamp and bush lay like a rumpled blanket. She tried not to look that way, but turned her face to the mountains. Soona sat beside her, holding her hand, sitting straight, but the make-up on the fishergirl's face was streaked with tears. Susan wondered if hers was the same. She did not know if she had been crying or not. It seemed important to try to appear brave.

It's a beautiful land, she thought, it's only the Temple that's ugly. A saying of her mother's came to her: There's a worm in every apple. The High Priest was the worm. His cart was rolling behind, pulled by priests too, and guarded by his deaf mute guards and followed by the Bloodcat. To Susan he seemed more terrible than the cat because he knew what he was doing.

She looked up into the clear blue sky. There were no Birdfolk there, and no Birdfolk coming from the mountains. She had never really believed Nick would succeed. But she knew that somehow Jimmy and Ben and Limpy would try to save them, and she wished there were some way of telling them not to try. There was no need for them all to die.

'I wish you hadn't broken your flute,' she said.

Soona made no answer but gripped her hand tighter.

The road climbed towards Deven's Leap and the priests hauling the cart leaned into their work. But instead of following the fork that led round to the front of the Leap they went towards an opening in the stands and pulled the cart through towards the centre of the arena. Susan felt the chill of shadow and saw a bank of white-clad priests shining in the sun. She heard the hideous chatter of Ferris bones. They came out into a baying like that of hounds. It beat on them and forced them back into the velvet seats of the cart, crushing their wings.

Susan looked up at the tiers of priests. Their faces were white, encircled by white leather, and their bones were yellow and hands yellow. She turned her face away, unable to look at them without feeling sick, and saw the townsfolk on the seats opposite. They were dressed in brown, in cloaks and robes with hoods turned back, and their faces seemed innocent and ordinary, even though they too were shouting for the spectacle to begin. The High Priest's cart, draped in black and silver, rolled into the arena, and the priests stood, with ritual high-pitched cries, and beat their Ferris bones. The sound was deafening, yet it had no weight, it was ghostly and unnatural and cold, seeming to come out of some fracture in the daylight world from places warmth and light would never penetrate.

The two carts rolled side by side down towards the open end of the arena, where the Leap had been smoothed and paved with marble, and a platform like a scallop shell hung over the drop. The High Priest, in leather too, with yellow bones and painted face, sat with his clerkish hands folded on his belly, looking sternly left and right. She felt her gaze drawn further round, against her will, to where the Bloodcat walked behind his cart, and found the animal's eyes fixed on her. It leaned towards her as it walked, keeping its chain taut.

The carts stopped and the High Priest climbed down and mounted a dais built on the paving. Beyond him the shell stretched away fifty metres – like a tongue, Susan thought, poking from the mouth of the arena. The guards arranged themselves four-deep about him, and the Bloodcat was led to the dais and fastened on a ring. On the highest tier above the crowd trumpeters sounded a fanfare. It stilled every other sound. When it was over the High Priest began to speak. His voice seemed to scrape against the silence – a thin voice, like a blade, a voice that cut and had the power almost to draw blood. Now and then he paused and the massed priests gave a roar. Susan did not listen to his words – they were part of a ritual and she willed it to go on so the next part should not arrive. She looked about cautiously for Nick and Jimmy. Soona gave a cry and gripped her arm. 'My father. I see my father.'

'Don't point. Speak softly. Where?'

'In the front row. Close to the end. My brother is there too.'

Leaning back in her seat, pretending to be faint, Susan looked at the row. At first she saw only brown cloaks, strange faces – then one stood out, two, as though their focus had changed. Nick and Jimmy sat there: and further along Limpy and Kenno. Jimmy had a grin on his face. He winked at her. But Nick gave a small shake of his head, warning her to look away. She turned back to the High Priest, who was now shrieking unintelligible words. Flecks of foam whitened the corners of his mouth. It seemed to Susan he was working himself into a sort of madness. Suddenly he fell silent and the only sound in the arena was his panting. A man in black and white robes, like a harlequin, advanced to the dais with an inlaid staff topped with silver wings, and knelt and offered it. The High Priest took it, held it at his side, and laid his hand on the man's brow. His voice was sharp, yet had an eager note.

'Susan grants you the gift.'

The man rose, a smile on his face. He walked past the dais, along the shell to its end, stood and raised his arms like wings. He was like a bat standing there. Then he fell, leaning his body to a point of balance, falling past it, vanishing as though he had never been. The crowd made a single throb, an exhaled breath of satisfaction.

Soona, pale, whispered, 'It is part of the ritual. Each

year the staff-bearer dies. The new one is coming.'

Another man, identically dressed, with the same look of expectation on his face, approached the dais. The High Priest laid the staff in his hands.

'What is the staff?' Susan said.

'The holiest relic. The wings are said to be the wings that grew on Susan's back when she flew.' Soona smiled faintly. 'When you flew.'

Susan looked at Nick again. His eyes were gleaming angrily, but he made the same quick shake of his head and she turned and found the High Priest watching her. The Bloodcat watched too – its eyes never left her.

'Now,' the Priest said – and he spoke to them alone – 'now my dears, you will discover the foolishness of opposing the Temple.'

Guards came to the cart and motioned them out. They climbed down and let themselves be led to the dais. The Bloodcat strained at Susan, but the High Priest spoke sharply and it cringed. He spread his arms and Soona and Susan found themselves placed one under each palm. He spoke in his grating voice and every word rang in the arena.

'A hundred turns have passed, and now we are in the holy time. A hundred turns, on this day, at this very hour' – no, Susan whispered, it was dusk – 'Susan came to this rock and flew. And in that very moment the Temple was born. Men belonged to her, and to it. To her Priest – that is, to me, her seventh High Priest. And on this day she is here again, though we do not see her, and if she favours us, then one will fly. She will grant it.

'You see two girls before you. This is the Chosen One.' He lowered his hand on Soona's head. 'She is chosen for holiness and purity and learning. If Susan wills it, she will fly, and she will sit beside me in the Temple and rule O in

162

Susan's name. But if you have sinned, then she will fall. And you must pay. Suffering and penance will be your lot.'

The crowd raised its voice: 'She will fly. She will fly.'

The High Priest smiled. Slowly the crowd grew still. 'This girl,' the Priest said, 'this second girl, we did not expect on this holy day. But she is a heretic and must be tested. And she will make holy bones – for she has said that she is', he made them wait, 'Susan Ferris.' As he spoke the name he lowered his hand on to Susan's head, and jerked it back as though it had been burned. A yell of rage came from the priests. They lurched forward in their seats, as though they would rush at her. Susan felt the weight of their hatred, she felt as if fists were striking her, as if she were burning and shrivelling up. She struggled to stay calm, and she looked for Nick and Jimmy and found their faces in the crowd. Jimmy winked again. That kept her standing straight. And Nick gave a derisive grin. But he was concerned with something else. He held his hand across his chest and pointed with his finger, and when she made a question with her eyes, pointed again, nodding his head. She understood. He was telling her what to do. When the time came he wanted her and Soona to walk down to the end of the shell, to the edge of the drop. Whatever they were planning would happen there. Perhaps – perhaps . . . But she could not think. Too many things were happening. The High Priest had raised his hands and stilled the crowd.

'We shall sing the story, we shall make the invocation. And then perhaps we shall take our gift.' The trumpets sounded again. When they were silent the crowd began to sing. Susan did not listen to the words, though now and then she heard her name, and Nick's and Jimmy's, and Otis Claw's. She looked at the horse-shoe arena and the banks of spectators – townsfolk brown and grey, somehow human colours, and priests bone-white – at the guards and their polished swords, and the Candidates, and the High Priest standing, singing, like a headmaster, and, always, at the Bloodcat, resting at the dais. It was only a metre or two away. Its eyes never left her, and every time she looked at it its claws unsheathed and its lips curled back from its teeth. She saw muscular tremors under its hide. The sun beat down, the crowd shimmered. Sweat trickled on her face. She knew if she stood much longer she would faint.

The song ended with what seemed to be a shout of triumph. Then came the invocation – cries from the High Priest, responses from the crowd, and a rhythmic beating of bones. They were asking, demanding, that Susan come to them. It ended with a prolonged rattling of bones, and the silence at the end was so deep it seemed to shiver.

'Now,' the High Priest whispered, 'now my dears, you must do your part. You saw how my staff-bearer fell. It would make it more impressive if you did that. More dignified. But of course my guards will throw you if you prefer it.'

'We'll do it ourselves,' Susan said. She tried to keep her voice from shaking. It was important to get to the end of the shell without guards.

'And you, Soona?' the High Priest said. 'Ah, how I wish you had played your flute one last time.'

'Yes, by ourselves.'

'Very well. You're two good girls. Off you go now. Walk slowly, it looks better. You can hold hands if you like.'

But they went down side by side, without touching. They walked very slowly, and a breeze began to play, moving their dresses, making the silver wings flutter on

164

their backs. In a moment Susan judged they were out of earshot.

'Soona,' she whispered, 'listen to me. Keep walking slowly. We'll be all right. Nick signalled me. They're going to rescue us when we're on the edge.'

'They can't rescue us.'

'Yes they can. Nick must have brought the Birdfolk. But we'll try to give them more time. I'll pretend to stumble and you help me.'

They walked a few steps more, then she faltered, held her arms out, sank to the ground, pretending to be overcome with fear. The crowd gave a bark, amused. It came, she thought, more from the priests than the townsfolk, and she took heart from that. Soona helped her up; and now the sound that came was a hum of approval. Soona was the central one in this drama, and it seemed compassion became her. As the fishergirl helped her up, Susan looked at the High Priest. He was watching them with interest and a small pleased smile.

'Keep on helping me,' she said. 'We'll go very slow.' She leaned on Soona and they went with shuffling steps, and many pauses, out towards the lip of the shell. It was like walking on to the prow of a liner, except there were no rails. And the sea was far away, shining like glass, as smooth as glass. As they walked, the coast came into view, sliding out from under the shell, and the brown swamp followed, featureless and still. It made Susan dizzy. She had never liked high places, but everything was shrinking to this one – the lip of stone, the curving edge – and the way back was closed tight behind them. When she turned, the hot arena and the horse-shoe banks seemed to strike at her and force her closer to the drop. She clung to Soona, not acting fear. They stood there, a metre from the drop, two girls dressed up to die, with wings upon their backs and painted faces. The time had come. Susan felt betrayed. She could not think of rescue. She could not think of anything to do. Her eyes went blind with tears. She felt her knees give way.

Nick did not see her fall that second time. He was looking out beyond the end of the seats opposite. Sheercliff, on its curve towards the sea, came into view several kilometres away, with the hill where the Birdfolk were hidden rising above it. Something was moving there, something heavy lumbered over the bush. He strained his eyes to see. It was like a giant insect with another tangled in its legs.

'They're coming,' he said to Jimmy.

'They better be quick.'

Nick looked at Susan. She wasn't acting now. Soona tried to help her up, but could not make her stand. He knew that soon the High Priest would send guards to throw her off.

'Jimmy, I'm going out. I've got to delay them.'

'Yeah. Play it cool, son. All we need is a couple of minutes.'

Nick climbed over the rail in front of his seat and dropped on to the floor of the arena. He ran, bent from the waist, keeping his eyes on the guards about the dais. But everyone was watching Susan and Soona and he reached the edge of the shell before he was seen. A yell of anger rolled at him like a wave. The guards started towards him, but he saw the High Priest signal and they stopped. He stopped too, halfway between the dais and the girls. He faced the arena. Slowly the crowd grew quiet; and he heard the voice of the High Priest, speaking in a friendly tone: 'Well boy, tell us who you are.'

Nick raised his voice. 'I am Nicholas Quinn.' Then he

shouted it. 'I am Nicholas Quinn. And she is Susan. We have come to end the Temple.'

A roar began in the crowd but the High Priest stopped it with a raising of his arm. He smiled at Nick. 'This gets better and better. All we needed was a Nicholas. Tell me Nicholas, or Nick, how do you propose to end the Temple?'

'We'll end it, you wait and see.'

'I am waiting.'

'Everything the Temple says is lies. We'll tell the people.'

'There's a better way than telling them,' the Priest said. 'Why not show them? Show them by flying from the cliff. They'll believe that. Do it now. Will you walk to the edge or shall my guards help you?'

Nick looked about him. Had he gained enough time? He could see nothing ttwards the hill. 'I'll walk by myself,' he said hoarsely. He turned from the High Priest and walked to Susan, who was leaning on Soona, watching him with blurred despairing eyes. He took her from Soona and held her in his arms. 'It's all right,' he whispered, 'it's all right. Ben's coming. The Birdfolk are coming. Look Susan, here they are.'

They burst from behind the tiers; they were in the sky, where it had been empty: ten giant birds with wings beating. Ben was sprawled in a harness of vines beneath them, with Dawn clinging to the fur on his back. A gale of wind struck the shell, almost knocking Nick and Susan and Soona into space. They fell to their knees, trying to find a hold on the marble. The Birdfolk seemed to tumble down, then released the vines, and soared, spreading like a star-burst. Ben pitched on the shell and rolled over twice, and Dawn sprang away to avoid being crushed. She had Jimmy's axe and Kenno's bow strapped on her back.

And Jimmy and Kenno were there, grabbing them, while Limpy threw aside vines tangling the bear. Ben rose to his feet. He rose on his hind legs and bellowed, with paws extended and claws unsheathed. And behind him, behind Nick and Susan on the shell, another flight of Birdfolk burst from below the rim and hung in the air, with arrows notched in their bows, facing the arena.

The guards had scrummed about the dais. They seemed to cover it in a mound. The High Priest was nowhere to be seen. Only the staff-bearer and the Candidates stood in the open.

Jimmy ran forward, holding his axe high.

'I'm Jimmy Jaspers,' he yelled. 'I'm the bloke yer been callin' the Terrible One. So lissen ter me, yer bunch of bloddy no-hopers. Yer Temple's done for. Finished! Kaput! Yer High Priest's finished. We'll give 'im a job cleanin' dunnies. That's all 'e's good for. So keep yer bums on yer seats. One move out of you lot an' them Birds up there is gunner let yer have it.'

A rage-thickened scream came from the High Priest. 'Never! Do not listen. Attack them! Kill them! This is heresy.' But he had no way of commanding his deaf guards. A few must have seen his signal, for they ran at Jimmy. Bows twanged in the air and they fell.

'Priests! My priests. Attack! Throw them off the cliff.'

But the priests on the seats were Temple priests and office priests, not hunters or fighters. One or two moved, and arrows thudded into their chests. The huge Birdfolk in the air, burning in the sun, and the bear, standing tall, coloured like the sky, were too much to understand or fight against, they paralysed them. As for the townsfolk, they watched and did not move. They had never had any love for priests.

Jimmy ran back to Kenno. 'If we can keep them guards pinned down, we got 'em.'

'We've got to get the High Priest,' Kenno said. 'I can't see for a shot.'

Another dozen guards broke from the pack. They charged, with out-thrust swords, and tongueless mouths in a silent scream. Ben moved and swatted three, but the others came past and the Birdfolk over the shell shot them down.

Kenno had not loosed his arrow. 'There he is.' He sent it speeding at the pack. But the High Priest jumped out of its line behind the dais.

'He's letting the Bloodcat go,' Nick yelled. He swung Susan behind him.

The Bloodcat came out of the scrum of guards as though propelled by a spring. His movement was too swift to follow – a flash, a jet of fire. Arrows fizzed at him, but he was gone from where they struck. Ben had fallen back on all fours. He half rose as the cat came at him, and the animal, changing from left to right, breaking speed and angle, launched himself on a jump that would carry him over the bear, over Jimmy and Kenno and Dawn and Limpy, and bring him down close to the lip of the shell, where Susan crouched behind Nick. But he had not allowed for Ben's height. And it seemed the bear was able to read his mind, for he rose on his hind legs in the instant the cat sprang, and raised his fore-legs and plucked the animal out of the air like a man catching a football. The fight was over in a second. Colours flowed together, a marbling of red and blue, a glint of tooth, a slash, a tear, and the Bloodcat went bowling away like a ball, back towards the dais. He sprang again, straight up, and arrows loosed from the air struck where he had been. Ben stood upright, swaying, with a wound bleeding in his chest. The Bloodcat was raked down its side, four parallel grooves. It gathered itself to spring a second time. Ben half-raised his front paws. Then neither animal moved. Jimmy yelled to the Birdfolk in the sky, 'Don't shoot. Ben's talkin' to 'im.'

Then, while the arena grew silent, and no one moved on the shell, and overhead the Birdfolk swept round and round, the two animals, the blue bear, the red cat, both dripping blood on the marble, fastened their eyes, locked their eyes together, with such intensity, such strength from one and hatred from the other, it seemed to some of the watchers that a thread, a white straight line was drawn between them. Susan saw it, and felt the force, the hatred, the confusion, running along it. Dawn slipped back to her side.

'Ben's breaking the High Priest's control of him,' she whispered.

The cat trembled and crouched close to the ground.

'He's breaking him free. He's telling him to go home. The Bloodcat – he doesn't know. The Priest has twisted him. But yes, Ben's getting him free. The Bloodcat's so savage. He wants to kill. He wants you, Susan. Ben's making him see his home – the Hotlands. He's telling him to go there. Susan, he's healing the wound they made in his mind.'

The Bloodcat lay watching Ben, unblinking, with his head resting on his paws. And Ben dropped back on all fours and ambled a few steps forward. Then Susan felt a pressure in her mind, a command that made her lean towards the bear. Nick kept his hold on her.

'Let go,' she said.

'Ben wants her,' Dawn said.

'The Bloodcat's there. She can't go.'

'The Bloodcat won't hurt her.'

'Let go, Nick,' she said.

She went forward, past Kenno and Jimmy, and stopped by Ben and put her hand on his neck. An image formed in her mind, and though it made her tremble, she nodded and obeyed. She left Ben's side and walked towards the Bloodcat. She felt the bear holding them, the cat as firmly as she, even as it came to its feet and drew its lips back in a silent snarl. She saw the muscles trembling under its hide, and its eyes burning. But she reached out and touched its head; and she slid her hand down its neck and let it rest on the studded collar. 'Quiet,' she said as the Bloodcat rumbled in its chest. She unfastened the collar and let it fall. Then she stepped back and looked the cat in its eyes. 'Go,' she said.

For a moment more the animal looked at her. Then it shifted its eyes to Ben. 'Kill,' cried the High Priest, but the sound was no more than a squeaking. The Bloodcat turned. It ran, and leaped the huddle of guards, and sped along the arena, and up the tiers, where the priests parted with yells. It gathered itself and jumped twenty metres across the gap from the top row of seats to the brow of the cliff, and stood there a moment, red on grey. Then it turned and vanished into Wildwood.

Susan ran back to Ben. The danger was not over yet, not while the High Priest was hidden in his guards. He had burrowed into them like a maggot, and they huddled over him, bristling with swords. But to Susan it seemed strength had gone out of them. Their minds had been twisted as cruelly as the cat's, and something had happened to them with the freeing of the animal.

Jimmy came up and stood with Ben and Susan. 'None of youse needs to get hurt,' he cried. 'Jus' chuck yer boss out, he's the one we want.'

'They can't hear,' Susan said. She made a movement

171

with her hands, as though parting them. A guard came rushing at her, and an arrow pierced him from the sky.

'No,' Susan cried. 'No more killing. I don't want anyone killed, not even the High Priest.'

'How are we gunner get 'im out?' Jimmy said.

'Tell Ben to talk to them. They're like the Bloodcat, they've been hurt. Tell them they're free.'

Ben had already understood. Again she felt the power of his 'speech' flowing out – broader this time, it seemed to enfold the guards. And it made them open their tongueless mouths as though they were trying to speak in return; and made tears flow from their eyes. It was almost as if they were being born. After a while, in threes and fours, they laid down their swords. They parted, and the High Priest stood alone beside the dais. He looked around him wildly, his hands went darting at this one, that one of his guards, to hold them at his side, but they freed themselves and walked away.

'Yer on yer own, matey,' Jimmy said.

'But I am – I am the High Priest.'

'Not any more.'

'There is no Priest,' Susan said. 'And no Temple. Kenno, put down your bow. I promised we wouldn't hurt him.'

'He must die,' Kenno said.

'I am the High Priest. Susan guards me. Arrows cannot touch me.'

'We'll see about that.'

'No,' Susan cried. She stepped in front of Kenno. 'There's no need to kill him. His guards are gone. He's got no power left.'

'He's got his priests. And his army down there.'

'I will go to my army,' cried the High Priest. 'I will lead them.' He advanced on Susan, a little man with a round

172

belly and a sharp nose and demented eyes. His bones clicked on his chest. 'I will fly to them. You cannot. But I can fly. I am Susan's Priest. My guards will return and worship me. I shall live forever.'

''e's flipped 'is lid,' Jimmy said.

'He's better dead.' Kenno raised his bow.

'No. Let him go,' Susan said. She looked at the High Priest with pity. 'You are free. No one will follow you again.'

The High Priest looked around wildly. Susan thought she had never seen anyone more alone. She almost felt the panic beating in him. He moved in a shuffling old-man's run. He ran to the staff-bearer, standing by the dais, and wrenched the staff from him. Then he ran back past Ben, past Susan and Jimmy. He pushed Soona aside, and stood on the edge of the shell.

'Susan,' he shouted into the void, 'hear me! I am your Priest. I have your wings. I shall fly.'

He raised the staff high over his head, and gave a little two-footed hop, and a yell of eagerness – and was gone with no more sound. Nick and Kenno and Limpy ran to the edge and peered over. They seemed to watch for a long time. Then Kenno turned and walked a few steps back. He looked at the silent priests and silent townsfolk, and raised his hand and pointed his thumb down. 'That's how he flew.'

The town side of the arena rocked with laughter. It went on and on, while the white priests sat in silence.

Then Susan walked forward. She had one more thing to do, then she could go home. She came to the dais and mounted it. She raised her hand and slowly the laughter stopped. When everything was silent she spoke clearly. Her voice filled the arena.

'I am Susan Ferris. And that is Nicholas Quinn. And

173

the one with the axe is Jimmy Jaspers. We come from Earth. We're human like you. We're nothing special. So stop worshipping us. And stop your Temple. The High Priest is dead. He was the last. There won't be any more priests.'

She felt very tired. She did not want to say any more. And she did not want to tell them what to do – except for one thing. She faced the priests.

'Take off your Ferris bones.'

They seemed confused, and some rebellious. It seemed for a moment they would not obey. But the Birdfolk swooped lower, and slowly they took them off and held them in their hands.

'Now put them down.'

They obeyed. The stand chattered like starlings as the bones fell on the floor.

'You're not priests any longer, you're men and women of O. That's all. I'm going back to Earth now. You won't see me again. I'm not going to tell you what to do. You can decide. O belongs to you, and the Birdfolk and the Woodlanders, and the others. You can make a new religion if you want to. It's up to you. But all I ask is – leave me out of it.'

She stepped down; and Kenno jumped up and started a speech. She did not hear it. It seemed to be words about a council and a government and an alliance with the Birdfolk and the Woodlanders and the Seafolk and the Varg, and everyone being equal, and learning from the lessons of the past. People cheered as he spoke. She did not take any notice, but went off to one side so she would not interfere with it, and said to Nick and Jimmy, 'Take these wings off me.'

Nick unfastened them from her back and threw them away.

'Now I want to find a creek and wash this stuff off my face.'

'They don't need us here,' Nick said.

'So we'll make ourselves scarce,' Jimmy said. He put his hand on Ben's neck. 'I want to get the old feller into the bush and make 'im lie down.'

Dawn came up and looked at the bear. 'He needs something for his wound.'

'I must say goodbye to Soona,' Susan said.

She saw Limpy and Soona walking towards her, hand in hand. Limpy's face was flushed with triumph, and Soona was happy too, but a shadow seemed to darken her eyes as she looked at Susan.

'Are you going?'

'Yes. Home to Earth.'

'It's time for us to go,' Nick said. 'We can't do any more here.'

'But there will be a celebration. You must show us how to govern.'

'No,' Susan said. 'O belongs to you. You can make it a good world now. You and the Folk.' She put her hands on Soona's shoulders. 'Let me take off your wings.' She turned her round and undid them. 'Now you're Soona the fishergirl. And Limpy, you can go to sea. You can be a fisherman.'

'First I must help my father. We must set up a government. And get an army ready. And I must sail to Stonehaven and bring my mother back.'

'Well,' Susan said, 'good luck with it.' She did not want to think about armies. She wanted to get into the quiet of the bush. She kissed Soona and brushed away her tears.

'Make a new flute, Soona. Promise me.'

'I will.'

'And think of me sometimes. I'll think of you.'

'Perhaps I'll have dreams of Susan Ferris.'

Susan smiled. She embraced Soona. She waved to the Birdfolk in the sky. Then she and Nick and Jimmy and Ben and Dawn went along the arena and out through the main gate and up the road that led to Wildwood.

CHAPTER TWELVE

Susan

They reached the banks of Sweetwater and turned towards the mountains. There was no need for hurry. They kept off roads and followed bush trails. Dawn found herbs and dressed Ben's wound and they travelled at the bear's slow pace.

In a village they exchanged Susan's robes for a simple dress. She smoothed the homespun-cloth on her hips and looked at the black and silver garment in the village woman's hands. It had the look of a dead thing, the skin sloughed by a snake. After that she walked more freely and sometimes hummed a tune as she went along.

From time to time Birdfolk passed overhead, flying down from the mountains. On the third day Nick counted more than a hundred. Then the Sweetwater turned north and they saw no more. Six days after starting out they reached a place where the river emerged from the base of a hill. 'Why did we come this way?' Nick said. 'We must be miles from the cave.'

'It's straight above you, half a day's walk,' Jimmy said.

'I'll find Shy for you in the morning,' Dawn said.

They made a fire and ate their evening meal. Ben slept with his head on his paws.

'He's like me, gettin' past it,' Jimmy said. 'But he didn' do too bad against that cat. Not bad fer an old age pensioner.'

'Will you go back to Mount Nicholas?' Nick asked.

'Yeah. We'll take it easy. One last trip fer ole Ben an' me.'

'What will you do then?'

'Build a little shack and see me days out. By the river, where we can catch some salmon, eh ole feller?'

The bear opened one eye, closed it, snored again.

'Dawn?'

'I'll go with them. Back to my friend.'

'And we'll go to Earth. I wish I could live in two worlds,' Nick said.

Presently they heard the sound of Birdfolk. Yellowclaw and Silverwing walked into the light. 'We saw your fire. We came to say goodbye.'

They brought news of a battle on the edges of the swamp. One of the Candidates had fled to the army and declared himself High Priest. But the army had defected and fought alongside the troops of the newly-formed Council. The new Priest was captured and executed. But the hunter priests and their dogs had fought on. The fight was fierce and many had died on both sides. 'Without the help of the Birdfolk the battle would have been lost,' Yellowclaw said. The priests were beaten. A few still roamed the swamp but they could do little damage. The religion of the Temple was dead.

'Was Kenno hurt?'

'He fought well. He sits on the Council now. Some say he will be President.'

'What about Limpy?'

'He has sailed to Stonehaven to bring his mother back.'

'Soona? Is she all right?'

'She sends her love,' Silverwing said. 'She has the stone-silk gloves and will take them back to Verna at Shady Home. And she said to tell you she has made a flute.'

Susan smiled. She felt that as long as Soona played her flute O would be happy.

In the morning, while the others made ready for the day, Jimmy took her walking in the bush. They went to the place where the river came from its cave.

'They reckon this is the source of Sweetwater,' Jimmy said, 'but it ain't, yer know. I found the source.'

He led her over a hill and down through bush into a valley. And there was the river again, running silently, as clear as glass. Pink and blue sand lay on its bed. The bush fell away and they came into a basin of hills with grass growing among weathered rocks. There lay a spring fifty metres across. Its surface stirred lazily with new water, and colours, pink and blue and green, shifted in it. Susan felt the water. It was cold as snow. It seemed to come from some pure source deep inside the mountains.

'This is where she starts,' Jimmy said. 'And this is what I named after you, Susie.'

'This?'

'I thought you'd like it more than a waterfall.'

She looked at it. She looked deep into it. 'Susan's Spring.'

'I just call it Susan,' Jimmy said.

He left her there, and she spent the rest of the morning by the spring. She drank from it, she washed in it, shivering with cold, and seemed to wash away the last stain of the religion that had been named after her. When she followed the river down and climbed over the hill to the camp she felt that she had said goodbye to O.

Dawn was waiting with two Shy flowers. When they had eaten it was time to part.

'You'll be home by dark,' Jimmy said.

'Goodbye, Jimmy.'

'I hope I don't have no more dreams. I'm not goin' inter deep freeze again fer anyone.'

'Goodbye, Ben.'

They rubbed the old bear's fur and hugged his neck. They hugged Dawn. She was the last Woodlander they would see.

Yellowclaw and Silverwing were circling overhead. All afternoon as Nick and Susan climbed into the mountains the Birdfolk kept them company. And when they came at dusk to the plateau in front of the cave, they dipped their wings, and cried their thanks, and dived like hawks down the flank of the land. They gleamed like sparks in the last of the sun, diminishing, dying out, against the dark of Wildwood.

Susan and Nick faced the cave. They held their flowers in their hands, and went inside to make their passage home.

The Fat Man
Maurice Gee

When people like Herbert Muskie take up residence in your mind, there's nothing you can do to get them out.

Colin Potter is a skinny boy, hungry for chocolate. Herbert Muskie is enormously fat, hungry for revenge. A dramatic encounter down at the creek forges an unhappy alliance between the vindictive man and the fearful child.

But who is the fat man and why does he hate the people of Loomis? What guilty secrets are hidden in the past and why are Colin's parents such special targets?

❀ Aim Children's Book Awards Book of the Year 1995
❀ Winner of Aim Children's Book Awards (Junior Fiction) 1995

WHAT MY HEART
WANTS TO TELL

WHAT MY HEART
WANTS TO TELL

Verna Mae Slone

PERENNIAL LIBRARY
Harper & Row, Publishers
New York, Cambridge, Hagerstown, Philadelphia, San Francisco
London, Mexico City, São Paulo, Sydney

A hardcover edition of this book is published by New Republic Books.
It is here reprinted by arrangement.

Decorative illustrations are from the Dover Pictorial Archive Series.

First PERENNIAL LIBRARY edition published 1980.

ISBN: 0-06-080510-2

80 81 82 83 84 10 9 8 7 6 5 4 3 2 1

For Sarah Jane Owens Slone and Isom B. (Kitteneye) Slone
—My father and mother

ACKNOWLEDGMENTS

THIS BOOK WAS written to honor my father. I loved him so much that I was not willing to let the memory of him die. I would have loved him even if he had not been my father. He is only one of many mountain people—proud, brave, sturdy, hard-working, god-fearing, and sensitive—living in a place and time so unique and different that its very simplicity is too profound to be fully understood and explained.

Also, I hope to dispel some of the myths and misunderstandings of these people soon to be forgotten.

Without God's help, I could never have written these things of my heart.

Isom B. Slone	Feb. 27, 1863 (dec.)
Sarah Jane Slone	April 25, 1872 (dec.)
Flora Belle Slone	Dec. 23, 1888 (dec.)
Frank Morrell Slone	Mar. 7, 1890 (dec.)
Arminda Slone	May 26, 1892 (dec.)
Vince Slone	Dec. 10, 1895
Jezzie Ann Slone	Sept. 4, 1897 (dec.)
Lorenda Slone	Oct. 7, 1899
Devada Slone	Jan. 10, 1902
Lou Frances Slone	Jan. 26, 1904 (dec.)
Edna Earl Slone	Feb. 4, 1906
Sarah Alverta Slone	May 12, 1909 (dec.)
Owen Slone	July 25, 1911 (dec.)
Verna Mae Slone	Oct. 9, 1914

Copied from the old family Bible.
Isom and Sarah were married on July 28, 1887,
by John L. Slone, the brother to Grandpa Jim.

A section of photographs follows page 64.

DEAR GRANDCHILDREN:

I am writing you this letter to be read later when you are older and can understand.

If you are the kind of folks who honor money and prestige, then I have very little to leave you: just a few handmade quilts and a few old silver coins, made and collected over my sixty years of life—not much to show for a lifetime of hard work. But I hope by writing this book, I can pass on to you the heritage my father left me.

Materialwise, he only gave me an acre of land, half of a house (the other half had been torn down), a few handmade chairs, a basket, and less than two hundred dollars in money. But, believe me, I would not exchange the memories I have of him for all the gold in Fort Knox. And the truths and wisdom of life he taught me, have been a staff and a rod to comfort me all the days of my life.

In this book I will try to pass on to you, all my memories of him.

He was a very wonderful man, wise beyond his own place and time, with a spontaneous wit and humor that was "meractious" for his limited education. He was always ready to give his neighbors a helping hand, whether it be to lay the "worm" of a stake and rider fence, square up the foundation of a building, help a sick cow, or prepare the dead for burial.

These stories will probably be like a large ball of string: made up of many small strings too short to use and too long to throw away.

Grandpa Kitteneye had so many sayings—little nuggets of wisdom and philosophy—that contain so much truth and basic principles of life. I shall try to remember and pass them on as I manage to work them into my story. I think his best was "prepare for the worst, expect the best, and then take whatever comes." He not only said this, but he believed it and used it to live by, and taught me to do the same. I have been influenced so much by his thoughts and truths that I sometimes wonder where his thinking leaves off and my own begins.

Grandchildren, this letter is not to be a sermon. In writing this, I will write as I remember it. I may make a few small changes, but basically it's all true.

So many lies and half-truths have been written about us, the mountain people, that folks from other states have formed an image of a gun-totin', "baccer-"spitting, whiskey-drinking, barefooted, foolish hillbilly, who never existed, but was conceived and born in the minds of the people who have written such things as *Stay on Stranger* and the *Beverly Hillbillies*. And as lies seem to be more easily believed than truths, no matter what we do, we can't make folks believe we are any different. These lies and half-truths have done our children more damage than anything else. They have taken more from us than the large coal and gas companies did by cheating our forefathers out of their minerals, for that was just money. These writers have taken our pride and dignity and have disgraced us in the eyes of the outside world. When our children go into the cities for work or are drafted into the army, they are forced to deny their heritage, change their way of talking, and pretend to be someone else, or be made to feel ashamed, when they really have something to be proud of.

God knew that it would take brave and sturdy people to survive in these beautiful but rugged hills. So He sent us His very strongest men and women, people who could enjoy life and search out the few pleasures that were contained in a life of hard work. They were an enduring people, who did not whimper and complain because their burdens were heavy. They loved each other and lived closer to God and nature than any folks anywhere.

So with God's help, I hope my brain can say to my hands what my heart wants to tell.

VERNA MAE SLONE
October 1978

WHAT MY HEART
WANTS TO TELL

It WAS SO cold that February morning in 1863, the wind almost bounced off the sides of the hills as it roared its way up Caney Creek and up the mouth of Trace, whirling the icy snow around the log cabin. It was an angry wind that bent its fury against the sturdy logs, trying to find a crack or hole between the wood so as to get to the woman and little seven-year-old boy inside. But the cabin had withstood many such winds. It was built in 1809 by Shady Slone, and was now owned by his grandson Jim Slone. Jim's wife Frankie and ElCaney were safe and warm inside.

Frankie had listened to the winds last night. She had not slept very much. The cabin seemed so empty with only the two of them. She was used to all three beds being full. Her older boys had gone to Walker Town (now Hazard) to swap her hand-tied lace to some salt and coffee.

She laughed at herself when she remembered the coffee and how she had cooked the first batch she had ever seen. The peddler had said, "It's good with fresh meat." And so she had used it as a spice. Of course the meat had to be given to the dogs and they did not like it either.

The wind whistled through the "noise maker," which Jim's great-grandfather had once helped him to make. They had clipped the hairs from a horse's tail and fastened them tightly between the logs, where they were pinned together at the corners of the cabin. The hairs were placed in groups of one, two, and three, and were so arranged that the wind blowing through them made a musical sound. Frankie did not like to listen to the whining, sad, musical tones. It reminded her of death and the scary stories Jim's great-grandmother had told of the "wee folks in Ireland."

Frankie reminded herself she must get up. ElCaney would soon be awake. He had been a little sick all winter, a bad cold that just would not go away. She had made catnip tea several times and ginger tea, adding a little whiskey to the tea, and had rubbed his chest and feet with the juice of a roasted onion. Nothing had seemed to help. The boy said the onion made him stink.

Frankie got up slowly and put her dress on. Going to the hearth with her shoes in her hand, she took the poker and pushed at the "fore log" that was now very near burned in two. By raising first one end and then the other, using the poker as a lever, she pushed the half-burned log back against the "back log" and then placed a fresh log across in front. She counted the logs left in the pile. Only three, but that would be enough; the boys would be home this evening or tomorrow anyway.

She picked up the water bucket and saw that the water had frozen solid.

"Well, it will take too long to melt that," she thought. She slipped her feet into her shoes and reached for an empty bucket. It was her milk bucket, but the cow was dry now, so she could take it and go to the spring for water.

As she raised up, a pain struck her in the back and moved on around in front, down low. She clasped her hands against her body and said, "Oh, no, it can't be that; the baby han't due till April or the first of May. Jest an upset stomach; we've been eating too much of the same thing."

All the "sass" had been gone since just after Christmas and there was no more hog meat, just a few more shucky beans. She wouldn't dare eat any more of the "taters"; they had to be kept for seed.

There was one more shoat to kill. That was why the boys had gone after the salt. She should have killed it in January. "Everybody knowed a hog did not mend any during February," but she had wanted to keep this one until Jim came home. But it did not look like he would come home soon, and if she did not kill the hog now there would not be enough of the cold weather left to cure the meat.

"Well, a good mess of fresh meat shore would taste good, Jim or no Jim."

As she lifted the heavy latch to open the door, she saw a long hickory stick leaning against the side of the house. Nick had cut that the other day for ElCaney to ride as a horse. She took the hickory stick in one hand and the bucket in the other, and using the "horse" as a cane, she braced herself against the wind and started to the spring.

As she looked up she saw a beautiful red bird sitting in a low branch of the "weepin' willer"; she hurriedly repeated, almost without thinking, "I wish the war would soon be over and Jim would be back home." Then she thought, "I wonder how many red birds I have made that same wish on. Well, a red bird shore is a purty thing. I have heard of some people eatin' them. I'd starve 'fore I would."

When she got to the spring, a thin sheet of ice had frozen over the top. She took her stick and tapped lightly on the ice and dipped her bucket in. Turning, she hurried back up the path. She saw that she had forgotten to close the door behind her after she had come out. As she set the bucket of water down on the side of the table, another pain hit her, much harder than the first. And as she grasped the edge of the table for support, she knew she had been fooling herself. It was her time, and the baby was saying, "Here I come, ready or not."

She filled the iron teakettle with water and set it before the fire, off to one side. Here it would soon be warm and out of her way, so she could bake some bread. She thought, "I will need all the strength I can muster, so I won't take time to fix a plum out-and-out mess; I will just make a snack for me and ElCaney."

The thought never entered her mind to be afraid; it was just something that had to be done. "Women were made to bear children; children, the Good Book had said. . . . in pain shall you bear them." Of course she did not enjoy pain, but it was something to be gotten over with. She tried to keep her mind on the great joy she would have when it was over.

She mixed a little cornmeal with a pinch of salt and soda, and mixed it with a little water, making a very thick paste. Then she took a board from behind the wood pile stacked in the corner of the room. This board was about three feet long, eight inches wide, and one inch thick. One side of it had been made very smooth. She placed this board at a forty-degree angle before the fire, propping it up by placing a smaller one behind it.

She divided the cornmeal dough into two patties and placed them on the hot board. On the other end of the board she put two large slices of dried beef, sprinkling them with the last of the salt. Soon the cabin was filled with the smell of food, a good appetizing odor that would have brought water to anyone's mouth.

It wasn't long before ElCaney woke up. "Oh, Maw, I smell

hotcakes and meat, and I shore am hungry."

"Well, jump up, son, and eat. Don't mind putting your shoes on, fer soon as you eat you have to go back to bed."

"Oh, Maw!"

"You know I mean what I say and I say what I mean."

After they had eaten, she made ElCaney go back to bed.

"Turn ye face toward the wall and don't look around till I tell ye," said Frankie.

"But, Maw, why?"

"Do as I say and no 'why' to it." She wished Caney wasn't here; he was too young.

"You know I told you how the ol' Hoot Owl was goin' to bring us another little'un."

"Yeah, but, Maw, you said it would be after we had our corn all dug in, and Maw, it's still winter outside."

"Well, Caney, me or that ol' Hoot Owl, one or t'uther got mistook, fer he is bringin' that young'un now."

Although Caney was only seven, he knew far more about births than his mother realized. A mountain boy lives so close to nature that he learns many things at an early age.

Another pain came so hard and sharp that she sank to the floor, caught her breath, and murmured, "Please God, let me keep my mind, so I can take care of this little'un You're sending me." She realized the baby was being born. She could not even get to the bed, and pulling Caney's pallet before the fire, she braced herself for the coming of her child.

In less than an hour, Caney, still facing the wall, heard a small, weak cry almost like a kitten and he said, "Can I look now, Maw?"

"Now listen, Caney, and listen good. Ye take that hickory stick Nick cut fer ye a hoss and knock down some of them wearin' things hangin' on that 'are pole and ye bring me my underskirt, that white'un, and bring me some twine from that wood box under the bed. And reach me the knife from the table."

"Shore, Maw."

"And hurry, son."

And Caney scrambled from the bed, feeling very important as he got all the things his maw had asked for. Still hearing the small whimpering voice, he could not believe it was a baby's, it was so low and weak.

It seem to him like hours before his mother called him to her side and showed him what she had wrapped in her white underskirt. And when he looked he almost gasped.

"But, Maw, it's so puny."

"Yeah, under three pounds is my guess, but ye know he has this whole big world to grow in. He is almost as small as a kitten."

And ElCaney answered, "Kitten, Maw! Why he han't as big as a kitten's eye."

And that, my dear grandchildren, is how my father became known as Kitteneye. Although the name written in the Good Book was Isom B. Slone, he was to be stuck with the name Kitteneye all his born days.

So KITTENEYE GREW. Although he was always small in size, he was hard and sturdy as the hills that stood protecting and imprisoning his cabin home at the mouth of Trace on Caney Creek. But he was as gentle as the cool summer winds that found their winding path up the narrow hollow.

He was walking by himself by the time he was seven months old. By his first birthday, he had learned to climb over the four-rail fence and get outside the yard.

I do not know too much about his childhood years, but he was a "smart young'un." I know he learned all the old folks could teach him. From his father he learned how to make the staves that became "picklin' barrels" to hold our sauerkraut, pickles, corn, and beans, and the "water barrels" for water (and I hate to admit it, but sometimes something much stronger). The washtubs and buckets were made from shorter staves. The iron to make the hoops that held the staves together was the only thing that had to be store bought.

Sometimes they used one-half of a log for a wash trough. It could also be used for a water trough for their stock. If they were lucky enough to find a hollow log, so much the better. Then they were saved the trouble of having to hew or burn a trench to hold the water.

Many times they would leave a hollow stump in the yard for the same purpose. They would also chip a deep hole in a stone or rock for a wash basin. These were always smaller and here they washed their hands or face.

Kitteneye must have helped his father to build a "kil," a place to dry apples and peaches. They dug a ditch about three-feet wide and five- or six-feet long. On each side of this hole they put a small wall made from creek rocks, cemented together with clay. A large flat slate rock (or two or three small ones) was used to form a roof. One end of this man-made cave was left open; the other end was finished with more creek rocks and clay, to form a very low chimney. The tablelike top was made smooth with about a two-inch layer of clay. Sometimes they built an open shed with a split board roof, to keep off the rain.

He learned to keep a slow fire burning in the opening on the ground inside the kil, before it was ready for the apples. The rocks and clay had to be slowly "seasoned out," for too much heat would cause the clay to crack or break.

The apples were peeled and quartered, the seeds and core removed. Sometimes they dried apples with the hull on, without removing any of the skin. Other folks preferred the "rung" process: Only a circle of peeling, around the center and another at each end, was taken off, leaving the remaining skin.

There is nothing in the world more tasty than a dried-apple pie. Eaten raw they are a kind of combination bubble gum and candy to nibble on. There were Horse apples, Johnson Winter Keepers, Black Twig, August Arch,

Virginia Beauty, Roman Beauty, Belle Flower, and June Apples. A sweet apple called Rusty Sweet was good for drying, as was the Roman Beauty.

Peaches were also dried, but although the hills were full of wild grapes and plums, I don't think they fooled with these fruits.

From his father Kitteneye learned to split rails and to make a stake and rider fence. It took a very skilled person to lay the "worm," or first row. They would try to follow the ridge, or tops of the hill whenever possible. Sometimes they'd go through a flat, or bench the small level footholds. But how they built the fences strong enough to hold up, when they were following an upgrade of a ninety-degree angle, I can't understand. It would seem as if the first wind would have sent them flying all over the place. But if the "worm" was laid right, the fence usually stood firm and strong until it decayed.

Kitteneye's father also taught him to lay the foundation for a house. It had to be on a "four square" to be solid and strong. The cabins were always low on the ground. This served a double purpose: It was warmer and the last logs didn't have to be lifted so high. The location of the cabin was determined by the closest spring of fresh water, usually in the middle of the only little bottom ground they had. Then the garden, or "truck patch" was planted all around the cabin.

With only a "straight axe" and a "broad axe" for tools, these cabins were built solid and strong, ugly and rough, but so snug and warm—sturdy as the men who were to spend their lives in them.

These mountain home builders had no gadgets to "count off" inches or feet, yet all the logs had to be the same length, and each corner at a forty-five-degree angle. They used the width of their hands for measurement of one foot. The hands placed downwards—open and with spread out thumbs meeting together—was one foot. Of course some folks' hands were larger than others. This was solved by learning just how far to lap your thumbs—to the end of the nail or up to the first knuckle. (Kitteneye's hands were smaller than most, so in order to get a true measurement he had to add the width of one thumb to the width of his hands.) Then they would cut a straight hickory stick to the desired length of several feet, and use the stick for longer measurement. And by placing the heel of one foot before the toe of the other foot, they could "step off" an acre and even miles, and were much more accurate than you would presume.

Kitteneye learned from his folks the different plants, the names and uses of all the trees that grew on the steep hills of Trace, Hollybush, Short Fork, and Bunion. He knew which tree made the best boards or shingles, that the chestnut was the best to use for fence rails because it split easy. The black locust was hard and sturdy and did not rot, so post and foundation logs were cut from these. The birch made good stove wood. Maple burned a lot longer, but the birch gave a pleasant odor when burned. Of course, the pine caught fire more easily, making good kindling and torches. Baskets were made from white oak, chair rounds (rungs) were hickory, the legs maple.

Kitteneye learned that cutting the bark off in a circle around the chestnut tree, about three or four feet from the ground, would cause the tree to die. The best time was in early spring, when the sap was in the tree. That way the wood had a better chance of seasoning or drying out and the tree would be ready for use later. If the tree had been cut down it would have decayed very quickly. There are some large chestnuts still standing on the hill above our house that bear these "rings." I love to think this was the work of my father's hand.

Of course all this work was hard, but to these mountain folks work came as natural as breathing. They loved to work. They began as soon as it was light enough to see, continuing until it was too dark.

Kitteneye's folks taught him about planting, gathering, and putting up food in accordance with the "signs of the seasons," or the signs of the zodiac. They did not use the astrological names, but the parts of the human body that represented each sign: Aires (head); Taurus (neck); Gemini (arms); Cancer (breast); Leo (heart); Virgo (belly, bowels); Libra (kidneys); Scorpio (sex organs); Sagittarius (thighs); Capricorn (knees); Aquarius (legs); Pisces (feet).

There were many rules that went along with the signs:

1. You must not castrate an animal when the sign was in Scorpio.

2. You must not wean a baby when the sign was in the head. If you did, the baby would cry until the sign went out to the feet. Also, you must not wean a calf in this sign.

3. If you planted your cucumbers when the sign was in Gemini, then they would grow two together and produce more. Beans were also planted in this sign so the blooms would not drop off.

4. Sweet potatoes were "set out" or replanted when the sign was in the feet, so they would "take root" better. All plants that were transplanted in this sign grew better. House plants made from "cuttings" should also be started in this sign.

5. You must not have a tooth pulled when the sign is in the head.

There are many, many more. When my father grew up, he did not believe any of these. He said, "I plant my stuff in the ground, not in the moon."

From his mother Kitteneye learned to tell time "by the sun." The length and the direction of the shadow cast by a tree or a large rock would determine the hour of the day.

You had to take into account the time of year, if it was spring, winter, or summer. And Frankie knew the stars in the sky by name, not the names you are familiar with, but the names she had been taught: the Seven Sisters, the Dog stars, and the Twin Brothers.

Because they had no calendars, it was hard for them to keep any kind of record. One thing I love to remember was the way they knew it took the same length of time for their fingernails to grow full length as the pregnancy period of a hog. When their sows got with pig, they would cut with a knife a very small nick or hole just where the nail began. When this small scar grew to the end—about three months, three weeks, and three days—they knew that the baby pigs were due to arrive.

Some folks did not know the months. I know one woman who could not tell you the month in which her children were born, but could always tell you if it was fodder-pulling time, grubbing time, or cold weather.

The way the smoke rose from the chimney meant rain or fair weather. This was not altogether a foolish saying. The heaviness of the air brought on by the moisture in the air caused the smoke to rise straight up or float out. Frankie did not understand the scientific reason for this but she had learned by watching and remembering.

Granny Frankie passed on to Kitteneye a vast store of knowledge of herbs: which ones were good for what ailment or sickness, whether for animal or person, and how to prepare them. Some would be used as a "pollus" and some boiled for tea. Oh how I wished I had paid more attention and learned from him what he learned from her. It was not all foolish.

I do remember a few things: Catnip was used for colds and to make you sleep; peach tree bark for vomiting. The bark of the possum bush (pussy willow) was good for headaches.

I remember my father once said, "I don't believe God would have wasted his time to create any plants or varmit or anything at all if it did not have some use or purpose. Us humans are jest to dumb to know what everything is fer."

I know there were some things that had no sense and were only superstition, like carrying a buckeye in your pocket to cure rheumatism. The buckeye is a brown nut with a yellow circle on one side. It's so named because it looks so much like a male deer's eye. There were a few people who believed in this cure; I know Papa did not. He always said, "The only thing carrying a buckeye will do is make a hole in your pocket." And he would rather have a hole in his pocket than in his head.

Kitteneye's only books were the *Blue-backed Speller* and the Bible. From these he learned to read. His favorite heroes were little David, the one with the slingshot, and a Slone, who held a high position in the English army when they told "them frog eaters a thing or two at the battle of Waterloo." There was also supposed to have been a Slone in the army that helped to win the Revolutionary War. I don't know if either of these Slones were real or not. Kitteneye believed they were.

There have been Slones living on Caney since 1790, when Alice Slone, better known as Little Granny, came from Virginia with her husband and three sons. They had a government grant to several acres of land here in Knott County. Slone could have been the Revolutionary soldier. The three half-grown boys, Shady Hall, Isom Adkins, and Isaac Stephens, weren't his sons, but as their stepfather, he gave them his name. He and Alice had one son, Hi, the only true Slone, and he moved to Texas. Shady Hall Slone married Katy Reynolds. One of their sons, Billie, married Sally Casebolt. They were the parents of Jim Summer Slone, my grandfather.

I love to picture in my mind Little Granny's long journey

from "somewhere in Virginia": all their "worldly goods" on two or more oxen-driven wagons; coops filled with squawking geese, ducks, and chickens; one of the boys herding the milk cow and mule.

What did Alice think when she saw these rocky hills, the new home for her family? They were sturdy stock and sufficient unto themselves. They were the first white people to live on Caney. For over 150 years, the Slones lived, loved, fought, and died undisturbed by the outside world, protected and imprisoned by the hills.

Someone once asked my father how far back he could trace the name Slone, and he answered, "Well, for shore I can only go back to Little Granny Alice," and then with a laugh he finished, "but by the way of one of Noah's sons, we go back to Adam."

There are three different ways of spelling our name: Slone, Sloan, and Sloane. We jokingly say that the richer ones spell it Sloane, the middle class, Sloan, and the poorest, Slone. The Slones resent having it spelled Sloan. I know for sure that a man who used an "e" lost many votes in an election on Caney because he had changed the way he spelled his name. It is his privilege to spell his name however he wants to, but it is our privilege to resent it.

I am glad that I did not have to change my name when I got married—although me and my husband are not cousins—and could pass on to my children the name my father gave me. As all my children were boys, all my grandchildren are also Slones. But now that one of my granddaughters is married, there is the first break in the chain.

IT WAS LATE May in the year 1872. It had been raining almost all morning, but now, about ten o'clock, the sun was trying to shine.

It had rained a lot this spring, and many of the folks up and down Trace were far behind with their corn planting.

Jim was down with the "rumatis" again, and Frankie and the boys were thinking about having a "working," if it ever cleared up enough. They did not like to ask other folks to help them, when everyone's corn was just as weedy, but maybe they would have to.

Kitteneye sat in the open door where the sun came slanting in. The warm sun felt good on his back. All the other boys and the two girls were pulling sprouts, the young shoots that came up around the stumps in the new ground. But Kitteneye had a sore throat. His mother came to the door and looked outside, anxiously scanning the sky.

"Well, the rain's over. Begin 'fore seven, quit 'fore eleven," she said, more to herself than to the small boy.

Then her eyes turned up the hollow. She saw someone walking slowly down the side of the creek—a woman with a bundle in her arms. When she saw the woman slow down as she approached the gate, she knew she was going to have a welcome visitor.

"Well, I do declare, here comes Cindy with the young'un. First time I've seen her out of the holler since last summer."

Kitteneye got up and pulled his chair out of the door, making room for her to enter.

"Come on in, Cindy, shore glad to see ye, and ye bring ye young'un. I been aiming to come up to see it before now, but with one thing and another, I jest kep' putting it off. Here, Kitteneye, give Cindy a chair."

"Yeah, I shore am out of breath. This child is a heavy'un to tote so fer." She sat down as she spoke.

"Here, give me ye bonnet and I'll put it here on the bed." Cindy pulled off her bonnet and used it for fanning her face. "Well, let me see if this one looks like all the rest." Frankie took the baby and unwrapped its bundle. "My land's sake, its almost growed up already. Look here, Kitteneye, look how purty."

Kitteneye gave a shy look and reached for the baby. Taking it gently in his arms, he placed it on the bed and sat down beside it.

"Well, you puny agin, Isom?" Cindy asked.

"Yeah," his mother said, not giving him time to answer for himself. "The palate of his mouth is falling down again. He's allus having trouble that 'er way."

"I heard tell that it was a present cure, if'n you tie ye sock around ye neck and sleep with it on." Cindy was fanning away as she talked.

"I already done that," Kitteneye spoke from the bed. "Maw pulled my ears and my hair straight up. She'll have me bald 'fore I get growed up."

"Jim feeling puny agin?" Cindy asked.

"Yeah, down with the rumatis. Nothin' does him a bit of good. He carried a buckeye in his pocket and turned his shoes with the bottoms up under his bed every night, but he aches and pains. This rain spell makes it worse."

"Oh, Maw, ye know Paw always gets better after we'uns get the corn laid by," Kitteneye laughed.

"Ye better'n let ye paw hear ye say that, he'll whup the hide off'n ye."

"Well, Maw, ye know everbidy says Paw jest has the rumatis in the summer. That's why they call him Jim Summer."

"It don't aggravate ye paw none to be called Jim Summer." Then turning to her visitor she asked, "What brings ye out in this here bad weather?" She wanted to keep Kitteneye from saying more about his father.

"Well, I wanted to see if'n ye could spare me some cabbage plants. Mine did not do one bit of good this year. They jest spindled and died soon as they come up."

"I got a'plenty. Already set out all I want. Ye can have all the rest of the bed, fer as I care. This is a good time to set 'em out. It's been raining; the ground's good and wet. Ye won't have to water 'em none hardly a'tall." Frankie reached for her own bonnet hanging from a nail behind the door.

Cindy put her bonnet back on and answered, "Well, I don't know if the sign's right or not, but I guess if'n I want any sauerkraut fer this winter I better git some cabbage plants in the ground."

"Well, I never thunk it mattered much where the sign was when ye sat 'em out. It all depended on when ye planted the seed. I heard tell if'n ye made kraut, when the sign was in the bowels, it would smell awful." As they started out the door toward the garden, Frankie looked over her back and cautioned Kitteneye.

"Ye stay with the baby while we go pull up them cabbage

plants. Be shore and don't leave it fer one minute, fer that old cat might climb up in the bed and take its breath."

"Shore, Maw, I know."

The two women walked off the porch and through the yard toward the garden.

"I see ye got a right smart of beans planted, got a sight of blooms on 'em. It will be a caution of beans ye'll have, if'n the blooms don't fall off too soon," Cindy remarked.

"Yeah," Frankie answered. "Cindy, I know ye have somp'um a'bearing on ye mind. What is it?"

They had been good friends and neighbors for years and could speak frankly with each other.

"Well, it's what happened yesterday. I 'speck ye knowed that Vince's paw had come back on the creek?"

"Yeah, I knowed, I seed him go up the holler yesterday mornin'."

"Well," Cindy went on, "he come up to our house. Quick as I seed him, I knowed who it was. He had been gone for a long time, but I knowed it was Grandpa Reece soon as I laid eyes on him. Vince takes after his paw a lot. He axed where Vince was and I told him he had took all the big young'uns way back up thar in the last flat to rake weeds. I told him to come in and sit a spell, but he said how he 'spected he would go find Vince. I axed him if he knowed the way and he said he had not fergitten the lay of the land. He kep' a'looking at everything like it pleased him to be back. Well, ye knowed Vince. He han't one to talk much, but the boys told me what happened. Poor old man. He axed Vince did he recollect him, and he said yeah, he had never fergit him. Then Reece axed could he come and live with us, said how he would give him his hoss and what money he had if he would take him in and keep him long as he had to live."

Cindy took the corner of her apron and wiped her eyes, and then went on. "Vince never even stopped working, jest said, 'Paw, ye never cared what happened to me and my brothers and sisters. When we was little ye left maw and went off. Now ye come to me. I don't want ye hoss nor ye money, and I don't want you.' That's what the boys told me."

"Well, I lay waid him as he come back out of the holler. He looked so pitifullike. I tried to git him to come in and eat a bite, but he wouldn'. I took him out a plateful of grub and some coffee. I know he treated his wife and family real mean, goin' off that way. But I still felt sorry fer him. Vince told him to go stay with his Indian young'uns. Well, anyway, I hate to go agin Vince. It sure is good to talk about it."

"Well, let's don't fergit the cabbage plants," Frankie said. "I hope they han't took the hard shanks a'staying here too long."

"They look alright to me," Cindy answered as she stooped to pull up the cabbage plants.

Frankie broke several large leaves from a "pie plant" nearby, and as Cindy pulled the plants up and handed them to her friend, Frankie rolled the rhubarb leaves around their roots. Each woman was in deep thought.

"Well, ye better go home with me. Guess I'll take this short cut through ye truck patch."

"Ye jest better stay all day," Frankie returned.

When the older woman entered her door she heard Kitteneye laughing.

"Well, what's ticklin' ye so. Ye are smiling like a summer possum."

"Why, Maw," Kitteneye said, "Cindy done and went off and fergit her baby."

"I do declare." She ran to the door and looked up the road. "Maybe I can holler to her 'fore she gits too fer. Oh, no, she is clear out of sight. Well!"

"Maw, can we git to keep her?" the boy asked.

"Well, ye know she'll recollect her 'fore she gets much

further. She was a'worrin' a'right smart. But to fergit ye own newborn baby. I never heard of such. She will sure be plagued when she comes back."

"Yeah, bet her face will be as red as her hair," laughed Kitteneye. "Oh, Maw, can I nuss the baby 'fore she comes back?" he pleaded.

"Yeah, don't see how it would hurt anything. Ye beat everything I ever seed, the way ye take to young'uns, ye being a boy child."

Frankie went to the bed and brought the baby to where Kitteneye sat in his chair.

"Now hold ye hand to its back and don't tetch the soft place there in the top of its head. Ye can kill a young'un by mashing that soft spot."

They both looked up as they heard the gate open and Cindy soon burst through the door.

"Say, did ye ever hear tell of such a person goin' off and fergitten their own flesh and blood baby?" She dropped on the nearest chair and began to fan her face with her bonnet.

"Kitteneye was a'hopin' ye wouldn't come back a'tall. He wants to keep her," Frankie explained.

After a few more moments of talking Cindy took her baby and again started for the door.

"Ye all go up with me," she said.

Kitteneye said, "Ye can take her now but someday I'll come git her."

"All right, son," Cindy promised, "some day I'll give her to ye when she is all growed up, puny as you are. If'n she takes after the Owens, she will catch up with you."

They both knew they were speaking in jest. Little did they know that these words would be remembered for many a day, repeated several times, and even told for generations to come.

For this was the first time my father met my mother, Sarah, his future wife.

You have also found out how we became known as the Summer Slones, a nickname that everyone in Knott County (who can lay claim to it), wears proudly, even to the fifth and sixth generations.

MY GRANDMA FRANKIE made "tied lace," a handcraft that is now a lost art. At least, no one in our family knows how to make it, though I have seen a few pieces. My stepmother had some sheets that were edged with "hand-tied lace." I remember it was a heavy, thick lace and must have been made from twine. She used no needle and simply made it by tying the threads together by hand. It was very beautiful. She used many different patterns: She made small edging for sheets, pillowcases, and underclothing for the women; and she also made a large curtain. Folks hung these from a pole just under the ceiling, in one of the back corners of the house. Behind it all their "wearing things" were hidden from view. They could also have a little privacy to bathe or change clothes by getting behind this curtain.

Grandma made the tied lace to sell at the small towns. She would work at these all winter. Then in the spring she would go and swap them for salt, coffee, and the very few things that her family had to have and could not raise or make themselves.

One morning in the early spring of 1874, way before daybreak, Frankie and Kitteneye started for Walker Town. They had a load of these spreads and some dried roots. They wanted to get an early start for they had a long walk before them. "Now it's sure chilly this morning," the small boy said.

"Yeah, but it'll be hot agin the sun gits up. Not backing out on me are ye son?"

"No, I am much pleased to go. And Maw, you did say you might git us some brown sugar?"

"Yeah, I shore will. Say, I tell you what us do, jest wrap these spreads 'round our head and shoulders. They will keep us warm. Be careful and don't let 'em hang down and get wet. They'll be ruint if'n ye do."

So up the road they went. Soon Frankie, who was in front, stopped and whispered, "Be quiet. I reckon I hear a mule comin'." Although it was still quite a while before daylight, these mountain travelers knew this road like the back of their hand and did not need much light. But the mule meant someone was coming, and if they did not get out of the narrow path that ran along side of the creek, the precious white spread would get splattered with mud when the mule and rider passed.

So they climbed up on the side of the hill, just out of the road, but back under the trees in the semidarkness. Frankie placed her hand on her small son's shoulder, and he knew she wanted him to be quiet, until they saw who else was out as early as they were.

Just as soon as the mule turned the bend in the road and came in full view, Kitteneye saw it was his Grandfather Billie. But when Billie saw them he gave a gasp and groan, "Oh, my God, I am seeing a haunt, two haunts."

Frankie dug her fingers into Kitteneye's back hard and said shush to him, as Billie raised his trembling hand up before his face and made a cross in the air.

"The Father, The Son, and The Holy Ghost, what do ye want with me?" he moaned.

Then in a deep, throaty voice Frankie said, "Your son Jim is sick and in bed, and has no meat for him or his young'un, while you have a'plenty. Go back home and git two of ye biggest middlins and a ham. Take them to him, or if ye don't I will haunt ye all ye born days."

Billie did not wait to hear anymore, but turned his mule and rode back home.

Frankie and Kitteneye could hardly wait until he got out of hearing distance to begin laughing.

"Don't never mention this to a livin' soul," Frankie finally said when she caught her breath.

"But, Maw, I don't see how you thought so fast."

"Well, maybe we are haunts," she laughed.

Next evening when they returned home, Jim met them at the door with the news that his father had brought two large middlins (sides of salt bacon) and one smoked ham. Jim could not understand why.

"Didn't he tell ye any reason fer givin' ye this meat? He han't much fer givin' ye anything. Allus has been tight as the bark on a tree." Frankie could hardly keep from laughing.

"Nah, 'spect it was 'cause I am his son and he is my father."

Kitteneye looked at his mother and whispered, "Yeah, the father, the son, and the holy haunts."

MY FATHER WAS not the only man on Caney to have a nickname, and he had more than one. He was also called Tow Wad. Tow was the thread left over from making cloth from hemp or cotton. A small wad of this tow was used to load their old "hawg rifflers." My father, being so small, was called Tow Wad. He was also called Lick Skillet, for the same reason. He said all the other boys ate the grub and he had to lick the skillet where it had been cooked.

Our mountain people love to "name after each other." It is a great honor to have the same name as an uncle, aunt, or grandfather. I even know several folks named for their own sister or brother. It did get kind of confusing to try and keep it straight, especially when we all lived so close together. So nicknames were a "must do," or necessity. Four of the first white people to live on Caney—Alice, Isom, Isaac, and Shady—have many namesakes. You will find these names in almost all the Slone families. At one time there were eleven Isom Slones on Caney: my father Kitteneye, Fat

Isom, Big Isom, Pot Stick, Stiller, Hard's Isom, Andy's Isom, Jailor Isom, Preacher Isom, Crazy Isom, and Salty Ice. Sometimes the father's name was added on, so as to tell just which one you were referring to, like Hard's Isom and Andy's Isom. Often using the father and grandfather's name, for example, we said, Hard's Billie's Pearce, though I could never understand why as he was the only man named Pearce that I ever knew. Of course the women had nicknames too, as they were also named after someone else. When a boy was named for his father, it would be Big Sam and Little Sam. This begins to get funny when Little Sam weighs over 200 pounds and is six feet tall. My husband is still called Little Willie by some folks, although his Uncle Willie has been dead for over fifty years.

Sometimes the last names were nicknamed. There were so many Slones that we had to have nicknames for the different families. Of course we are all Kitteneyes. Grandpa Jim's were the Summer Slones, my husband's folks were the Jim Bows.

Almost everyone enjoyed their nicknames, although there were some who got angry if you called them that to their face. I know one man who killed his nephew over a nickname. I was an eyewitness to this, and I will tell it as I remember, changing very little except the names.

Hank, the nephew, was an orphan. His father had been killed in a shooting accident just a few months after his mother had died. He and his youngest sister stayed with their grandparents; his twin brothers, who were about five or six, stayed with Uncle Josh. I don't think Josh was very good to the twins. I know of one time when my father stopped him from giving them a whipping, but then father would not let anyone whip a child. He said there "was not a place on a child big enough to hit." So there might have been "hard feeling" between Hank and his Uncle Josh, even before the nickname began. Josh had gotten burned in the face when he was a child. The burn had not been deep enough to leave a scar, but it did cause no beard to grow on almost all his chin. There was a very small patch on one side. For this reason someone called him Nine Beard. When Hank found out that it upset his uncle to be called this, he would call him that all the more. The more Hank said it, the madder Josh got. Soon all the kids began yelling at him every time they passed his house or met him in the road. They would sing, "Nine Beard, Nine Beard, split one, make ten."

My father's house was next door to Josh's. In the night sometimes we would hear Hank and his friends yelling as they passed, "Nine Beard, Nine Beard, split one, make ten." We would hear Josh yelling back insults. My father tried to talk to him. He would say, "Don't let them know it bothers you and they will hush." But Josh would only say, "I'll hush 'em if I have to kill 'em."

One night a lot of us young folks had been to the Community Center, for a play or show—something to which all the Creek children had been invited. After it was over we had gathered in the post office, all laughing and having a good time. I saw Josh stick his head in the door of the post office. He looked like a wild man. I did not see a gun in his hand, but some of the other kids said later that they did. He just looked over the crowd and left "without saying a word." Somehow we none felt like fun any more so we started home. One of Josh's daughters and I were the last to leave. I had kind of wanted to wait until father came in with the mail and walk home with him, but the other girl seemed frightened and asked me to go with her. There were perhaps twenty, more or less, of us—all grouped off in twos and threes. My own young nephew was just ahead of us; he was holding on to Hank's hand. I heard Hank begin "Nine

[27]

Beard, Nine Beard." I remember thinking, "Oh, no, not tonight." And then I heard the gunfire. It was only then that I noticed Josh. Hank stumbled, staggered, and started running across the creek and into Manis Slone's house as the gun kept blasting. Everyone began screaming. That has been almost fifty years ago, but I still recall it all. For awhile I was so stunned I could not move; I did not even think to see about my small nephew, but began running back toward the post office. I must get to my father (as always I thought he could make everything alright again). He had just left the post office. I ran into his arms and sobbed, "Papa, Josh has killed Hank."

"Are ye shore?"

"Yes, I saw it. I saw the bullet hit him. I saw his shirt jump."

"Where is he?" my father asked, and I told him that I saw him run into Manis Slone's house. "Well, if he can still walk, then maybe he is not dead. Let's go see. Don't tell anyone what you saw. There was plenty of other witnesses. I know what lawyers can do to a witness, and if you are really needed you can be used later."

When we got to Manis' house a large crowd had gathered; everyone was talking in whispers. I stayed in the yard and did not go in. After my father looked at Hank he said, "Hank, can you hear me?" He answered, "Yeah, Kitteneye, I can." Father said, "Hank, have you made peace with God?" And he answered, "Yeah, I know I am dying; tell Uncle Josh I forgive him." Hank lived only a few more hours. Father prepared Hank's body for burial, then went home. Josh "gave himself up to the law." He was tried and pronounced insane and sentenced to the prison for the criminal insane, where he died a few months later.

I did not have to be a witness, but my little nephew was, and he won the hearts of the whole courtroom. Because he was so young he was not allowed to be "sworn in." The judge took him upon his lap and talked to him.

"Well, Hal," the judge began after asking him his name and where he lived, "How old are you?"

"Six, might nigh seven."

"Do you know the difference between a lie and the truth?"

"Shore, Grandpa Kitteneye learned me that."

"What would happen to you if you told a lie?"

"Why, Grandpa would be awful plagued and mad to me."

"Would he whip you?"

"No, he never whup any'un."

"If you are not afraid of him, then why do you obey him?"

"Because I love him."

"Did he tell you what to say here today?"

"Just to tell the truth, like allus."

"You and Hank have the same last name. Are you kinfolks?"

"If we are, Grandpa never did learned me that."

"Was Hank your friend?"

"Sure, Hank was a friend to everyone."

"How long have you known Josh?"

"Why, a long, long time," Hal answered, "ever since I was a little boy."

You couldn't hear the judge's next question for all the laughter.

CHAPTER SIX·

I KNOW THAT my father carried the mail when he was only seventeen. He was chosen by his parents to be the mailboy because his other brothers were larger and more able to do the heavy work. Also, because he was small, he was a less load for the mule to carry, not that there was ever much mail. Sometimes there were only a few letters in the "mail pockets."

He made only one trip each week, going somewhere near Harlan. He started out early Monday morning, getting to the end of his route on Wednesday evening. Then on Thursday, the journey home would begin. Sunday was spent at home. He must have spent the night with folks along the way, sleeping on the floor or sharing the bed with some of the menfolks. The mail pockets he had to keep with him always. That was his sworn duty. He would place them under his feet when he ate, even at the table, and under his head at night. It wasn't that he did not trust the people he came in contact with—this was a requirement by the government. And before you could become a mail boy there was a swearing-in ceremony. One of the things you promised to do was keep the mail bag that contained the first class mail with you at all times.

A mountain boy might not respect the laws of his government and even have contempt for anyone who enforced them, but his word was his honor. That he would not go back on. To call someone a liar to his face was putting your life in danger. So when Kitteneye "took an oath" to keep the mail with him at all times, that was just what he did.

He had many stories about his first job as a mail boy. One night a very bad storm came up all at once and he had to spend the night under a cliff. This cave had two separate rooms, divided by a large rock, which probably had been part of the roof at one time. But it looked safe enough and having no other choice, he and his horse were soon bedded down. He slept sound. He remembered waking up a few times during the night and hearing someone snore, but did not get aroused enough to pay attention to it. He slept very late the next morning and when he looked under the other side of the cliff, he found some footprints that told him he had spent the night with a bear.

Another time Kitteneye was delayed for some reason and had to find shelter with an old couple, who shared their only food with him, green onions. They had only one bed, so he slept stretched out before the fire. Next morning after chopping them some wood and piling it in the corner of the cabin, he continued his journey. He often worried how these old folks made out that winter, or if spring found them still alive.

He often carried his lunch—a piece of corn bread and saltback. He said he never knew how this grub could take up such a small place in his pocket and fill up such a big hole in his belly.

And once when his mule broke though the ice he almost

drowned trying to save the mail. Some way he managed to get out of the water and onto the mule's back. He did not remember anything else until he woke up in bed at the post master's house several miles away. He had not been able to call out when he arrived before the door and just by chance did they find him. His feet were frozen to the stirrups and and they had to "prize" his fingers loose from the mail pockets.

The winters were much colder back then. Sometimes the creeks would stay frozen over for weeks at a time. Then the mule would have to have "ice nails" in his shoes.

One such cold spell caught a snake in the middle of the stream as he was crossing from one side of the creek to the other. There he stayed, frozen stiff for many days. It happened to be close to the trail that Papa and his trusty mule, John Barney, were ambling along. As the long hours spent in the saddle were lonesome, looking for this frozen snake each time he passed became a pasttime and a small break in the monotony. He wondered what would happen when the water thawed.

As luck would have it, he chanced to be there when Mr. Snake finally was released from his prison and slowly but surely climbed the bank. Kitteneye saw, understood, and remembered.

Grandchildren, you get your education one way and he got his another.

KITTENEYE COULD TELL it was going to be a very beautiful day. He had been awaken by a crunching sound from the kitchen and a flopping beat, beat, which came from the direction of the fireplace. Both told him that breakfast was on the way. Maw was grinding coffee, and one of the girls was churning. He thought how good that fresh butter would taste with the molasses. He sure was hungry. He remembered he had not eaten a "plum mess" since breakfast the morning before. That nickel's worth of brown sugar and round crackers he had bought at the grocery store could hardly be called a snack. He had eaten them on his way back home.

He knew that Maw had left his supper for him on the table covered over with a cloth. He could have eaten, but he did not want to risk waking her up. He knew she would ask him why he had gone to town. He knew she would have to know sometime, but knowing how she would fret, he wanted to wait as long as he could.

He glanced over in the other beds. No one except Maw and the girls were up. He would wait until everyone else was getting up and maybe Maw would forget to question him in the confusion and noise. With some putting on their clothes, some at the washbench dousing their faces in the cold water, others using the comb, he might get by.

Soon they were all settled around the long table. Along the side next to the wall was a long bench. Here sat all the young ones side by side like crows on a fence. Chairs had been drawn up against the other side and here sat all the "big children and grown-ups." Paw was at one end near the bread. He would be the one to pass the bread. No mountain man would break bread from a woman's hand. The Good Book spoke against that. Maw was at the other end, near the stove, where she could reach the coffee pot, when someone wanted a second cup, or the one that needed to be "hit up" if it became cold.

There was a large square of corn bread, from which each person broke a chunk. Paw would break a piece and hand it to the ones who could not reach it themselves. A big platter of fried meat swimming in its own grease, a bowl of gravy, some fried potatoes. The fresh butter and the ever-present jug of molasses—maybe not so fancy but very nourishing.

Kitteneye finished his breakfast real fast, then, pushing his chair from the table, he hurried for the door.

"Wait, son, I want to talk to you," Frankie said.

"I am in sort of a hurry. Be back in a minute," he answered. He sure did not want her to ask him now, for he had never told her a lie in his life and he did not want to talk before the whole family.

As he went toward the barn, he thought, "I will just go on now." He was still wearing his best clothes and the piece of paper was in his pocket. So he caught his mule and put the saddle on it. No one had come outside. He turned the mule and started up the road.

When he got to Vince Owens' house he stopped and got off his mule, tied the bridle to a fence post, and went in.

He knocked at the door and a voice from within told him to "Come in, if your nose is clean." He pushed the door open. Sarah and her mother were sitting before the fireplace. The young girl's lap was full of wool, with a full basket by her side. They were carding the wool, which would later be spun into yarn.

When Sarah saw who had entered the room, she put her hand up to her mouth, then dumping all the wool into the basket, she got up and made a fast retreat for the kitchen.

"Well, well," laughed Cindy, "you sure have plagued Sarah. She thought it was one of the young'uns a'foolin' us. She never dreamt it was someone a'comin' in. She would never a'said that to you. Well, git ye a chair and sit a spell," she finished. Kitteneye sat down in the chair, now vacated by Sarah.

"Where is ye old man, Cindy?" he asked. He did not really want to know, but good manners demanded that he ask.

"He took a turn of corn to the mill," she answered, still working away with her wool and wooden cards.

"Yeah, I fergit it was mill day."

"Isom," she asked in a very concerned voice, "what fer are ye all dressed up in your Sunday go to meetin' clothes and it be a weekday?"

"Well," he said, "that's why I stopped. I wanted to tell ye I am git'n married today."

"Kitteneye, are ye goin' to marry Jane Hughes?" she exclaimed.

"Yeah, I went to town and got my license yesterday. I am on my way to her house now."

"But son, do you like her a whole lot?" she asked. They had always been real good friends and Cindy knew she could speak freely with him.

"Well," he mused, "I 'spect it is more for Cleveland's sake, and I am twenty-four years old. Most everybody else has been married a long time, agin they are that old. You know she lays Cleveland to me," he blushed when he said this.

"Yeah, I jest about know he is your'n. If ever a child daddied itself, he shore does. He is jest the spittin' image of ye. But I shore hate to see ye marry her."

They sat there for a while, both lost in their own thoughts. Finally, Cindy began to laugh.

"Anyway, I thought I had been raisin' ye a good girl. I have teased Sarah about you and told her how that I fergit her that time, and went off and left her at ye maw's house. You shore had made ye mind up to keep her then."

"Well, it's not altogether been a joke with me, but I just got mixed up with Jane, and anyway there's Cleveland. Sarah would not want to be bothered with him."

"Well, Kitteneye, I told ye I was raisin' ye a good girl. If ye want to wait a few more months, I believe everything will work itself out. Lay them license there in the fire."

"Alright," he said, and taking the paper from his pocket, he slowly placed it in the fire and watched as it curled, then caught, and soon became ashes.

"A long trip to town and two dollars all went for nothin'," he laughed. "but less ways I won't haf'n to tell Maw after all."

Then he turned to Cindy and said, "Well, ye are willin', the preacher is, and I am. I guess I will just have to talk Sarah into being willin'."

Sarah, who had been eavesdropping during all this talk, whispered to herself, "That's not goin' to be as hard a job as you suspect, Kitteneye."

And it must not have been too much trouble. In the year 1887, and on the twenty-eighth day of July, John L. Slone, an Old Regular Baptist minister, pronounced them man and wife. And they loved each other until they were separated by death.

I DON'T KNOW very much about their courtship days, but I don't think my story would be complete unless I told you of one happening that almost brought an end to their friendship before it had barely begun. They were planning on going to church that day, around on Hollybush. Sarah was to wait before the house, near the "chop block," while Kitteneye went to catch his mule. So while Sarah stood there in all her best clothes and a with a blanket folded to use as a cushion, Kitteneye took the bridle and started for the pasture.

He soon located Old Barney. But a large patch of ragweed, now in bloom, stood between him and the mule. He took one look at those weeds and then thought what they would do to his nice new britches. His mother had sewn them from cloth she had woven herself. She had even raised the flax and spun the thread. She had not dyed the cloth, so they were a kind of cream color, almost white. Those weeds were damp with dew and loaded with yellow pollen. If he walked through there, his pants would be ruined.

He glanced back over his shoulder and saw he was well out of sight. Pulling his pants off, he hung them on the pasture fence and went after the mule in his shirttail.

The mule did not want to be caught. He had found some very nice tasty grass and he preferred eating to going to church. It took Kitteneye quite a while, but he finally won out and put the bridle where it belonged, on Old Barney, and led him back to the fence where he had left his britches.

He looked and looked. He knew this was the right place, where he had climbed over the fence. He could still see the path of trampled-down weeds. What he could not see was his britches.

Then, he glanced over on the other side of the pasture fence, and lo and behold, there stood a two-year-old steer a'chomping away at his new pants while he stood there in his shirttail.

He rescued what was left, which was very little, not even enough to wear.

"Now what a mess I've got myself in," he said to himself. "Devil take that old calf."

The only way out of the hollow was right past the house, where Sarah was waiting. He hoped she had given up and gone inside. There was only one thing to do.

He mounted his mule, and started him running at a very fast lope. He did not even glance at the house. He saw Sarah through the corner of his eye, as the astonished mule went flying by with Kitteneye on its back, without saddle or pants.

I don't know how he ever explained it to her, but I guess they had many a good laugh about the time they did not go to church together.

CHAPTER NINE

I DON'T KNOW if they had a "workin'" when there was a log cabin to be built for my parent's first home. If so, all their brothers decided on a given day. Everyone on Caney was invited or asked to come. Bringing their own tools, they built a one-room cabin, to which more could be added later. The trees had been cut and hauled to the site before by Kitteneye, with a pair of oxen.

Each man did what he was best at; some hewed, and some notched the ends of the logs. Then everyone helped to place them on top of each other. The ridgepole was the hardest one to get in place, and even the womenfolk sometimes helped when there weren't enough men present. The roof was made of split boards, with the space between daubed with mud and clay taken from the creek banks. A chimney was built on the side, a door opening on another side. The door "shutter" was also made from split boards. Split logs were smoothed on the flat side to make the floor, and were called "puncheons." To keep these floors clean, they were scrubbed with beat-up sand rocks and a scrub broom.

I guess Kitteneye built his own chimney. I know he was a good hand to build chimneys. They used slate rocks, which were easier to chip and form. Stuck together with clay, they were not so heavy to stack. There would be a large open fireplace for heating and cooking. A large "back log" big enough to burn for several days was placed in the back of the fireplace, and a "fore log" placed in front, each end laying on a rock, or on a block of iron. This was so the fire could get air. Smaller pieces of wood were stacked crisscross so they would catch fire easy. The kindling would be put under this and lighted with a spark, made by beating a piece of steel against a flint stone. Many times when the fire had gone out, one of the kids would be sent to a neighbor to borrow some burning pieces of wood. So if someone seems to be in a hurry, we use the expression, "What did you come for? A shevilful of fire?"

At the working the women would be busy cooking a good dinner: chicken and dumplings for sure, plenty of fried eggs, meat either cooked or fried, large stacks of gingerbread and sweetcakes, egg custards, apple pie, maybe shucking beans or corn field peas, blackberry dumplings, and pots and pots of coffee.

These folks worked hard and ate hearty. There was always plenty to eat. If it was summertime, someone's job was to keep the flies from getting on the table. This was accomplished by waving a small branch or twig broken from a tree, backwards and forwards, over the food, while everyone was eating. Someone else took her place with the "swithin'" while she ate.

The men were fed first, then the women and children, but there was always enough for everyone and a lot of jokes and plenty of laughter. They worked together, ate together, and loved each other as neighbors were intended to do since time began. I think a lot was lost when these old ways were changed to so-called better ones.

I am not going to say that everyone got along together in love and fellowship. There were quarrels and disputes, even ending in fights and gun battles. Some men were killed. That has been told and written about, but I hope to show you another life, one that was more real and true: people who joined together to help their neighbors. A working was a social event that was enjoyed by everyone. A lot of work was done, a lot of food eaten, and a lot of enjoyment had by all.

Some folks had a dance the night after the working, but I am almost sure Kitteneye and Sarah did not. Both Sarah and Kitteneye's parents were Old Regular Baptists, and music and dancing are not allowed by our church.

I guess there would have been some drinking of "good corn liquor." Drinking moonshine, so long as you did not get drunk, wasn't thought of as a sin back then. I have been told that even the preachers would take a drink now and then. My stepmother said her parents always kept a large barrel of moonshine sitting inside their cabin door, with a cup on a nail above, so anyone, even the small children, could take some whenever they desired. Moonshine whiskey was used a lot for medicine.

I do not know if Sarah's first home was built by friends and neighbors, or by Kitteneye himself. I don't even know just where it was. I do know it was somewhere on the head of Caney Creek, near Trace. He once told me how he made their first bed out of poles stuck into the cabin logs, in one corner. Then he laced the poles together with strips of leather for springs. The mattress was a cloth bag filled with shucks, and I am almost sure my grandmother gave them a feather bed and pillows. All mountain girls had a supply of quilts made by the time they were old enough to get married, beautiful quilts, an art in their designs and with stitches so small you had to look close to see them, patterns such as Double Wedding Ring, Robbin' Peter To Pay Paul, Drunkards' Path, and many, many others. These patterns were exchanged with neighbors and friends and were regarded as very precious.

In a like way, mountain people would help each other butcher their hogs. Even the small kids and women would do what they could. From the beginning, when the fire was built to heat the water, until the hairs were cleaned up and burned, much work had to be done. The chickens must not eat the hairs. If they did, they would take the "squalks" and die.

There was a lot of fun. Someone would be asked to measure the hog's tail. If he had never heard the joke before, he would be told to place his finger along the underside of the hog's tail to see how far it would reach up his arm. Then with a quick push the poor unsuspecting guy's finger would end up in the hole under the hog's tail. As the now wiser embarrassed fellow went to wash his hands, everyone would laugh. This was childish and simple, but it made life more enjoyable and changed what would have been hard work into play.

As soon as the liver was removed from the hog, great chunks were thrown on the fire to "brile." These the children would eat just as soon as they were cooked enough to be edible.

The bladder was saved and made into a balloon. Even the intestines or "guts" were used. They were cleaned, washed, and dried to be later made into soap.

The small pieces and scraps left over from rendering the lard were called "cracklin's." These were used to make soap. They were also very good mixed with cornmeal and water, to make "cracklin' bread."

My father always said that all of the hog was used except the "squeal," and if he could find a use for it, he would try to save that. Anyway his children squealed enough to suit him.

A large kettle of the meat was cooked and after everyone

had eaten, each neighbor was given a "mess" to take home. The rest was "salted down" or made into sausage.

It's better not to feed your hogs just before killing them, since they are easier to clean and the feed is not wasted. But my father always fed his. He said he did not want anything to die hungry.

Another happy time was a "molassie stir-off." Every family had a crop of cane that had to be harvested just as soon as the seeds became ripe. If left standing any longer, the stalks began to dry. If cut too soon, the molasses would have a sour taste and would not keep. There was usually just one person in a community with a gin mill and a molasses pan. Kitteneye owned one.

He would take his equipment, set it up near the crop of cane, and begin his work. All the neighbors would gather to help. The seed pods were saved for chicken feed. The blades were dried for fodder. The stocks were cut and run through the gin mill. The juice was then boiled in the large pan placed over a fire.

When it first begins to boil, a green slimy scum is formed on top. This must be dipped off with a long-handled skimmer. This scum was thrown into a large hole dug in the ground. It was always a big joke if someone slipped and fell into this messy hole. They would use any trick to get each other into this hole.

When the molasses had boiled enough, a plug was pulled from a hole in one corner of the pan. The fragrant foamy liquid was caught in barrels or empty lard cans.

Eating molasses foam is one of my most pleasant childhood memories. We would take a stalk of cane and dip into the molasses, twirling it around until it was covered with a thick layer, licking it off while it was still hot. Everyone ate from the pan or barrel; maybe not so sanitary, but real enjoyment—better than marshmallow.

My father received some of the molasses in payment for his work and the use of his gin and pan. Every visitor was given a bucket or jarful, to take home.

One of my cousins told me that he found a barrel of molasses on his porch one morning. He knew it had been left there by Uncle Kitteneye. He and his brothers and sisters were very pleased with this gift. Their father at that time was being detained against his own will at the government's expense at Frankfort. He had been caught in the wrong place at the wrong time by the wrong people.

My father also made chairs. I don't know when he first began or who he learned this trade from, so he may have made the first ones to have been used by Sarah in her new home.

As I have said, these folks thought nothing of working twelve hours a day. Kitteneye told me that one day after they had worked all day hoeing the corn, he and my mother came home at the edge of dark, very tired. While she prepared their supper, he sat down in the door and laid back on the floor to rest. When she got her bread in the dutch oven and placed it before the fire, she also came and sat down in the door and stretched out beside him. They soon fell asleep and were awakened the next morning when their cow decided it was milk time and stuck her head in the door and gave a loud moo.

I wish I knew a lot more about their life together. I know they worked hard. As for "book learnin'," my mother knew only one letter, the letter "O." But she was educated in the things she needed to know: how to raise a family; how to card wood, and spin it to yarn; how to dye the yarn with bark and roots gathered from the hillside, which of these to use to get the color she wanted; and how to knit this yarn into stockings and caps for her husband and children. With some help, she sheared wool from her own sheep.

She knew when to plant her garden, which plants grow better in one soil than another, when to fertilize—using manure from the barn and chicken house, and rotten cinders and ashes from the fireplace—and how much was needed.

She loved to make her rows of beans and peas as straight as an arrow, dragging up large "ridges" or beds for her sweet potatoes, beets, and parsnips. She had artistic interest in how pretty she could make them look. She knew how to grow all the different vegetables, when to plant, to hoe, and gather them. She knew how to dry the green beans, to make shuck beans, and how to dry the "punkin" and cushaw (crookneck squash) for winter use. She sliced them into rings, about an inch wide, and hung them from a pole over the fireplace. She would have large barrels of shelled beans for soup beans. She knew how to make sauerkraut and pickled corn and beans.

She had a very large garden—row after row of vegetables—but the very best, with the richest soil, she used for her flowers: fall roses (zinnias), marigolds, bachelor's buttons, and touch-me-nots, and many others, too many to name.

My mother had no education, but in the things she needed to know, she had a master's degree, given to her by the greatest Master of them all. She knew the value of prayer, and how to serve the Lord. She joined the Old Regular Baptist Church when she was very young. In fact, she was one of the first eight to form the Mt. Olive Church.

She never went further away from home than five miles in her whole life. She had gone to the Lower Caney Church house and had crossed the hills to the Reynolds Fork Church and Carr's Church. She had even gone to visit her daughter that lived in Mallet. But she had never gone to see her oldest daughter living in Ball, no more than twenty miles away.

I know she had rambled all over these hillsides as a child

and young woman, hunting her cow and sheep, and bringing them in from the pastures. She had gone to dig roots, and gather barks and leaves, to make her dye and medicine, picking berries and gathering stovewood. I am almost sure she also went with my father to "fight fire," when the woods would get on fire and all the neighbors would join together. There were two ways a fire was "let out." First, every spring the "sage" grass was burned off the pastures to give way for the new grass to come up. Second, when a new ground was cleared, meaning all the trees cut down, the large logs were hauled away for use as firewood or buildings, and the smaller limbs were then piled up and burned. We called it burning brush. This was a get-together for all the neighbors, but sometimes the fire got out of control. The greatest danger was to the split rail fence. Many times Sarah and Kitteneye would pitch all the rails down the hill in advance of an oncoming fire to save them, later going back and carrying them, one at a time, to rebuild the fence.

My mother loved to cook, and fed everyone who came to her door. If anyone passed the house near mealtime, she would ask them to come in and eat with her. She often said she hoped no one had passed her house hungry.

They had a large family, so the table was extra long. My mother always had this big long table filled with bowls and platters of food, more than enough for her own family.

My sister told me of one time when seven men stopped in out of a rain storm. They were on their way from Carr, going to Wayland to work in the coal mines. When the men came into the house, my mother had dinner on the table. She asked the men to eat with them. All she added extra on the table were the seven plates and seven knives and forks. Yet everyone had all they wanted to eat.

The mountain folks took the words in the marriage

ceremony, "What God has joined together let no man put asunder," for what they were meant to be. No man talked very much to another man's wife unless the husband was present. On entering the house for a visit, he asked at the door where the "old man" was. If he wasn't at home, he would not come in. If the man of the house was working somewhere near, he would go find him. If the job was something at which he could help, he would do so, while talking.

If it was cold weather and there were some of the "big young'uns" at home, the visitor might stay for a little while, even if the husband was gone. The woman would always ask about the other's wife, and ask him to bring her and come see them sometimes.

When two mountain people met, they always asked each other to go home with them, and when anyone passed the house he was asked to come in. The one who was passing also asked the other folks to go home with him. This was a very strict code of the hills, and it was very bad manners if you did not observe them. Another rule is to always follow a visitor who is leaving to the door and talk with him until he is outside and always ask him to come back soon.

If a woman or man was said to be "clever," that meant they were unselfish and anyone was welcome to eat with them. If a woman or a girl was called "honest," it did not mean she would not steal, but that she had high moral values. Of course, there were a few "mean" women or "ridge runners" who were free with their favors, and gave themselves to any man who asked. These women were always shunned by all the "honest" women. A bastard or "wool colt" was fed and clothed, but never fully accepted. I remember being scolded by my father because I walked up the road one evening after school with a boy who did not know who his father was. This was a "double standard," for father had two children of his own without being married to their mother. As this is a true story, I must tell the bad as well as the good. My half-brothers were a part of our family, as much as anyone. The oldest one, Cleveland, is now buried in our family graveyard.

We people of the mountains are very clannish, with a family unity and closeness hard to understand and still harder to explain. You cannot help but notice how the same name will appear on mailboxes and business fronts: a few miles through the mountains and there will be only Halls, then Collins, to be replaced by Gayhearts. From all the old folks who obtained grants to land you will still find some bearing the same name, living on the same land. My own grandchildren are the tenth generation of Slones who were born, lived—and the first seven generations died and buried—here on Caney, within two miles of the same place where they settled in 1790.

MY MOTHER WAS one of the very few on Caney who could not read and who had no learning at all. The eight grades were all that were taught. You could then go to Hindman, where George Clark had a teacher training class. If you completed this and could pass the exam given by the state, you were qualified to teach.

I know the eighth grade is far from a college education, but it can not be classed as illiterate. In reading, spelling, arithmetic, history and geography, the grades were more advanced than that which is taught in school now, though in science and arts, they knew very little. If you had completed the fifth grade under these old teachers, you would have known about the same as an eighth grader does now.

Much more than half of our Caney folks finished the grades before 1916, and many became teachers. My oldest sister, Flora Belle Fugate, was one of these teachers; her husband was also.

We also had some very good lawyers, not on Caney, but in

Knott County. My uncle ElCaney Slone was one. He had always been the sickly one of the family and so he got more education. Sickly as he was, he lived to be over 100 years old.

There were many people who had talents. Some made beautiful chairs and fern stands with a "handmade lay" turned by a foot-powered pedal. Charley Huff made beautiful baskets accurate to size, holding either a peck, half-bushel, or one bushel.

Sarah Reynolds and Martha Watson wove beautiful blankets. I remember my mother had some of these. I have a small coat made from a piece of this hand-woven cloth. They raised the sheep, processed the wool, even dyed it with a dye made from roots and bark. They had intricate patterns of checks and stripes.

When my mother died, her home contained many pieces of furniture made by Preacher Billie Slone, a shelf for dishes called a cupboard, and a writing desk with several small drawers, expertly made. He had decorated them by making a notched edge using only an auger and handsaw. I still have the quilt shelf he made for my mother in payment for two bushels of "shelled-out" beans.

Their love of beauty was shown in the many beautiful quilts. They raised the cotton to pad these, though I don't think they spun any cotton. They did grow hemp and spun a crude kind of linen that they called homespun cloth.

Their shoes were moccasins made from leather, skinned from a cow or mule that had died from old age or disease, or a cow killed for food. My father said he was grown before he owned a pair of store-made shoes. He worked three days hoeing corn at twenty-five cents a day for some old man who lived at Jone's Fork. The shoes cost seventy-five cents a pair and the brand name was "stronger than the law." These heavy, awkward shoes were made in the same style for men and women, and in sizes for children also.

Some children would go barefoot all winter, staying in the house all the time except for the few moments each day when the call from nature came. When this happened, a large smooth board was heated before the fire and carried along to supply a warm place for the feet. The board was taken back to the house to be used again next time.

My stepmother told of using a "hot board" to stand on when they were washing clothes, or working at the loom. She said they were so careful with their "stronger than law" store shoes that they carried them with them to church, stopping just outside the door of the meeting house to put their shoes on. Sometimes the boyfriend would have the pleasure of carrying a girl's shoes for her. They used sheep tallow for polish.

That they were artistic and loved beauty is shown in so many ways. Mountain people grew "corn beads" or "Job's tears." The seeds are very pretty, with a hole through the center, and can be strung like beads. They decorated beautiful "comb cases" and picture frames for the walls of their homes with these beads.

For wallpaper, they pasted up newspaper and magazines. I taught my children the alphabet from my walls. My kids also invented a kind of "hide-and-go-seek" game. One would describe a picture or repeat a sentence seen somewhere on the wall. The first one to discover it got to choose the next. Living in these magazine walls gave you a feeling of being inside a storybook.

I always tried to read everything in these papers before I "papered the house." If not, I would sometimes get so interested in something I saw I would stop to read, and my paste would all dry up.

Almost every housewife knew how to sew and made clothes for her family. I have a picture of a large group of men and women who lived on Caney. They are nicely dressed, in the styles that were popular at the time—somewhere near 1890. I am sure their clothes were "homemade." A few had sewing machines; most sewed by hand.

They were intelligent folks, skilled and educated well in what they needed to know, because they had to make do with what they had.

That was a lesson I grew up with. We threw away nothing. To us a patch was not a bright colored swatch, placed "haper-scaper" on our jeans to make them look fancy. We patched our clothes to prolong their life and to keep the wind from whistling through a hole. Sometimes we even patched the patches.

There was not much we could do to make our shoes last longer except "half-sole" them and replace the strings with a strip of groundhog hide. When the hole in the crown of a man's hat became so large that it would no longer stay on his head, the brim was cut into strips and used for lamp wicks.

When quilts had outgrown their usefulness for the beds, they made saddle blankets, covers for a chicken coop, a dog bed, or they were hung over the opening of the outhouse or barn in place of a door shutter, or placed on the floor as a pallet for the baby. Our dish rags and wash clothes were from worn-out wearing things. An old meal sack became a towel. No Pampers hung from tree limbs along the creek. We used old bed sheets—after they became so thin you could sun bees through them—for diapers or "diddies" as we called them. A tick, a large cloth bag filled with corn shucks, was a mattress. For folks that did not keep geese or ducks and did not kill enough chickens to get feathers for pillows, the seed pods from milk weed did just fine. A man's shaving brush was also made from shucks. The razor strap was a good "chastising rod." My father always said, "if used enough it makes children walk straighter."

Even our toys were "make do's." A few gravels placed in an empty tobacco can became a rattle for baby. Empty thread spools strung together were another plaything. Jackstones were small chunks from a broken churn or crock. I was in high school before I knew you were supposed to have a small ball to go with the game of Jackstones. There were many games to be played with corn: Fox and Geese, Five Up, Hully Gully. Toy animals were made from cornstalks and everyone knows about the corn shuck dolls. Corncobs were made into pipes and also burned as fuel.

A washtub could be kept from leaking for a while by sprinkling cornmeal in it. After burning tar paper over the hole, some people used homemade soap to plug up the leak. Put on wooden "runners," a tub became a sled to haul manure and cinders for the garden, or to haul off rocks. It could be a home for baby chicks to protect them from rats, or a feed trough for Old Bossie. It might be filled with dirt and planted with flower seeds. An old dish pan was often nailed to the roof, where the stove pipe came through, thus protecting the boards from the heat, and also keeping the rain from running down the pipe onto the stove. An old saw too dull to cut wood became "laid hoes" or "fire shevils." Did you know you could use a dead turtle's shell for a soap dish?

Empty lard buckets became lunch pails, water or milk containers, and when there was more company than plates to "go around," the younger children could "eat off" the bucket lids for plates. An empty cream can made an unbreakable cup for little children.

Ashes from the fireplace made a fine polisher for pots and pans and silverware. Sand was used to scrub our floors and wooden chairs.

We were always glad to get wooden boxes or crates, such as the ones packed with fruit. We nailed them to the walls for bookshelves, or for dishes or clothes.

Potatoes and apple peelings were saved and fed to the chickens or pigs. Sometimes if apples were "scarce," the hulls, or peelings, were cooked in water and the juice made into jelly. The rest was run through a sifter and became applebutter when mixed with sugar and spices.

Even the eggshells were not wasted. They were browned and fed to the hens, or strung on the twigs of a tree in the yard to become an "egg tree." All food not eaten by the family was fed to the farm animals. Once an "outsider" lady came to Caney to spend the summer. She rented a small house from my father. She asked him what she should do with her garbage. When told what we did with ours she bought a pig from him. That fall when she started home, she came to him and said, "I would like to sell the pig back to you. I have only used it for six months. I think I should get back at least half what I paid you for it. Don't you?"

MY FATHER AND mother had a very large family. On October 9, 1914, she gave birth to her last child. Five weeks later she died.

She was never "out of bed" after I was born except once. My father had gone over "in the head of Hollybush" to bring sheep home. During the summer they were turned loose, as all stock were, to forage for themselves. There were no stock laws then. Everyone kept a fence around their crops and gardens. The animals ran loose. In the fall, they were rounded up and put in the barn lot or stall, where they could be fed and watered. As my father went past the house with the sheep, my mother came to the door to see them. This was the last time she ever walked.

Just a few nights before she died, she spoke to my father. He had pulled his bed up by the side of her bed so she could awaken him if she needed anything during the night. "Isom," she said, "Are you asleep?"

"Well, I was before ye spoke, but I am awake now. What do ye want?"

"I just want a talk. I wanta tell ye I han't goin' to get well."

"Now Sarah, don't talk like that. You're gettin' better every day."

"I've been showed I han't goin' to get well. I am kinda glad to go. I am so tired of bein' sick and I want to go home, and be with my little ones that have gone on to live with Jesus. I just hate to leave you and my children, especially this baby one. Will you promise me you will never have her whopped?"

Kitteneye could hardly speak for the tears, but he tried to talk jokingly.

"Ye know I never was one for whoppin' the young'uns. I allus left that up to you."

"I know, but I want you to promise you won't ever let anyone whop her."

And he answered, "I promise."

There were many times when this promise was to be remembered in the future. And this is why I never got a spanking in my life. Kitteneye would go to the teachers and tell them that if they could not teach me without spanking me to send me home. You would think that I would have been very naughty, but it worked the other way. I was afraid I would get home, so I was real good at school.

A few days after this talk, Sarah was feeling a lot better. The weather was warm for November. Elizabeth Slone had stopped in for a visit and to see "how Sarah was doing." Sarah had a piece of cloth from which she wanted some caps made for the baby. Little ones always wore caps, night and day, through the winter. Elizabeth had said she would be more than glad to sew the caps if Sarah could cut them out first.

Edna remembers that she was sitting, holding the baby on her lap. She was only seven years old herself. One of the older girls was looking for the piece of cloth.

Kitteneye had taken Frances with him to gather a sled of corn, just enough to feed on for a few days. He had been "putting off" gathering the whole crop until his wife got well enough to be left alone with just the girls. He had just got part of the way up the hollow when he heard someone ringing the dinner bell. He knew by the low mournful sound of that bell what had happened. He left his mule and sled and ran home just as fast as he could. But he was too late. His wife was dead. He always said he believed she recognized him standing at the foot of the bed, for she seemed to smile at him.

"She was jest a'sittin' there, laughin' and talkin' to us and all at once she put her hand up to her face and said, 'Oh, my head,'" Elizabeth told him.

In a daze, Kitteneye prepared his own wife for burial. This had to be done before the body became stiff. He placed her straight in the bed, tied her feet together, crossed her hands on her breast, and, using a cloth, he caught it under her chin and brought it up over her head and tied it. Two pieces of money were placed on her eyes, so the weight would keep them closed. This was a work of love; he would not have allowed anyone else to do this had there been anyone there. It was the last thing he could do for his wife, and a task he had performed for many a neighbor and friend.

Dora Bell Taylor bathed and dressed the body. Some of the children remembered that their mother had expressed a desire to be put away wearing her favorite black satin dress. Over this dress was put a white shroud made by Sarah Reynolds. Preacher Billie Slone made the coffin from seasoned wood, lined it with white cloth, and covered the outside with black cloth. The edges were trimmed with lace. Some folks used cotton to pad the inside bottom, but Sarah had a beautiful quilt she had made herself for this purpose.

Both the coffin and shroud were made in the home where the corpse lay.

We sent for all the children who were married. Flora Belle had married Sam Fugate and lived on Lower Ball. She had three children. Square Slone, one of our cousins, went after her. It took one day to make the trip there on a mule and another day to come back. Usually a body was only kept up one night after death, but Mother wasn't buried until the third day, because it took that long to get Flora word and bring her home.

Arminda said she remembers that another cousin, Isaac Slone, came to get her in Mallet. My mother had asked that the funeral be preached before she was buried, and not a year later as most folks then did. She did not want any drinking going on at her funeral, and she was afraid there would be, if it was delayed for a year.

This practice is still honored in some families. It probably began back in the days of the circuit rider preacher, who only came once a year in his round of visits.

Everything was done out of love and friendship: the grave was dug, the coffin made, the sewing done. None of these mountain friends thought of it as work and would have been insulted if anyone had offered them pay. To have paid for these services as we do today would have seemed to these folks like paying someone to kiss you.

When my mother was buried there was a small house built to cover the grave. These are now a forgotten part of the past. The lower part of the house was latticework and the roofs were made of rough board shingles. The tombstone was of slate rock with the name and dates crudely chipped in with handmade tools.

These houses protected the graves from the wild animals, and kept the rain from falling on a loved one's grave.

I remember my Grandmother and Grandfather Owens

had a larger house covering both their graves. It had a small door. Many times when my troubles and sorrows became too heavy for my childish heart, I would crawl through this door to cry in private. I always came away comforted.

These little gravehouses were torn down about 1940, very much against my wishes. The old board sign—whose words were burnt into the wood by using a hot poker—is gone from above the gate. It said, "God bless them that sleep here."

I guess my scribblings are like my crazy quilts, without any form or unity. The more I write, the more I remember. There are just so many things I want to say, maybe some are interesting only to me. Our young folks have lost so much without ever knowing they had it to lose.

CHAPTER TWELVE

Of ALL THE things my father taught me, I am thankful that I learned from him the enjoyment one could obtain from work. I did not know until I was grown that there were people who did not like to work, and not until my children were grown did I realize that some folks thought it was shameful to do manual labor. (I must admit, though, I do not like to do housework. I like for a house to be a home, a comfortable place to live, not a "show room.")

I wish I could pass on to my grandchildren how I feel about growing our own food. All good things come from God. But you seem so close to Him, one with nature, when you plant the tiny seeds, in faith that they will grow. Later there is the joy of gathering and storing away these results of your partnership with nature. The food you grow yourself tastes much better and seems a lot cleaner to me. It may not be "untouched by human hands," but at least you know whose hands they were.

Mike was once helping me to dig a mess of potatoes for

supper and asked, "Granny, why do you put your potatoes in the ground? Is it so your chickens can't get at them? Mother gets hers at the market."

I've always been thankful we owned a farm of our own, to grow corn, for example. A "new ground" (pronounced as one word) was best. This meant the ground had been cleared of all the trees and underbrush, and was now ready to be planted.

If you were lucky enough to have a new ground you would be assured of a good crop but a lot more work. It had to be all done by hand, using only hoes. Although most of the larger roots and stumps were removed—either by burning or dynamite, or sometimes pulled out by oxen—there were still too many small roots and sprouts to make plowing possible.

So, early in the spring, sometimes as early as January or February, we would begin "grubbin'," digging the young sprouts that were beginning to grow around where the trees had grown. After these were all dug, they were raked into piles and burned. Then we took hoes and shaved off the weeds. Each one working would take a "swith" and distance themselves as long as they could reach with a hoe, one above the other, each one just a little ahead of the one above. Around the hill they would go, raking a very small layer of the topsoil along with the weeds onto the row below. After this was finished, they would "dig in" the corn, about every three feet, in rows about four feet apart. A small loose hole was dug, with three to five grains of corn dropped inside, and the dirt spread over it. My father always said to plant five,

> One for the ground squirrel,
> One for the crow,
> One to rot,
> And two to grow.

[61]

When the corn was about a foot high, you began to hoe it, cutting all the weeds, and thinning it to two stalks to a hill. Someone would always joke and say, "Pull up the large ones and give the little ones room to grow." We replanted any missing hills and a few weeks later we hoed it again. This second hoeing was called "laying it by," because this finished all the work with the corn until time to save the fodder and gather the corn. The fodder was gathered in September and the corn brought to the barns in November. When we "layed by our corn" it called for a wild celebration. Folks on adjoining farms were always in friendly competition. Each would rush to beat the others. Our hills are so close, many different family groups could see and hear each other. When the last "hill of corn" was hoed they would begin to yell, beating their hoes together or against rocks, thumping on the dinner bucket, anything to make a noise. Someone at the house would ring the dinner bell, telling all their friends that they were through with their corn. An extra good dinner or supper, as the case might be, would be cooked, and everyone had at least one whole day's rest. Even the mules got this one day without working.

Another little saying of my father's helped us remember what happened when you waited too long to plant your corn:

> In July, corn knee-high,
> In August, he layed it by,
> In September there came a big frost.
> Now you see what corn this young
> man lost.

Fodder also had to be saved. All the blades from where the ear of corn grew down were stripped from the stalk, leaving the one on which the corn grew. Every few handfuls were placed between two stalks close to the ground; here they would cure out. After a few days, these would be tied into bundles, and stacked in a shock, or hauled to the barn. The remaining stalk was cut off just above the ear of corn, and tied into bundles and placed together in smaller shocks. These were called "tops" and were not as valuable as the blade fodder. The tops were usually fed to the cows, and the rest kept for the horses. Taking care of fodder was one work I could never do. I know now I was allergic to the smell, though I did not know what was wrong then. I just knew I always got sick when I pulled fodder or cut tops, but it never seemed to bother me once it was cured out, and I could help put it away.

My father's generation had no glass jars, so they did not can fruits or vegetables. They filled large crocks or churns with applebutter. When boiled down very stiff and sweetened with molasses, it would keep fresh for many weeks. Big barrels were filled with smoked apples; a few holes were made in the bottom of the barrel so the juice would run out, then filled up a few inches with apples that had been pared and sliced, with the core removed. On top of these a dish was placed in which a small amount of sulfur was slowly burned by placing a heated piece of iron inside the dish. A quilt over the top kept the smoke from escaping. Next day, another layer of apples and more sulfur was burned and so on, until the barrel was full. The sulfur gave the apples an "off" flavor that took a little getting used to, but was supposed to be good for you. I loved the taste myself, and always served them topped with blackberry jelly.

The late apples could be "holed away" in the ground. Often the floor of the house was removed and the hole dug there. It was lined with straw, the apples were poured in, and more straw and dirt were mounded over the top. You had to be very careful that none of these apples were bruised or rotten. Some were kept in barrels, each wrapped separately in a piece of paper. Sweet potatoes were also kept this way. Many times these barrels were left all winter in a corner of the bedroom, hid from view by a curtain or quilt. Apples were fried, or made into pies and dumplings.

Peaches were canned in syrup. We had a "cling stone" peach, so small that the stone could not be removed as in other peaches. Often we would peel these and can them whole—the stone gave them a very nice flavor—sometimes using sugar, and some in sugar, vinegar, and spice. We had a few pears, and I remember my sister, Frances, had a quince tree. Some folks, not many, had cherries and plums, but almost everyone had a gooseberry patch, and strawberries grew wild in many places. We picked and canned huckleberries and raspberries, but we used blackberries the most; from these we made jelly and jam. Dumplings were made by bringing the sweetened, cooked berries to a boil and dropping in fist-sized balls of biscuit dough.

Berry "sass" was a breakfast dish. The boiling berries were thickened with a little flour and water—not quite as heavy as the sauce used for a pie filling—sweetened and served like a pudding. I always loved to pick berries. No one ever went alone, because of snakes. The huckleberries grew on the tops of ridges. Every year, when they began to ripen, someone would start a rumor that a bear or wildcat had been seen on such and such a hollow, or maybe the story would be that some crazy man or desperate criminal was loose. Moonshiners started these tales so as to scare the women. They were afraid the women would find the moonshine stills while hunting huckleberries.

No one picks berries anymore; almost all the old orchards are gone. Of the fourteen apple trees that grew in my yard when I moved here, only four remain, too old for fruit, giving little shade, and almost dangerous to let stand. In fact, during the severe cold weather this past winter we reopened our fireplace, and chopped one of our apple trees into

Jim "Summer" Slone and his wife, Frankie Slone.

Grandpa Vince Owens and his wife, Lucinda Owens.

Right. This picture was taken of my father and mother about 1905. The building in the back is the schoolhouse where my sister Flora Belle taught. In the back row are Vince Slone, Morrell Slone, Flora Belle Slone Fugate, and Arminda Slone Thomas. In the front are Frances Slone Jacobs, Isom "Kitteneye" Slone, Devada Slone, Sarah Slone, Edna Slone Pratt, and Lorenda Slone.

This photo was taken around 1885. In the first row are Liz Slone, Nancy Owens Slone, Beth Slone, Sally Lee Slone, Elizabeth Lee Slone, Phoebe Jane Lee Slone, someone I don't know, and Margaret "Sis" Sparkman. In the second row are "Fat" Isom Slone and (third from left) Preacher Johnny Slone. The woman with her hand over her eyes is my husband's grandmother, Fairy Slone. The old man in the right-hand corner is Grandpa Owens. At his left is my half-brother Cleveland.

Verna Mae at nine months old.

Verna Mae with daughter Irene.

Left. This is the house where I was born. It was built in 1802 by Shady Slone, my great-great-grandfather. My great-grandfather Billie Slone lived here and it became my grandfather's, Jim Slone's, in 1876. My father bought it in 1901 and lived here and then gave it to my brother, Vince Slone, in 1923. It was torn down and moved from the mouth of Trace and rebuilt at the mouth of Short Fork. Some of the logs are still in use in a barn.

Kitteneye Slone and Morrell Slone, making chairs for Mrs. Lloyd.

Left. Miss Constance, a nurse who was on Caney between 1916-
1922. She is riding Little Beck, my father's mule. She often
borrowed him when her work took her up the hollows and across
the hills. Some of the women criticized her for riding "astraddle";
our womenfolk most always rode behind their men, using a quilt or
blanket for a cushion, or else they used a sidesaddle.

Kitteneye Slone.

firewood. I almost felt like I was forsaking an old friend.

All fruits and berries were eaten raw, or cooked in syrup, and made into jelly and jam, but most were used for dumplings or pies. For peach cobbler the slices were baked with layers of biscuit dough. Apples were used in fried pies, apples or applebutter, folded into small thin sheets of dough and fried in deep fat. I have also heard these called half-moon pies or moccasin pies. We also used vinegar as a substitute for fruit, making pies or dumplings flavored with vinegar, sugar and spice. A "barefoot dumpling" was when the balls of dough were cooked in boiling water, containing only salt and lard. Of course, they were better in chicken broth or fresh meat "sop."

We grew corn for feed and bread, but we also used it as a vegetable, canning it and pickling it in brine salt water for winter use, while the kernels were still young enough to be soft. Pickled corn is good fried in a little sugar, but it's best to eat as a snack, sitting around the fire at night and biting it directly off the cob. "Gritted bread" (probably from the word grater) was made from young corn; a gritter was made by driving holes in a piece of tin, maybe an empty peach can, with a nail, then fastening the tin to a board. The ears of corn were rubbed over the sharp edges made by the nail holes, to make meal. If the corn was young enough, no water needed to be added, just a little salt and baking soda, baked in a greased pan. Eaten with sweet milk, it was a meal in itself. You can use corn to grit until it gets old enough to shell from the cob. After the juice or "milk" on the inside of the grains begins to dry, the water must be added, to make a soft dough before baking.

I guess of all vegetables, beans were used the most. There were many kinds of seeds, from the "bunch" beans grown in the garden, to field beans planted along with the corn. The stalks of corn make a place for the bean vines to grow. Beans were pickled in brine salt water in large wooden barrels. We also canned them. Many times we placed the closed glass jars full of beans in a washtub filled with water allowing them to cook for several hours on a fire outside.

Then there was a "tough" bean. The hull was too hard to eat. These were used for soup beans, cooked by themselves or mixed with the dried beans. Salt pork or hog's jowl was added to the beans while they cooked. A friend once told me how every night, before being allowed to go to bed, he and his brothers and sisters each had to shell enough beans to fill a large cup.

We always raised two crops of cabbage. The later one was planted in early July in the hill and not transplanted. These were "holed away" for winter use. A long trench, or "fur," was made with the plow. The fully grown cabbages were pulled up "by the roots," with a few of the bottom leaves broken off. The remaining excess leaves were wrapped around the "head" and placed side by side with the roots turned up in the hole made by the plow; then dirt was thrown up around the cabbages, leaving part of the stalk and the roots exposed. This way they were easily found and removed. They would stay all winter and keep fresh. Cabbages kept this way have a sweet wholesome flavor that you can get no other way, and far exceeds anything you can buy in the supermarket.

And then, of course, there was sauerkraut: cabbage pickled in salt. I also use a little sugar and vinegar. We now put kraut in glass jars, but "back then" we used large churns or crocks or wooden barrels. Our folks would sometimes put the cabbages in the barrel whole, a layer at a time, and cut them up with a shovel. (I have known of people that dried cabbage. I remember watching an old man, when I lived at Dwarf, drying cabbage leaves on his housetop. I never did eat any.)

Beets were cooked and canned in sugar, spice, water, and vinegar; they were eaten no other way. We served them with shucky beans or as a snack. I love to pickle boiled eggs in the liquid where the beets were cooked; the bright red color makes the eggs pretty and gives them a nice flavor. This is a must at Easter for my family.

Tomatoes were thought to be poison by our grand-mothers, and were raised only as a flower. We canned the ripe ones to be used in vegetable soup; some added sugar and used it for dessert. Of course, during the summer they were sliced and served with green beans, or added to slaw. Green tomatoes are good sliced, rolled in meal, to which a little salt and pepper is added, and fried in deep fat. My husband likes them sweetened, I don't. There is a small variety which we call "tommy toes." Green tomatoes were also canned in sugar, spice, and vinegar, sometimes by themselves, sometimes with peppers, cabbage, and other vegetables. We also mixed green tomatoes, green pepper, and green cabbage, and pickled them in brine salt water; we called this "pickle lilly" or "chow chow." No matter what you called it—fried in grease and eaten with beans and corn bread—it was good. We ate corn bread for at least two meals each day. Very few people do this anymore. It's easier to use the toaster, I guess.

Next to the beans, I guess more potatoes were used. They were "kelp over" by holing them away. They were "fried, baked, cooked, roasted in the ashes under the grate, added to soup, and boiled with their jackets on." Sometimes we would take them to school with us and boil them in an empty lard bucket, on the coal heating stove. The teacher would help us eat them at recess.

We "bedded" our sweet potatoes in a "hot bed" made from shucks, manure, and dirt, and covered with fodder and an old quilt. After they began sprouting, the fodder and quilt were removed. When large enough, the plants were then transplanted to hills or ridges. Sweet potatoes were baked, roasted, fried in sugar and lard, or cooked with some salt and sugar added. We canned them by cooking them in jars, like the beans. We kept them through the winter in barrels or boxes, each wrapped separately in a piece of paper.

Sweet peppers were eaten raw; stuffed with sausage and other meats; canned in sugar, spice, water and vinegar; mixed with other vegetables to make "pickle lilly" or mixed pickles. Hot pepper or strong pepper was eaten as an additive to other vegetables. We also canned it in vinegar, or strung it up on twine, and allowed it to dry for winter use. Some folks like it added to fresh meat when cooked. We put a few pods of hot pepper on the top of our barrels or churns of salt pickles. It kept the gnats from bothering them, and also gave a good flavor. We added red hot pepper to our paste when we were lining our houses with newspaper and magazines. This kept the mice from eating the paste and ruining the paper. I remember once I had made a large kettle of paste from flour and water, to which I had added a large amount of pepper. I had set it on the back of the stove to cool. One of my boys come in from school, took a large spoonful, thinking it was his supper. It really gave him a hot mouth; I was sorry for him, but I had to laugh. He said he knew why the mice refused to eat it.

Cushaw and "punkins" were planted in the corn, every fourth hill, every fourth row. The small ones were fed to the hogs or cows. The hard-shell cushaws were chopped into small chunks and cooked, then placed in a pan, covered with sugar and spice, and baked. The soft-shell ones were peeled, sliced, cooked and mashed with sugar and spice to make cushaw butter. Some folks added cooked cushaw or pumpkin to their cornmeal dough, and baked it. "Molassie bread" was made this way also. Cushaws are better if molasses is substituted for sugar. And, of course, there were "punkin pies." Many cushaws and pumpkins, along with squashes, were dried. A green pole was hung by strings over the open fireplace. The cushaws were sliced into large circles or rings, then hung on this pole. In a few days they were dried, and more were hung up. This way they could be preserved for winter use, cooked with sugar and lard, or maybe salt pork or hog's jowl—very good. I have seen bushels of dried cushaws and "punkins" hung up in the smokehouse in the winter. By spring, it would have all been eaten.

Asparagus was only grown as a shrub in the yard, never eaten. The full-grown bush, with its green fernlike leaves and bright seed pod, is very beautiful. I have heard the old folks say, "You know, there are folks who eat 'sparegrass' when the sprouts are little." Yet, I never knew of anyone trying it.

Artichokes to us are the potatolike roots of a tall plant that have beautiful yellow flowers that resemble daisies. They were only eaten raw, as a snack.

Cucumbers were sweet-pickled and canned, used with other vegetables for "mixed pickles," pickled in brine salt, eaten raw, sliced and served with green beans or slaw.

Peas were one of the earliest seeds to be planted, sometimes as early as February. We grew a tender-hull kind that could be cooked like string beans, hull and all. We very seldom shelled them. Peas are delicious cooked together with very small young potatoes.

We grew two crops of turnips: a few were planted in ridges for summer use, and then in the fall we planted a larger crop, "broadcasting" the seed over the now empty garden. The tops were cooked for greens; the roots were holed away or put in the cellar. The cold weather does not hurt turnips; they keep growing almost all winter. I like to cook them together—the tops and roots—when the turnips are small.

Rhubarb we called "pie plants." Every garden had a long row, used for pies or dumplings, fried as apples, or mixed with strawberries to make jelly. It "came in" just as most of the winter food was used up, and the new garden was still too young to use. It was supposed to be good for you and help to cure "spring fever."

Some of us grew a few gourds just for the fun of it, but our forefathers grew them to be used. The larger ones would hold lard, salt, soft soap, meal, molasses, or whatever. The small, long-handled ones were water dippers. We called the small round egg-shaped kind "hen foolers," because we used them for nest eggs.

There were many different kinds of onions. Fall and winter onions grew through the winter, and could be eaten green. "Tater onions" got their name for the way the new ones grew in a cluster around the old one; they were kept for the roots. "Spring shallots" were very early and very small.

Onions were eaten as a dish, not an additive. They were fried either while green or after grown, but not as "onion rings," as they are now prepared. To keep for winter, they were pulled while there was still some top remaining, tied in bunches, and hung from nails in the barn or smokehouse. They become better after being allowed to freeze. Onions were used as a medicine, roasted, mashed and made into a "pollus" placed on the chest, to help "break up" a cold. Onion soup was also used for a cold or tonsillitis.

Then there were wild greens or "salet." There are many different kinds; sometimes the same plant was known by a different name by different people. "Plantin" is the one used most, a small thick-leafed green with a very distinct flavor, a little like cabbage. Then for cooking there was "sheep's leg," "groundhog ear," and "speckled dock." Poke salet had to be used very carefully, because it could be poison; it was cooked in one water, washed and cooked again, then fried in a lot of lard. If eaten too often, it can become a laxative. The stalks were also good peeled, rolled in meal, and fried. "Crow's foot," "shoestring," "chicken salet," and "creases" were eaten raw, cut up, sprinkled with salt, and then "killed" by pouring real hot grease over them.

In my father's time hogs were allowed to run wild. Each man had a "mark" so as to tell his own. The pig's ear was either notched or split, some used both, but no two exactly alike. When a sow mothered a "gang" of pigs, if the owner did not catch the small ones and mark them before they were weaned, and they had quit running with the mother, they were then accepted as "wild pigs": anyone who caught them was the owner. He could put his mark on them or butcher them for food. Wild hogs grew very fat on "mast": nuts and roots they found in the woods. I thought this gave the meat a good flavor, but I have talked with some folks that said this was not so; they were better if brought in and fed corn a few weeks before butchering them.

The older generations used more beef and sheep for meat than we did, but chicken and dumplings was counted the best dish of any. I have seen my folks cook as many as sixteen grown hens at one time, in an old-fashioned iron "mink" kettle, when there was a big crowd at a wedding, funeral, or family get-together.

Our folks on Caney, in the past, had plenty of good wholesome food. I don't see how they ever ate all these many barrels, holes, cans, and sacks full of beans, corn, cabbage, and many other fruits and vegetables that they called "sass." But they did. Maybe they knew nothing about vitamins or a balanced diet, but they worked hard to grow and put away food.

My father taught me to love nature's beauty as well as her

benefits. I remember how he would listen to the thunder. He would say, "God wouldn't want any of his children to get scared at something He made." I have always loved to listen to the thunder.

He also loved to look at the pretty sunset and rainbows. He often would call me to come outside to enjoy the view with him. The valley would be lit up with bright colors, as the sun set behind the hills. And he would say, "This is the way Eden must have looked before sin entered the world." He would not have known what you meant if you had mentioned any of the masterpieces of paintings. But he enjoyed the pictures painted by the greatest Master of them all. There is nothing more beautiful than a rainbow that seems to form a bridge from one hilltop to the other, or the snow-covered world early in the morning, before man has destroyed it by making paths. The many colors of the autumn leaves remind me of my "crazy quilts," such a blending of colors that the absence of any scheme or pattern makes a beauty or system all its own: a picture you will never forget if you have seen it once.

IN MY FATHER'S time, dinner bells were a necessity. Kitteneye and his neighbors used them for everything from celebrating election returns to telling the family that dinner was ready. We soon learned the different tones of each bell and could tell just who was ringing it by the sound it made. The children were not allowed to ring it just for fun except on Christmas; then everyone rang their bell. There was one old man who every Christmas morning, "let off a blast." The night before he went up on the hill above his house, bored a hole in a tree, and filled the hole with gunpowder and a fuse. Then early Christmas morning, he climbed the hill and lit the fuse. We were all awakened by this loud noise, rang our bells, and shot firecrackers. I guess there is nowhere in the world where folks celebrate Christmas with fireworks, except here in the hills. It's now a violation to use or sell fireworks, but it has not stopped us. Every Christmas our hills ring with the sound.

The birth of a new baby was another glad time for using

the bell. What a time to have a party! That was one occasion when the women took over. No men were allowed; even the father must leave home after bringing the "granny" and letting the kinfolks know. This happy time was known as a "Granny Frolic," and the expecting mother prepared for it in advance by making piles of gingerbread and fattening some frying chickens. In some homes there would be a few pints of moonshine. Every married woman friend and relative was welcome; no young girls were permitted. Anyway they were needed at home to look after the small children and menfolks. After the baby was born, bathed, and powdered with powder made from dry clay taken from between the rocks in the chimney, someone would remove the ax from under the bed. (It had been put there to cut the pains.) After ringing the dinner bell to let everyone know the baby was born and both mother and child were alright, the party began. They always cut up the father's hat, if he had not hidden it. I don't know why—maybe it was supposed to bring good luck.

Mountain children knew nothing about a stork; they were taught that babies "were brung by the Hoot Owl." In the evening when the owl began to call "who, who," the children thought he was saying who wants a baby. They would all run out in the yards and answer, "We do, we do." Maybe that's why our families are so large. Nowhere will you find people who love their children more than we do. No matter how large the family or small the house and income, a new arrival is welcome and loved.

Mountain men show a lot of respect for a pregnant woman. It's a law that if a woman asks for help when her baby is due, a man cannot refuse. Once a friend of mine used this to her advantage. She and her husband were "makin' moonshine." They had a large washtub full of the finished product sitting on their kitchen floor and were adding the spring water to "temper" it. Then they poured it into half-gallon mason fruit jars, ready for sale. The woman went to the door to see if everything was alright, and "fer down the holler" she saw the sheriff coming. She was very frightened, and very pregnant. She told her husband to be very quiet. She knew what to do. When the sheriff came to the door, she went outside and met him—looking just as large as she could—and said, "Oh, am I glad you came. I am here by myself, and my baby is being born. Will you please go git Granny for me?"

"Shore. Where does she live?" he answered, never suspecting a lie.

"About half a mile down the creek. Any'un can tell you where, and please hurry."

"Want me to tell any of your kinfolks?"

"No, she's my mother-in-law."

When the sheriff left, the husband begin to carry the whiskey outside and hide it in the "tater hole." He worked as fast as he could but there were still ten jars left on the kitchen floor when they saw the sheriff returning. He had made a fast trip.

"What will we do?" the poor husband wanted to know. His wife got into the bed and said, "Put those jars here with me." He placed them up and down by her side and then covered them with the quilt and made a fast retreat out the back door just in time.

The sheriff had a search warrant; he looked everywhere for whiskey except in the tater hole and in the bed. A few weeks later he ran into the husband at the courthouse and asked him, "Oh say, which was it, a boy or a girl?" He did not know why everyone laughed when the other man answered, "Oh, a gal, in fact, there were five gals."

Everyone in the hills, if they made whiskey or not, "hated the law," especially revenuers. They all joined together to outdo them when one was seen coming. The person who saw him quit whatever he or she was doing and quickly began ringing the dinner bell. "Dong-dong-dong," then a small pause, and then three times again, never stopping until they heard an answering bell from the next neighbor. That neighbor did the same until he heard the next bell. In a very short time the news had traveled up and down every hollow, giving the moonshiners time to get away and hide.

There were small bells worn on a leather strap by the cows and sheep, and one with a short handle that the teacher rang to "take up books." With all these bells you would think that we would have had a church bell, but us mountain folks have a different feeling about our way of worship—very hard to explain to outsiders. Maybe what my father said will help a little: "We don't need a bell to tell us to come to church, for that call is heard with the heart, not the ears."

CHAPTER FOURTEEN

UNCLE JOHN (SUMMER) Slone ran a small grocery store near the mouth of Short Fork. He was a very small man and as long back as I can remember him, he was drawn over in his back, so crippled with rheumatism that he could scarcely walk. But he kept his wife and kids and "lived good" from what he made in his small store.

My Uncle Milton Owens had the next store, near the mouth of Hollybush. Every two weeks a salesman or a "drummer," as we then called them, would come from Paintsville, Kentucky. Verne Stumbo, a very good friend of mine who is now dead, was a drummer. All his life he came riding a mule and carrying large saddle bags filled with his salesbooks and samples. It took him all week to visit the stores up the many small hollows in his territory. I guess he spent the night in the only hotel in Hindman. But he always ate dinner with some of his customers. I also ran a store for many years and he was still a drummer, but by that time we had a rough sort of road and he drove a car.

After the drummer took his orders back to Paintsville, the groceries or goods were shipped by freight to the depot at Wayland. From there they had to be brought in on a wagon.

My father's job was to take his wagon and team of mules and meet the train, every two weeks, to bring this load of groceries for Uncle John. He had to start long before it was daylight and never returned until after dark, for it was a long journey and mules have to rest every now and then when they have a very heavy load. Some weeks he would have to make two trips. If the groceries were left too long in the depot, he would have to pay a "storage charge." So he tried to meet the train.

During the summer my father would also take a load of vegetables and fruits with him to sell to the folks who lived in and around the coal mining camps in Wayland, Lackey, Punkin Center, Garrett, and Glow. Some of the things that he peddled were from the surplus his own family had grown. But much of it was bought from his neighbors. Sometimes a wooden coop was nailed to the back end of the wagon and filled with young frying chickens.

The stuff was loaded on the wagon the night before and he would get up real early and start on his trip. There were lots of other folks who were doing the same thing, and of course the folks were going to buy what they needed from the first "peddling" wagon who came to their door.

On one particular day he was real early, and he thought to himself, "I have got here before anybody else; I will have good luck in sellin' all my load soon." But he was very surprised when no one would buy anything. Up and down, between the rows of houses he went, knocking on door after door. He sold no food that day except to the doctor's wife and the people who lived in the best and richest homes that the bosses of the mines owned.

He could not understand why no one would buy anything. The day before had been payday at the mines. He knew everyone had plenty of money. His vegetables were fresh and good, and he knew no one had been there before him to have sold to them.

At last he came to a little old shack where an old black woman lived all by herself. He had often given her some of his vegetables for free. This day he stopped before her door and called, "Aunt Mary, come out here. I got something fer ye." And going to the back of his wagon, he caught one of the young chickens, and when she came to the door he gave it to her.

"'Lo, Kitteneye," she said. "It has been many a year since I have had a fryin' chicken—not since my old man got mashed up in the mines. I see ye han't sold much of ye stuff today, and I am a'goin' to tell ye why. Ye know ye fellers allus go down to the side of the river and dump what ye don't sell."

This was true, because they had so many vegetables and fruits at home, it wasn't worth the trouble to haul them back, and anyway, he had to have an empty wagon so as to return with Uncle John's "goods" from the depot.

"Well," Aunt Mary went on, "these trifling folks allus goes down there and gits the stuff and takes it home and eats it. They all made up that they would not buy anything today, and then ye would have to dump ye whole load. Don't let on I told ye, or they would be awful mad to me. But ye are allus good to me Kitteneye and I wanted ye to know."

"Well," he said, "I'll have to dump my whole load, but they won't git any fun atter eatin' it."

He went to the store and bought two gallons of kerosine or lamp oil. After unloading his wagon, he poured the oil over all the fruits and vegetables—except what he gave to old Aunt Mary.

Next week when he brought another peddling wagon, everyone was eager to buy from him.

VERY FEW OF our mountain folks ever stole anything. If you went by a man's apple tree, turnip or watermelon patch, and you took some, it was not counted as stealing, it was the custom. Anyone was more than welcome to what he could eat that belonged to his neighbor. Of course, like everything else there were a few exceptions.

My father owned a little black mule named "Little Beck." He had raised him from a colt. He was almost like one of the family and as gentle as a kitten. He would come from anywhere in the pasture when he heard my father whistle for him.

One evening one of my cousins and her boyfriend, Dick Patton, came to stay all night with us. The girls were very pleased, for we had few visitors and they thought a lot of their cousin.

Papa did not think it strange when Dick offered to go help him feed the stock and milk the cow. This was a common rule. If you were visiting anyone, you helped with the chores. But he knew why the next morning when he got up, for Dick and his girlfriend were gone. So was Little Beck.

My father began asking the close neighbors if they had heard anything during the night. He soon learned enough to know they had gone toward Wayland.

When he stopped at Joanar Slone's and learned someone had stolen a saddle from him during the night, he knew he was on the right track. When he reached Wayland, he heard that a man and a woman bearing the description of the two he was after had gotten aboard the train going toward Allen. He knew they had sold Little Beck to someone near Wayland. He began going from farmhouse to farmhouse giving the whistle that he had taught his mule to answer. It was almost evening. Tired and worried, he had almost given up, until at last from a stall, away down in a hollow, he heard an answer to his call. He ran to the barn and looked through the cracks between the logs, and sure enough, there was his mule.

The man who had bought the mule refused to give him up. My father came back with the sheriff and a warrant. Kitteneye gave a complete description of his mule even to the few white hairs on his left hip. All the rest of his body was black. The sheriff looked on the mule's hip and could not find the white hairs. My father took his hand and ruffled the hairs up, and sure enough, there were the stubs of white hairs, showing where they had been cut off. The law gave Little Beck back to his rightful owner and put out a twenty-five dollar reward for the arrest of the thieves.

A few weeks later my father and another man, both sworn in as deputies, learned where the two were staying and surprised them one morning while they were still in bed. When my cousin saw who it was she said, "You know you han't goin' to arrest me, are you Uncle Kitteneye?"

"Don't you uncle me now," he said. "You fergit I was your kinfolk when you helped steal my mule. You rode Little Beck then, you can ride behind me now to the jailhouse." But he must have forgiven her because Dick was the only one who went to jail and I think he escaped and was never heard of around here anymore.

At his trial, the judge asked Dick if he stole Kitteneye's mule and he answered, "No, I stole his bridle and the mule happened to have its head in it."

It seems as if every family clan had at least one "bad man," but I think many had more fame than their just due. The only one that had any connection with my life was Bad Amos Fugate, or Little Amos, as he was called by his friends—and he had many more friends than enemies. The story goes that his sister had a fight with some neighbor woman, and the other woman was killed. Amos confessed to the crime to save his sister and was sentenced to prison. Before his sentence was up, he dressed in women's clothes and walked out with some visitors. A price was placed on his head, to be brought in "dead or alive." Whenever he saw one of these posters he would mark out the word "alive," saying that he would have to be killed before captured.

He was a cousin to my brother-in-law, Sam Fugate, and a very good friend. My sister and their children really loved Amos. They helped him by giving him food while he was hiding from the law.

One day my father was going to visit his daughter, Flora Fugate. As he was going across the hill to Ball, where she then lived, he came upon a group of men sitting by the narrow bridle path. The men were drinking and playing cards. My father said he was upon them before he knew who they were. He said he was really scared when he recognized one of them as Amos Fugate. At first he considered the idea of turning back, but then thought better of that. The men moved back out of the path and let him ride on by. Just as he thought he was getting out of sight and all was well, Amos called and said, "Hey, are you Kitteneye?"

My father turned back and said, "Yes." Amos said, "Come back here a minute." Father really got scared then, but he turned his mule around and went back.

"Did you want a drink of good corn liquor?"

"Shore would." And Amos handed him his bottle.

"Do you know who I am?" Amos asked.

"Yeah, I think I do," Father replied.

"Well, you are Flora's paw, so go on, and don't tell a livin' soul you saw us here." And Father promised.

That night after supper at Flora's house, and after Father had gone to bed, Amos came to the door. Sam let him in and gave him his supper. Amos asked Flora if my father told them about seeing him, and he laughed when she said no. "Well, I didn't mean for him to not tell you, but I guess when I said to tell no one, he sure meant to keep his promise."

A few days later, Amos was coming back to visit Sam again, and some men "lay waid" him and riddled his body with bullets from a machine gun. His own folks kept the killers from getting his body, then they guarded his grave for one year, keeping a lighted lantern sitting on his tombstone at night, with a "'round the clock" guard. Those bounty hunters received no reward.

CHAPTER SIXTEEN

THERE MUST STILL have been a few Indians living in this part of Kentucky when our first settlers came—and a few intermarriages. The Thomases and the Mosleys both are proud to lay claim to being part Indian, and the look of this Indian blood still shows up in some of their appearances. My own granddaughter has the long black hair, high cheek-bones, dark eyes, and stately way of walking that would remind anyone of an Indian princess. I know I see her through the love of a grandmother's eyes, but she is still a pretty girl to anyone.

The story I want to tell is about an old Thomas man who showed how much like the Indians he was in his ability to walk for many miles without "givin' out."

In those early days the closest courthouse was at Catlettsburg, Kentucky. My father and a few of his friends were to appear there in a famous murder trial as witnesses. Mr. Thomas was one of these men. They had all agreed to meet at Hindman, so as to make the journey together.

Everyone was there, riding their mules or horses. When Mr. Thomas came walking, one of the men asked him where his horse was. He quietly answered, "I am going to walk." All the men gave a loud laugh and told him he should know better, that no man could walk that many miles, and if he did, he would be too late for the trial that was only three days away. Mr. Thomas said, "I bet I can walk as fast as any horse you got. I will keep up with any of you." One of the men who was very proud of his horse called the bet and started out. The man walked beside the horse. My father and the rest of his friends followed, but they did not catch up with the two men until nightfall, when they reached a town where they all had agreed on staying together for the night. They found Mr. Thomas calmly eating his supper as if he was not one bit tired. But the horse the man had ridden was not as strong as the "part-Indian" walker, because the next morning the horse was found dead in its stall. Mr. Thomas finished the rest of the trip walking fast enough to keep up with the crowd and was always, after that, referred to as the "man who walked a horse to death."

Something else happened on their way back that my father loved to tell. As folks made these long journeys, they would stop along the way to get water to drink. Sometimes it would be at some cabin, where they were always welcome because visitors were so few and people were always glad to hear any news. In many places the roads would only be "bridle paths" through the woods. Then there would be springs of water where the men would bend over and drink without any cup, drawing the water into their mouth, somewhat like animals do.

When my father and his friends were coming back from Catlettsburg, the day was very hot and they were all very thirsty. Just as they were coming around the bend in the road, there stood an old woman beside a spring of water. She had just dipped her bucket full of water and started back to her cabin. The men stopped and asked her for some of her water and she answered, "Shore."

My father said he looked at her, and she was so dirty her clothes and face were covered with soot and grime, and tobacco juice was dribbling from the corners of her mouth. He wanted the water so badly, but the thought of placing his lips on the side of the drinking gourd where he knew her mouth had been several times, made him feel almost sick. So when it came his time to take a drink, he turned the gourd upside down and drank from the hole in the handle. As he handed the gourd back to her she said, "Well, I declare, you are the first man I ever did see that drunk water out of a gourd like I do."

FROM THE RECORDS of old deeds I have found with their names, I know my mother and father lived in different places on Caney. Only once in my mother's lifetime did my father move his family "off of Caney."

In the years around 1895 they lived on Bunyun, where I now live, in fact in the same house where my husband and I first lived. Three of her children were born under the same roof where my two oldest were born. I love to think when I am working in my garden, "This is the very same soil my mother once turned over with her hoe." There used to be an Old Belle Flower apple tree in the yard my mother set out. I got a double pleasure using those apples, as I was sharing something with a mother I never had.

In the year 1899, my sister Jezzie Ann died at the age of two, just a few months after my mother had lost another premature baby. My father was gone from home and the older kids buried the small child on the hillside across from my home. Losing Jezzie Ann so close after this other tragedy upset my mother very much. My father thought it would help her if he could get her away from all the unpleasant memories. He swapped land with one of his brothers and moved to Possum Trot. But this only made matters worse. So in 1901 he bought the old family home from his father and moved to the mouth of Trace, close to the family graveyard. There they remained until my mother's death.

Around 1930, my father, stepmother and I moved to Dwarf, a distance of less than thirty miles, but in that day and time, it seemed like a long way.

We loaded our "house plunder" on wagons pulled by mules and drove to Hindman. There it was loaded on a truck and taken to Bear Branch, and then up the hollow in sleds. We loaded the wagons the night before and started long before daylight. I remember eating dinner just outside of Hindman, from a bucket. We had packed and brought along boiled eggs, fried side meat, corn bread, and onions. When we drive through there now, I try to remember how it looked then. We sat there on the side of the creek, drinking water from a spring, feeding and resting the mules, visiting with everyone that passed. After sharing our lunch, the men with the wagons returned home and we went on with the truck.

I never will forget that first night at Dwarf in our new home. The house was little more than a barn, one room about twelve-feet square, with a chimney made from picked-up creek rocks, and the logs of the walls nothing but poles. We had bought the place from a Emery Halland, who wanted to sell so as to move to the coal mines at Harlan. My father was building a new house, but he wanted to move before cold weather, so we lived in this shack for a few weeks until the new house was finished. That first night, there was only time to put up one bed, so I slept on some fodder placed on the floor with quilts, sheets, and pillows. I was awakened the next morning when an old mule began pulling the fodder through the cracks between the small logs of the wall of the house.

When my father and my brother-in-law Sam Fugate got three sides of the new house finished, we moved in. The old house had to be torn down to make room for the new one's fourth side. Before a chimney could be made, cold weather set in. I remember my father kept a large fire made of logs in the yard, and believe it or not, it kept us warm, even though the house was open on one side. The only thing was, we had to take turns sleeping, so as to guard the fire.

I had never seen such big trees as those that grew on Bear Branch; the woods on Caney had been timbered out a long time before I was born. My brother-in-law and my sister owned almost half of the hollow. He had bought a saw mill and was cutting the logs and selling the lumber to some of the mining camps. Everytime I think of these years, I can still hear the hum of that saw and recall the smell of the sawdust, in which my nieces and I used to play.

He had several men to help him. Some cut trees, some worked at the mill, while others drove the teams that hauled the finished lumber to the mouth of the hollow, where it was picked up by trucks. Many of these men boarded with my sister. Some were blacks. The white men slept in the house with the family, but the blacks had a small shack close to the mill. They all ate together. The table was not large enough for everyone, so first the white men ate, then the blacks, and last of all the family. There was a hired girl, whose last name was Richie. How that girl could sing! The girls would help her do the dishes, if she would sing for us. When she got tired—because we never got through listening—she would say, "Sing a little song, won't take long. Duddle up, duddle up. Now it's all gone." We knew it was all over for the night.

I don't think my father was ever completely satisfied at Dwarf. He moved back to Caney, then back to Dwarf so many times that it became a family joke. Once he said he had made the move so many times that the chickens had gotten so they would "lay down on their backs and cross their legs so as to be ready to be tied." And once he asked my brother Vince to help him with his wagon and mule, and Vince told him, "Well, Paw, I am kind of busy this week with making my molasses. You get some of the others to help you. I will be free next week and help you move back."

Sometime between 1901, when my father moved his family to the old home place at the mouth of Trace, and the year 1909, when my sister Alverta was born, a large lumber company named Cole and Crain came to Caney Creek to buy up all the trees that were eighteen inches in diameter "or up."

Their foreman's name was Hayes Johnson. He built a shanty at the mouth of Hollybush for those men who lived too far away to go home at night. He also had a store and sold dry goods and notions (I don't think he sold groceries) near the shanty.

He had the men that he hired to work for him build a dam just below where the waters from Caney and Hollybush meet. Then they built a "trom road" from the dam up to the mouth of Trace. Here it branched out and became two tracks—one going up Trace as far as Bill Owens', and the other up Caney onto Short Fork. It ended where Short Fork is divided into two different branches of water. Henry C. Short lived there.

This trom road was made somewhat like a small railroad track. Logs about four feet long were placed about every two or three feet on the roadway, in a straight line. Then running lengthwise along the top of each tie the rails were "spiked down" with iron spikes. The rails were also made of wood, but had an iron coating on the top side.

The logs were carried to the dam along the trom road on small flat cars, also built of wood, with three wheels on each side. The outside of these wheels were iron, with a groove in the middle to fit on the rails of the trom road.

Each car could carry four or five logs. It was all downgrade from the end of the road to the dam, so there was no power needed to operate them. They did have some kind of a "hand brake" for stopping the cars. I think the empty cars were pulled back up the hills by oxen or mules.

After the water had been caught in the dam and enough logs had been hauled and dumped ready, the gate of the dam was opened and the logs floated to Maytown, where they were then taken by riverboats to Catlettsburg. I don't know where they went from there. There may have been a large sawmill there, or they may have been sent somewhere farther on.

G.C. Huff was living in Trace then and owned several oxen. He and my father hauled most of the logs out of the hills using these "beasts of burden." One of these oxen had an accident that resulted in a broken leg. It was killed and fed to the workers. My father did not approve of this; he said it was "eatin' one of his friends." When the men were called to eat their dinner, they were surprised when Kitteneye expressed a wish to say the blessing. He always said you should give thanks to God every hour of the day from your heart. A memorized prayer repeated automatically came only from the lips and did not please God. Kitteneye's blessing that day may not have met with the approval of his Maker, but it caused the men to laugh:

Poor old steer, what brought you here,
You been beat and banged for many a year,
Beat and banged and given abuse
And now brought up for the table use.

Almost everyone on Caney sold their timber to Hayes Johnson. My father sold his and helped to cut it. Hayes paid so much a cubic foot for the trees and sixty cents each for cutting and hauling them to where they were loaded on the flat cars. This job lasted for five or six years. My sisters said they could remember when my mother sold vegetables and chickens and eggs to Hayes Johnson. He bought them to feed the men who lived in his shanty. In exchange she received cloth and other things from his store. Vada said she could remember that mother "swapped cabbage to the cloth to make the dress she is wearing in the picture I have of her, which is in my living room now."

After Hayes Johnson got all the trees he wanted, and, maybe became a rich man from the profits, he left Caney. Soon the shanty rotted down. The dam was used no more and soon washed away. The trom road was covered over by soil with each new spring flood, or "warsh out" as we mountain folks call it. Another part of Caney's history was forgotten so completely, that when the flood of 1937 uncovered some of the old trom road, many people wondered what it was.

MY FATHER DID not, nor would he let us believe in ghosts. We called them "haunts" or "buggers," but many of our neighbors would "sware right down to ye" that they had "seed things." There were certain places where more than one person had encountered something that did not comply with the laws of nature, and heard voices or sounds when there was no reason (or so they said). We even still have a Bugger Branch on Caney and a Bugger Hollow just across the hill on Watts Fork. I wonder if any of our old folks really believed these stories. There were many great storytellers. We had few books, and listening to these stories were our only entertainment of this kind. Father would tell us it was alright to listen, but to never tell the person that we did not believe them. When we would hear some "bugger tale" from one of our schoolmates and come home and repeat it to him, he would make a fanning motion with his arms and a blowing with his lips and say, "Now, there, you see, I have blowed it all away. No more bugger."

When he heard or saw something strange he never stopped until he found out what it really was. When he was a child, folks believed a cow could lose her cud. They had noticed how cattle would burp up their food and chew it the second time. They did not understand, and thought the cud was a special thing belonging to cows. If a cow lost this cud they thought it would die. They would make them another from an old dishrag and a salty meat skin, maybe adding something else. This would save the cow's life. One day Father was watching a small calf. His job was to see it did not get into the corn or garden patch. When the calf began to chew its cud, he held its mouth and made it spit it out, to see what it was.

Some of the folks also believed in witches. Some even said they were a witch themselves. To become one you had to go up on a high hill on the first night of a full moon, spread a white sheet on the ground beneath an oak tree, kneel on this sheet, shoot a gun toward the sky, curse the Lord and bless the Devil. Three drops of blood would fall on the sheet. Then you would have the powers of a witch. But when you died you would belong to the Devil.

Once there was this old woman who thought someone had bewitched her cow, causing her milk to "turn" and to taste awful. Father knew the reason was because she was not a very good housekeeper and did not sterilize her churn and milk bucket. So he told her to go to the north side of her spring where she got water, choose three small "gravels" or stones, wash her churn real clean, put the gravels in the bottom, then rinse it with boiling water. This would break the spell.

One story told and believed by some of my husband's folks was about the Devil. Some men had a habit of going to an old lonely shack every Saturday night to play cards, gamble, and drink moonshine whiskey. This one time, about midnight, a stranger rode up on a very fine black horse, hitched it up outside to the fencepost, and came in. He spoke to each one and called each by name, although none knew him. He asked if could he sit in on their poker game. No one refused. Very slowly, as the game went on for hours, he began to win all their money. One man dropped a card on the floor. When he stooped down to pick it up, he saw that the stranger had hooves where there should have been feet. This scared him so much that he jumped up, turning the table over, and ran out the door. All the other men ran after him, leaving all their cards, money, and jugs with the stranger. As they ran out of sight, they heard the stranger laughing, a strange high crackling sound, like the wind through a forest fire. The next day when it was daylight some of the men were a little braver and came back. The shack was burned to the ground. They looked in the ashes and found the silver money, melted and formed into the shape of a cross. None of these men ever played poker again.

One old lady gained a lot of fame because she had a "knocking spirit." Anyone who spent the night with her could hear it, ask it any question, and it would answer two knocks for a no, three for a yes. This was a great mystery, until someone found out that one of her sons had tied a thread spool to a string, and pulled it through a knothole near his bed.

There was another woman who heard a knocking in her loft, every night, three knocks—the second one not as loud as the first, the third one still fainter—only to begin again. She was a "wedder," living by herself. She asked my father to come and find out what this knocking sound was.

Now these old-fashioned lofts were much more than just a space beneath the roof. They were more like a second story to the house—not high enough for a bedstead, but feather beds or straw ticks were placed on the floor for the children or extra company. Some had a stairway that went up by the chimney inside, some, not so nice, had a ladder on the outside. In my father's house, this upstairs was very nice and comfortable, but I remember staying all night with some friends. We had to climb up an outside ladder. There was no shutter to the opening where we went in. The next morning we awoke to find a two-inch snow covering us, where we were warm between two big feather beds and many quilts. I would be scared to death for you, grandchildren, to sleep like that, but we thought it was a lot of fun. We put our clothes on under the covers and hurried, laughing, down to the fire and breakfast.

In these lofts we also kept our dried beans, cushaw, onions, and seed corn. Almost everyone had an old trunk or two full of the dead folk's clothes, and anything else that needed storing away. So it was up in a loft like this that the old woman heard the strange knocking sound. As luck would have it that night the moon was full, not a cloud in the sky. After supper and before dusk, my father went up the ladder and settled himself in a corner. It was very hard for him to keep from going to sleep. The light came in from a small opening where the wind had blown a board off. He thought, "Tomorrow I will nail that back on fer her." He tried counting the rows of boards, the strings of popcorn, the bunches of dried beans. He would first rub one eye, then the other—anything to keep himself awake. He could hear the squeak, squeak, of the old woman's rocking chair. At last there was something moving in the other corner. There was a board across a barrel, probably filled with dried apples. Next to this sat a large churn. Like a flash something ran across this board, made a dive from the end, and landed in the churn. Whack, whack, whack, three times went the other end of the board. He went over and looked into the churn. Mr. Rat gave a fast retreat. The churn had been full of cracklin's, kept there until the "right time of moon" to be made into soap.

When one family went to stay all night with another (as they often did), after supper and the dishes were washed and put away, and all the other "work done up," everyone would get together. We'd gather around the fire, if it was winter, or on the porch, around a "gnat smoke" made by burning rags, if it was summer. The older folks would sit in chairs with the young children in their laps, or huddled around their feet. That's when we would hear all these scary bugger tales. By the time we were ready to go to sleep, it sure was nice to know the small ones would be stuck in at the foot of the grown-up's bed, or so many of us in the same bed that we would have to sleep sideways so as to have room for us all.

These stories lose a lot in being written—the facial expressions, the movement of the hands, the bending forward of the body, the lowering and raising of the voice by the storyteller—cannot be captured on paper. They added much to the enjoyment of listening to these bugger tales.

There was one story my father taught me that I have told my grandchildren so many times I know they will never forget it. It's kind of a poem, or maybe you would call it a chant. There is no end to it, and each line must be followed by a long, low moan:

There was an old woman all skin and bone—mo-o-an
She took a notion she would not stay at home—mo-o-an
She got up—she walked down—mo-o-an
To the village churchyard ground—mo-o-an
She saw the dead a'laying around—mo-o-an
She saw the grave of her only son—mo-o-an
She thought of all the crimes he had done—mo-o-an

And on and on until you had your audience really listening. Then, very suddenly, maybe right in the middle of a word, you would jump and scream *boo*. Even after telling it over and over again, and they knew the loud boo was coming, I would still be able to scare them. Just think what it would do to someone hearing it for the first time.

I think some of the parents used bugger tales to scare their children just to make them be good. It seems as if every family had a "Hairy Mouth" or a "Bloody Bones" that would come and get you if you were not good. My father would not let us be told anything like this. We were taught to be good because that was what Jesus wanted us to do. He told us there was a Devil, but not one you could see with your natural eyes. And so have I taught my dear grandchildren.

Kitteneye knew a lot of fairy stories, some different and some very similar to your versions today. Rumplestiltskin was named Tom Tit Tot, and the girl with the glass slipper was Cinder Ellen. He knew hundreds of songs or rhymes all by heart. I can't recall all of them, but this story would not be complete unless I gave you at least two: "The Bird Song" and "The Fox Song," my favorite ones.

The Fox Song

It was a moon shining night
The stars shining bright
Two foxes went out for to prey.
They trotted along
With frolic and song
To cheer their lonely way.

Through the woods they went
Not a rabbit could they scent
Nor a lonely goose on stray.
Until at last they came

To some better game
A farmer's yard by the way.

On the roost there sat
Some chickens as fat
As foxes could wish for a dinner.
They hunted around
Until a hole they found
And both went in at the center.

They both went in
With a squeeze and a grin
And the chickens they soon were killed.
And one of them lunched
And hunched, and bunched
Until his stomach was fairly filled.

The other more wise
Looked around with both eyes
He would hardly eat at all.
For as he came in
With a squeeze and a grin
He noted the hole was quite small.

The night rolled on
And daylight down
Two men came out with a pole.
Both fox flew
And one went through
But the greedy one stuck in the hole.

The hole he stuck
So full of his pluck
Of the chickens he had been eating.

He could not get out
Or turn about
So he was killed by beating.

The Bird Song

I use to kill birds in my boyhood,
Black ones, robins, and wrens.
I hunted them up on the hillside,
I hunted them down in the glen.

I did not think it was sinful,
I did it only for fun.
I had such sport of royalty,
With the poor little birds and my gun.

One bright day in the springtime,
I saw a brown thrush in a tree.
She was singing so merrily and sweetly,
Just as sweet as a birdy could be.

I raised my gun in a twinkle,
I fired, the aim it was true.
For a moment the little bird fluttered,
Then off to the bushes it flew.

I followed it softly and closely,
And there to my sorrow I found,
Right close to a nest full of young ones,
The mother bird dead on the ground.

The young ones for food they were calling,
Yet how could they ever be fed?
For the dear darling mother who loved them,

Was laying there bleeding and dead.

I picked it up in my anger,
I stroked the motherly bird.
Not never again in my lifetime,
Would I kill a poor innocent bird.

Kitteneye was a good hand at making up his own rhymes
or pieces. I am sorry to say many were about his friends and
neighbors, and he would picture their character so quaint
and real that I would be afraid to repeat them. He used his
imagination in using swear words and expressions. Some of
his sayings he must have made up, because they seem to
belong only to him:

If you don't stand for something, you will get knocked
down by everything.

Cooked potatoes are easy to eat, but you have to do some
gnawing to get meat off the bone.

There are no "little white lies." They are all black, trying
to hide from the truth.

When you become discouraged, think of the hole a little
ground squirrel makes in the side of the hill. It does not
bother him how large that mountain is.

Don't be concerned about something that don't concern
you. It won't make your bed any softer, or your meat fry any
faster.

Two things I love to hear, but seldom do: truth and meat
a'fryin'.

I think the one he used most was "Devil take it." He told
about the one time when he came in from picking blackberries without his shirt. His mother asked him why he had
no shirt and he answered, "Well, you see, I kep' git'n caught
in these blackberry briars. And ever'time I would say, 'Devil
take it,' and I guess the Devil, he just come and took it."

CHAPTER TWENTY

SARAH ALVERTA WAS my sister's name but I always called her Sissy. She was born with a normal mental capacity, but when she was eighteen months old, she had a fever that lasted six weeks. The doctor called it a brain fever. When she recovered she could not talk and her mind never grew anymore, but remained as the mind of a two year old. She might have been taught some if she had had the right teacher. We ourselves could have done more for her, if we had been rash with her; but we loved her so much we gave her her way in everything. The whole household was run to suit what we thought was best for her. My sister Vada was the one who loved her the most and took constant care of her, sleeping with her at night, washing her clothes, even diapers.

She was a few years older than me, but I soon learned that whatever she wanted of mine, I was supposed to give her. I did not resent this because I had been taught that she was someone very special. I remember once I had a fried egg in my plate and she reached with her hand and took it and ate it. I thought it was a big joke and laughed.

Once we were playing near the chair shop where my father was making chairs. The little nobs or ends of wood that were left as scraps from the ends of the finished chair post, made very nice playthings. With a child's imagination they could become anything from a father and mother with a whole family, to a table covered with pots and pans. To me they could be anything. All Sissy liked to do was beat them together to make a loud noise, or pile them up in a large heap and then kick them over.

I can remember many happy hours playing with Sissy and these wooden scraps. But what I am going to tell you next was told to me by my father.

He heard a loud noise, looked out, and found me pulling and tugging at Sissy. She was hitting me and kicking but I would not let go. Both of us were screaming and crying.

My father came running and parted us and demanded, "What are ye doing? Ye know ye must never fight with Alverta."

"But, Papa," I said, "There was a big worm. It might bite Sissy."

He went back to where we had been playing and he found a large copperhead, which he killed.

We did not get much candy, but each time my father went to the store he always brought back three large red and white peppermint sticks of candy, which were called "saw logs." There was one for each of us: Alverta, Edna, and me—the youngest of all the kids. Sissy wouldn't eat candy. I don't know if she just did not like the taste, or if it hurt her several decayed teeth. But she loved the red and white striped color, so she always wanted one, mostly to play with. My father would always tell me, "Now don't ye take Alverta's candy, but ye watch her and when she gets tired of playing with it, you can have it to eat." I would follow her around for hours, and sometimes wait until she took a nap, but sooner or later, I got her candy.

Alverta loved anything that was red. One Christmas my sister Vada got a large apron, which was then known as a coverall. It was something like a sleeveless dress that opened up and down the back. The color was a bright red with a small, springly, flowered design. Alverta fell in love with it at once and Vada cut it up and made a dress for Sissy. She had this pretty red dress on that Easter morning that had such a sad ending.

Several boys had met in the large "bottom" or meadow just across from our home at the mouth of Trace to play a game of "round town," a game somewhat like baseball. Lots of girls had come to watch from our porch and yard. Everyone was having a good time. It was Easter and everyone had on their new clothes for the occasion.

When we heard a terrible scream, everyone ran in the house and found Alverta's clothes on fire. Lorenda ran for the water bucket, which was empty. Vada began tearing at the burning clothes, but before Renda could get a bucket of water from the well, all Alverta's clothes were burned.

My father had just been gone for a few hours on his way to Wheelwright, where he had a job as a "planer" in a carpenter shop.

Someone sent for a nurse who stayed at the Caney school. Someone said, "Who will go overtake Isom?" Hazy Caudill said, "I have the fastest mule, so I will go."

In my childish trusting mind I thought "everything will be alright again, when Papa gits here." The next thing I remember was running to meet him, when I saw him coming, and he hugged me until it hurt. I did not know until later that he had been told I had been the one who got burnt.

Sissy lived until about midnight. I can still see my father

as he pulled the sheet up over her head and told the nurse, "It's over."

I REMEMBER THE first time I ever heard of Mrs. and Mr. Lloyd, who founded the center and school that are now Alice Lloyd College. My father and Frances had gone to the corn crib and shucked two "coffee sacks" full of corn for the next mill day. Alic Jacobs had a mill house. He had built a dam across the creek to catch the water. The power of this water, when the gate was opened, would turn the large millstones and grind the corn into meal. In payment for this service he took part of the corn for himself. There was a kind of wooden dipper called a "toll dish," a small one for his portion of one-half bushel, and a larger dipper for a full bushel. Each man's corn was ground in turns, depending on his arrival. (I guess this is where we got the nickname a "turn of meal," meaning a sackful.) This gathering of a group of men was enjoyed by all. It was a time to catch up on all the news, and enjoy a lot of joking and laughing. Every young boy thought himself grown-up when he was allowed to go to the mill.

All the women took great pride in seeing how nice and clean their meal sack looked. Some would stitch their name or initials on the sacks so as not to get them mixed up. Others, who did not like to sew, would tie their sack with colored string. These meal sacks were of very heavy material, a cream color with a small red or blue stripe running lengthwise along each side.

This particular time Papa and Frances came back from the crib with the corn. Renda went to the quilt shelf and got a clean quilt. After sweeping the floor and moving everything out of the way, she spread this large quilt on the floor, and Papa poured the corn on top. Father and the older girls placed their chairs around the corn, close enough so that they could pull the edges of the quilt up over their knees, somewhat like an apron. Then they began to shell the corn, letting the grains fall onto the quilt. The smaller kids sat on the floor around the edges and shelled too. Sometimes Papa would have to start ours for us by shelling two rows of grain. This was called "rowin' it."

We would throw the cobs in a pile in the corner of the room to be used later for fuel to burn in the grate or cook stove. After a while the younger ones tired of working, and anyway, by that time there were enough cobs for us to play with. Edna would place them on top of each other in the form of a square that looked a lot like a log cabin. When it was very tall, she would let me or Sissy give it a push, to watch them all tumble down. Sissy loved to do something like this. Sometimes we would build houses, fences, and roads. We had just as much fun with our cobs, as children now do with electric trains and tinker toys.

After a while I began to listen to the grown-ups talk. Renda said, "Did you know Bish Johnson went over on Reynolds Fork and got them strange people, who come from off yonder, to come here on Caney to live? He give them some of his land, if they would come over here. Why do you think he did that Paw?"

"I don't know fer shore, but it may be fer the best," Papa answered.

"I can't see why they want to come here. Some people think she is goin' to bring in teachers. If she does, our own teachers will lose their jobs."

"Well," Papa said, "let's wait and see. Don't try to judge the other feller until ye know all the facts."

Then Frances said, "Well, some people think they are working for the government and will find out where all the moonshine stills are and report them to the revenuers."

Edna looked up and asked, "Well, Papa do ye guess these strange people believe in God like we do?"

And my father answered, "Well, I think everyone in the whole world believes in God. These folks don't believe exactly the same beliefs we do, but they have promised to not interfere with our religion, politics, and our moonshine stills."

Everyone was silent for a few minutes; then Frances spoke up and said, "Some of my cousins at school said Mrs. Lloyd has been givin' people some clothes and things, not new store-bought clothes, just old clothes."

Renda said, "'Lo, I would not want to wear somebody else's clothes, if I did not know whose they were. Why, they might be dead people's clothes."

"Or even been wore by some old nigger," Vada said.

Father said, "Vada, why do you hate niggers so?"

"I don't know; just 'cause Granny Frankie did. You know Granny said a nigger did not have a soul like white folks do."

"Your Granny did not believe that. She just talked to hear her head rattle. A nigger is just like anyone else; some good, some bad. I would druther be a black man with a white soul, than a white man with a black soul."

Renda said, "You know all I can remember about Granny Frankie is: one day I asked her why the rusty spots were on the Rusty Sweet apples and not on other apples, and she said, 'Nature.' And when I asked her what nature was, she answered, 'Hair on a nigger's nabble, that's nature.' Granny shore loved to joke."

By this time all the corn was shelled. My father made a three-cornered opening by catching the edges of the meal sack with his teeth and both hands. Renda got a plate from the shelf and using it as a shovel, she scooped the corn up from the quilt and placed it into the sack. Then she folded the quilt and put it back in the shelf. While they were doing this, Edna and Frances had put all the cobs into an empty coffee sack and placed it behind the stove.

Soon, we were all in bed asleep.

I shall never forget one Christmas when I was about five years old. I had been looking forward to the holiday eagerly, ever since Preacher Billie had gone from house to house all up and down Caney Creek, even to the very head of each hollow, making a list of everyone's name and age. We had all been promised a "Christmas gift" from the Center school.

Even all the baking and stewing and cooking of all the good things to eat, did not make as big an impression as the thoughts of this package soon to be mine. I talked about it by day and dreamed about it by night.

At last the day before Christmas arrived and Father went to get our gifts. It seemed like hours and hours before he returned with two large bags with his name in big letters and a "Merry Christmas from C.C.C.C." written on one side.

We never even thought of waiting any longer, but tore into the bags at once.

Inside were smaller packages in bright colored wrappers,

one for each member of the family. As luck would be, mine was the last, the very bottom one in the bag.

It was a large brown package tied with a heavy twine. I was so eager to get into it, I tried to break the cords. All the other girls were busy with their own, and were shouting, "Look what I got."

My father soon came to my rescue and cut the strings with his knife, and I hastily dug in. I will never forget, until my dying day, what I saw.

It was the remains of a large faded brown teddy bear, no eyes, one ear gone, a dangling leg, and a mangy-looking covering from which the straw stuffing was protruding in more places than one. I gave one look, threw it on the floor, and ran screaming to my father's arms for comfort. I think the angry look on his face frightened me more than that hideous monster. In a voice I had seldom heard from him, he said. "Well, I guess them folks from off yonder think we are in a hard place to think a little child would be tickled with a thing like that for Christmas."

He threw the whole thing, wrapping string and all, into the fire. My enjoyment for Christmas that year was not completely restored even with the poppa doll and cap-pistol he had bought for me.

In all fairness I must say I don't believe anyone connected with the school had anything to do with this. I believe they had sent it on to me, wrapped as it was, from "our good friends" up north. Mrs. Lloyd herself sent me another present when she heard of my bear. I do recall a new silver quarter, which was doubly precious; she had "sent me word" that this coin was a present to me from her.

I THINK ONE of the best times I can remember is "eating around the fire." Sometimes it would rain and we'd be caught without dry wood for the stove. Sometimes it would just be cold and the girls would "dread" to cook in the kitchen. Then they would get us something to eat by using the fire in the grate.

They might make mush, which is cooked in a large kettle hanging from an iron bar fastened to the cracks in the chimney-rock, high above the fire. Water, to which a little salt has been added, is brought to a rolling boil. The cornmeal is slowly poured in with one hand, while you stir it constantly with a large spoon in the other hand. You have to be very careful or the mixture will get lumpy. But if made just right, it will be of a very mushy thickness. This is then dipped out in spoonfuls into your bowl and covered with milk—a very delicious meal.

Maybe it would be beans or fresh meat the girls would cook in the big iron kettle. Sometimes they hung it from the iron rod or placed it directly on the grate. Then the bread would be baked under the grate in the hot cinders. You have never in your life eaten anything that tastes as good as corn bread baked this way. You add a little soda and salt to cornmeal and just enough water to make a thick paste. The skillet must be preheated and the inside covered with a small layer of lard or grease. This is so the bread will not stick to the skillet.

The fire must not be too hot. The cinders under the grate are hollowed out to form a place for the skilletful of dough. Some folks put a lid over the skillet and then knocked more hot coals on top; I prefer to let it bake without a lid. Maybe a few cinders did fall into the dough, but what did that matter? They could be picked out, and anyway, a child is supposed to eat one peck of dirt in its lifetime.

We would sometimes roast sweet potatoes, Irish potatoes, apples, and eggs under the grate in the hot cinders. The eggs had to have a small hole made in them and a straw stuck in the hole. This was to keep them from bursting or exploding when they got hot. If they did burst and got a few ashes or cinders on them, we just rubbed it off and ate the eggs anyway.

Of course there was always a big supply of popcorn. Every family owned a big long-handled wire "popcorn capper." If you pop corn over a fire made from burning willow wood, you get a flavor in the corn from the burning willow that is very good and different from anything with artificial flavors you buy now in the markets.

We also parched the regular white corn, normally used for feed or meal. To parch corn, you shell it first, then you put it in a skillet containing a large spoonful of lard or butter and a small amount of salt. The skillet is kept real hot, either on the stove or grate, and the corn must be stirred constantly. It becomes very brown and brickle, and very good.

We always gathered a large supply of nuts to be eaten during the winter: black walnuts, chestnuts, and hazelnuts, or "hazenuts" as we called them, to name a few.

In the summertime there were always plenty of berries and apples. And in the spring when the sap or watery liquid began to form under the bark of the trees, we would tap the "sugar trees" and get a sweet woody tasting drink. But I think the most fun of all was to "go sappin'."

My father would take his ax and we would each have a spoon. We would climb the hill until he found just the right-looking birch tree (you could also use beech, but birch is much better). My father would cut the tree down and then take the bark off in large slabs by cutting rings around the tree about every two or three feet. Then he would split the bark between the rings and it would come off in two large half-circle pieces. The inside of this bark had a very juicy lining, which we scraped out with our spoons and ate. Some people added sugar and let it sit overnight, but we most always ate ours there in the woods.

There was also a small, thick leafed plant with red berries that grew close to the ground on the tops of hills, which we called "mountain tea." We gathered and chewed the leaves and ate the berries. There were some roots of plants we also ate as a snack, like "sweet anise" and "pop paws."

There is a tree that blooms real early in the spring. It has beautiful white flowers and later, a small red berry that we used to eat. I don't know what the real name of this tree should be, but I do know why we mountain people called it a "sarvis berry."

Back in the early days we had no church house and people lived so far apart that the only religious connection with a church was the "circuit rider" preacher: a preacher who rode all over two or three counties, up hollows, and across the hills, stopping to stay a few days at someone's home where he performed a service. All the neighbors would gather at this house to hear him. There would usually be a few couples of young people that had been waiting for him, so they could get married. He would also preach a funeral service for all folks who had died since his last visit. He had a certain time to visit a community. The time he was to come to our part of the county was in the spring when these "sarvis"—for service—berry trees were in bloom. The mountain people had no calendars back then, but when this tree began to bloom, they knew it was time to watch for their preacher.

My father used to tell a funny story about going with some young girls, about his age, to gather some of these sarvis berries. When they got to the tree they found that all the limbs were too high for any of them to reach. My father decided he would climb the tree, and, by swinging from the limbs, the weight of his body would bow the tree over, close to the ground. But the tree was very large and he was small, and the tree only bowed a little and left him hanging halfway between the top of the tree and the ground. He asked two of the girls to get hold of his feet and pull, so with their combined weight the tree would bend over. As no mountain girl would touch the body of a man before they were married, the girls got hold of his pants legs instead. Everything would have been just fine, but when they tugged his pants legs, his "gallous" (suspenders) broke and his pants fell off. Folks did not wear undershorts back then. The poor girls were so embarrassed that they dropped his pants and ran, leaving him to drop several feet to the ground.

Watching for the sarvis berry was natural when you hiked along the creeks like we did—we grew up close to nature and partook of all her changing seasons.

I remember how we used to walk—not like those "brought on" people who jog, trotting along like a stiff-kneed mule, their eyes looking straight ahead like they had been used to wearing a blind bridle, half-naked, their elbows sticking out like the wings on a picked chicken. I mean to need and want to go somewhere, and having no way to get there except on "shank's mare."

You get out early, while the ground is damp with dew. The sun is creeping slowly into the valley. You are in no hurry, so you take your time, just so you get home in time to do up the work before dark. You breathe deep the nice clean air, taking time to notice the odor of flowers, and to listen to the rejoicing voice of the birds. (That's the trouble with the world today; we just don't take time to enjoy ourselves with the entertainment God gives us free.)

As you pass each house you look to see if there is anyone you could holler at. All ask you where you are going. One woman says, "If you stop at the post office, please see if I got any mail." A man is building a fence. He is afraid he is going to run out of nails before he gets done. Would you please bring him a nickel's worth of eight penny nails from the store.

When you come to a place where the road crosses the creek, you place rocks in the water to step on. As you jump from one rock to another your foot slips and you baptize one of your feet. You laugh and look quickly to see if anyone saw you. Had it been winter you would have stopped at the next house, gone in and had a nice long chat, while you dried your shoe and sock in front of the fire.

Soon you come to a place where a woman has a fire built under a washtub. She is dipping up water from the creek to heat, so she can put out a washing. Again and again the road and the creek interwind, and you place more rocks to step on, jumping across when you can.

You meet a mother who is taking her children to see Grandma. She is carrying a baby in her arms and leading one almost as small. The largest boy has another little one on his back. The kids are very shy and keep hiding their faces in their mother's skirt as she talks a few words with you.

And then you overtake the school kids, noisy and still shining from their morning bath, shuffling along, walking in the dustiest part of the road, letting the soft dirt squish up between their toes, each swinging a bucket that once contained four pounds of lard, and now is full of "crumble in milk." The smaller boys and girls are in separate groups. The larger ones are walking in couples. By the time they get to school they will have walked off much of their excess energy and will be tired enough to set still and listen to what the teacher has to say.

We also walked to and from church, sometimes as much as four or five miles. A lot of nice, clean "sparkin'" went on in these walks. It's so nice to walk your best girl to church, no matter what age you are: just met, just married, or if you both walk with a cane.

You have been musing to yourself and would have passed the next woman, without speaking, an unpardonable slip of good manners, had you not heard her hoe hit a rock. She is hoeing her garden. You lean against the fence and discuss with her the wisdom of doing the cabbage first, waiting until the sun dries the dew from the leaves of the tomatoes and cucumbers.

There is just one thing better than taking a walk along a country road, among folks you know and love—and that is going the same journey with a friend.

BY THE TIME I was about six years old, my father got a job making chairs for Mrs. Lloyd. About this time he "divided his land" and gave it to his children. My brother, Vince, got the "old home place."

My father bought a small "lot" or plot of ground from my Uncle Sam, near Alice Lloyd College. He built a "boxed" house made from sawed lumber, four rooms with lots of windows. It was very much in style with the changing times, but I loved our old log home much better.

Most of the chairs my father made were used in the school. There are still a few left now. He made lovely flower boxes or "fern stands"; I have two of these, and I see several yet in the home of my neighbors.

By this time all my older sisters had married and left home, one by one. There was just Edna and me still at home when we moved to the new house, and very soon after, she too was married.

For a while there was just Father and me. I remember this

as being the happiest part of my childhood. Looking back now, I know my father was having a very hard time taking care of me, with all the cooking and housework, after his day's work in the chairshop.

I stayed with one of our close neighbors from the time school let out until he got home from work.

Every few weeks he would take a wagonload of chairs to Wayland, to be shipped by freight up north. This was why he was so late getting home on this particular evening. It was summertime. There was going to be some "big doing" at the school that night. All the community had been invited to come. The neighbors, my baby-sitters, were busy doing their evening chores and getting supper ready. I crawled up in a big chair on the porch and went to sleep.

When the large bell was rung by someone at the school, telling everyone the show was about to begin, my friends forgot all about me in their hurry not to be late.

It was dark when I awoke all alone. I was so scared! There wasn't a light in anyone's house. Everyone had gone; not a soul but me in the whole neighborhood. I knew how to light the old-fashioned oil lamps, but I had never been allowed to use matches. So I just sat there in the dark and cried and cried. Oh how glad I was to see my father when he came to get me! I remember running into his outstretched arms. How safe I felt when he lifted me up and carried me all the way home.

As he put me in the bed he said, "Well, Junner, looks as if I am goin' to haft to git ye a stepmom to take care of ye, when I'm gone to work."

As far as my life was concerned, that was the worse decision my father ever made: not his wanting to marry, but in his choice of a second wife.

I know I was a spoiled brat. I had never been spanked, but was always petted and given my own way by my father and older sisters. But looking back now through the eyes of a grown-up, I don't see why she did all the things she did.

A code of the hills is "never to speak ill of the dead," and one of my father's sayings was, if you can't say anything good about anyone, don't say anthing "a'tall." But then I would have to leave my stepmother completely out of my story.

The first few weeks everything was just fine, but soon something happened to change that.

One day some older boys were going to take a mule and sled to get a load of apples from the orchard at the head of Sparkman Branch. All the younger kids, the ones who were about my age, were going along to help pick up the apples. I asked my father if I could go along. It would be a lot of fun and then, of course, they would give me all the apples I wanted to eat, even a bagful to bring home.

My father told me I could go if my cousin Denny went with us. That was another code of the hills. No female was allowed to go far from home without the protection of some male of the same family. They had this respect and reverence for their "womenfolks," even when they were very young.

For some reason, Denny did not go with us, but my stepmother gave me permission to go anyway.

When I came home my father met me at the door very angry and demanded, "Why did ye go atter I told ye not to, if'n Denny didn't go?"

"But Barbara said I could," I told him.

"Well, she told me she didn't," he answered.

I had always been taught to tell the truth. I had never lied to my father in my life. I looked at my stepmother and said, "You know you said I could go. You know you did."

She looked me straight in the eyes and said, "No, I didn't."

I turned to my father and said, "Believe whichever you

want to, but you can ask the other kids; they heard her."

I think he knew who was telling the truth. I don't think he bothered to ask anyone else. A few days later he told me that I did not have to "mind" my stepmother, but to always get permission from him when I wanted to go somewhere.

I wasn't allowed to touch anything that belonged to my stepmother. Even worse, if I wasn't there when she and my father ate, everything was thrown out and I got nothing to eat.

I remember well the night when things finally came out in the open. I guess—looking back now—my father had noticed a lot, and was just hoping everything would work itself out.

We did not own a cow then; my stepmother could never learn to milk. Each evening after school I walked up to my sister Renda's home on Short Fork to get a small bucket of milk, which she gave us. I was having so much fun playing with her children that I forgot it was getting late. At last Renda came to the door and said, "Ye better go, honey. Paw will be worrying about ye if ye are atter dark git'n there."

So I got my bucket of milk and ran almost all the way home. Sure enough, they had eaten and gone to bed.

My father grumbled a little at me and told me to hurry and eat and get to sleep.

I went into the kitchen and looked, but as always there was nothing left from their supper. I put the milk away and slipped into my bed.

My father heard me and said, "Now don't be all mad because I quarreled at ye, and not eat any supper."

I told him, "I am not mad, I looked and there weren't anything to eat."

"Ye could have drunk some of the milk with corn bread."

"But there weren't any corn bread," I answered. "I looked fer some."

"I know there was some left. I didn't eat all I wanted myself, so as to leave some fer ye. What did ye do with it Barbara?" he asked my stepmother.

She did not answer him, so he got out of bed and went to look for himself. He found it in the bucket of scraps, that was saved for the pigs.

"Barbara," he said, "why did ye throw out everything? Ye knowed Verna Mae had to have something to eat?" This made me forget my fear of my stepmother and gave me courage enough to tell him, "This han't the first time; she does it all the time."

"Put ye clothes back on. Ye are goin' to have supper tonight," he said. I did not know what he meant, but I did as he asked.

He took me across the road to where Joe Jones had a store, which was still open.

"Now buy anything ye want to eat and I'll pay fer it." I did not have to be told but once, and I don't remember what I got, but to "eat out of the store" was a treat.

He and Barbara must have had a big quarrel, or racket as we say, for she moved out and they stayed separated for over six months, but they got back together after a while. Maybe she promised to treat me better, but by that time I had learned to stay out of her way. My father saw I always got something to eat after that. But she never would do anything for me.

As I got older my relationship with my stepmother did not improve, and finally, I just quit home altogether. I stayed with different folks; my father would pay for my board and I went to school. At last I went to the Center school to stay.

Mrs. Wheeler ran a kind of boarding house, called "Practice House," for girls. It was connected with the school in many ways, yet we were kind of a separate home. There were about ten or twelve of us. We had to obey all the rules Mrs. Lloyd had made. We were not allowed to have boyfriends, not even to walk along the campus with a boy. We had to wear white pleated skirts, long-sleeved middy blouses, long white hose, and white flat-heeled oxford slippers. The girls of Practice House did not eat at the school dining room, "Hunger Din."

We paid ten dollars a month. Some, like myself, paid cash. Others brought vegetables and fruits from home.

Mrs. Wheeler taught us to cook and keep house. She was a very strict and stern old lady. We had to obey her. I don't think any of the girls ever got close enough to her to ever like her very much. But you had to admire her. We secretly called her "Big Chief."

I loved my home at Practice House, but eventually it closed. Mrs. Lloyd made room for Mrs. Wheeler and us girls in her already crowded dormitories. I was placed in the downstairs of the girl's old dormitory, a place with such small rooms and little heat, that we gave it the nickname "Pig Alley."

Mrs. Lloyd got most all of her teachers from outside the mountains, or as we say, from off yonder. Some were good and came with kindness and understanding in their hearts, wanting to help. Some had formed their opinions about us from what they had read before they came.

One such person was a lady whom I will call Mrs. Parks, because I don't want to use her real name. She was a large, pompous woman, who's very walk seemed to say "God made me of better material than he did you, and I was privileged to be born up north."

She was in charge of the dining room. Four or five of us girls worked for her cleaning up the tables and washing the dishes. She was always telling us how to walk, how to talk—

to be a lady like her. The advice was great, but it was the way she went about it and the way she made us feel—so cheap— not any of the girls liked her.

One night something had happened on the creek, a bit of news that I knew the whole school had heard. Everyone was being very nice about it, not saying anything to me.

But not Mrs. Parks. I was at the last table in the very end of the room, when I saw her coming toward me.

She began asking questions about what she had heard. At first I tried to answer as politely as I could, without really telling her anything.

She was determined to know all the details. When she said, "Well, I don't see why the law does not do something about it," I looked her right in the eyes and answered, "You need not have any fear Mrs. Parks, for as low as these women are, they would not have anything to do with your husband or son. They hold themselves above that."

Letting her breath out in one big "humph," she wheeled around and started marching back toward the kitchen. One look at that retreating back and my anger overcame me. I let fly one of the plates I had stacked up, at her broad backside. As the plate crashed at her feet, she turned in time to dodge the second. Then she began running as, one by one, I threw all twelve plates at her, before she made it to safety inside the kitchen door. She was no lady then. Neither was I.

I went to my room and did not attend classes that day. I was almost sure I would get expelled from school. That evening when I was called to Mrs. Lloyd's office, I went expecting the worst. But her words were, "Why, Verna Mae, why? This is just not like you at all."

"Well, Mrs. Lloyd," I answered, "she was talking about my folks, and I have always been taught that you don't talk about anybody's folks to their face."

I am almost sure I saw a twinkle in her eyes, but all she said was, "Go back to your room. We will do something about it."

I was not punished in any way. I was given another job and someone else helped with the dishes.

Miss Cline showed us how to be a lady by being one herself. She was a small birdlike woman with red hair, which she always wore cut real short and straight. She taught French and Sunday school and played the piano. She introduced me to my first cup of tea, a habit that I still enjoy. I know you grandchildren will always remember the green mug that I drink my tea from.

CHAPTER TWENTY - FOUR

I LOVE TO think that the name hillbilly was derived from our way of talking, that "billy" meant William, because we still retain the words and expressions used by William Shakespeare.

The outsiders did not seem to realize that they sounded just as different to us as we did to them. We could understand them better than they could understand us, because we have so many quaint expressions that are meaningless to anyone but ourselves.

I remember a Mr. Moorehouse who taught history in high school. We were discussing the "Lost Colony" of Roanoke. I said, "No one knows what went with them," a mountain expression meaning that they were lost. When we don't know where something is, we say, "we don't know what went with it." I know it sounds very funny to a stranger. Mr. Moorehouse laughed and made me explain, which was all right.

He must have been a native of New England. He had a

very funny northern accent, and he talked through his nose.

Maybe he had embarrassed me, or I might have just "had a mean spell on me" that day, but the next question he asked me, I answered by using his same tone of voice, saying all the words so much in an imitation of his way of talking that all the other students in the room burst into a loud laugh.

Did that man get mad! He really ruffled me up good and put me out of the room by dragging me by my hair, but what hurt most was what he said.

"I would love to look your father and mother in the eyes. I would like to know something about the parents of a girl like you."

The next day school had just turned out when my father was returning from the post office, after delivering the mail. He was riding his mule and carrying a pistol as all mail carriers are required by law to do.

My father had some of the school children "point out" Mr. Moorehouse to him. After learning who he was, he rode his mule up beside him and stopped.

"Are ye Mr. Moorehouse?" he asked.

"Yes, I am. What do you want with me?"

"Well, first, I want ye to look me straight in the eyes." Mr. Moorehouse looked up. My father had his gun in his hand by then. When the teacher saw this, he turned very pale.

"Well, ye said yesterday ye would like to look into the eyes of Verna Mae's paw and maw. Well, ye are looking at her paw; her maw's dead. I had it in mind to give ye a good whoppin', but seein' ye are an old man (my father was past sixty-five at that time) I don't want to hit ye any. But ye get up on that rock wall and start runnin', not walkin'. And ye run every step 'till the end of that wall."

After the big washout or flood of 1927, when over half of the school had been destroyed by high water, Mrs. Lloyd had a wall built of split rocks from one end of the school to the other, as a protection against the future flood waters. This wall was about four-feet high and about two-feet wide.

Mr. Moorehouse took one more look at my father's face and the gun in his hand, and he climbed up on the top of the wall and began running. My father had to make his mule go real fast to keep up with him. Of course, everyone was laughing, fit to burst, except Mr. Moorehouse.

When he got to the end of the rock wall, my father put his gun back in his pocket and said, "Now I think we're about even. Ye go on about ye own business." And my father turned around and went home.

Mr. Moorehouse went directly to Mrs. Lloyd's office and told her what had happened.

She listened quietly until he was through talking, and then she said, "Well, my advice to you is to leave Caney at once. Don't stay until tomorrow. Pack your things and leave your address; I will ship them to you. Walk across the hill and go out by way of Hindman. I know Kitteneye, and he loves his children. We must remember, although we are here to help these folks, this is their home. We are the intruders."

FOR MANY YEARS my father drove a wagon and brought the mail from Wayland to Pippa Passes. Mrs. Geddis, the mother of Mrs. Lloyd, was the postmistress for many years. She did not keep the office open from eight until four, as is done today. She stayed in her own room—a building quite some distance on the hill above the post office. She came to the office only when she was needed, which wasn't very often.

My father and Mrs. Geddis became very good friends. I think she had more understanding of us folks than anyone else from the outside. I know all the older folks loved her more and thought more of her, than other outsiders.

One evening, when my father came in with the mail, he hollered to her, "Oh, Mrs. Geddis, mail boy." She must have been very busy at something, with a lot of noise in the room. He called in a still louder voice, "Mrs. Geddis, mail boy." Finally she came to her door and said, "Oh, Kitteneye, do you want me?"

"Why, Mrs. Geddis, ye know I do. I been a wedder so long, I would take anybody I could get."

She understood that he only said this as a joke and meant no disrespect to her. She enjoyed the laugh as much as he did.

The mail wagon, going to and from Wayland, was our only connection with the outside. My father did many errands for the school and the folks who lived on Caney. It also served as a bus. Folks coming in or going out rode in his "jolt wagon," and the twelve miles in that wagon was no pleasure trip. He took folks to the dentist, doctor, or to catch the train for a longer trip, and brought folks back, coming in.

Everyday someone was sending him to get something from the drugstore, or other business, for things our small stores did not carry. He only received fifty cents a day from the government for his job as mail carrier, but the dimes and nickels that folks gave him for these little extra jobs helped to boost his income. Each rider gave him twenty-five cents as fare for the ride.

On one such trip, Mrs. Geddis sent him to the drugstore for some medicine for herself. At the same time, one of the teachers sent for some medicine for her pet cat.

That evening when my father delivered the packages to Mrs. Geddis, she asked him what she owed him for his trouble. He answered, "Ye don't owe me anything fer your medicine. I never charged anything I did fer a sick person. But I want a dollar fer that cat medicine. I think if some fool can give five dollars fer medicine fer a cat, she can give me a dollar fer bringin' it. There are too many little children on Caney that need medicine, than to waste it on a cat."

I never saw my father drunk in my life. My older sisters said that they knew he got drunk when he was young, but up until just a few years before he died he always "took a sip or two of whiskey" every day. During the winter months, when he would be driving to and from Wayland, he would drink a little whiskey. He thought it would keep him warm. Of course it was against government regulations for him to drink on the job.

Several times someone sent in a report to the Post Master General. But they could never get anyone who could say they saw him drinking. So without definite proof, there wasn't anything the law could do about it.

Once a year a postal inspector visits each post office, and so my father was driving the mail wagon when he made this yearly visit. The inspector rode from Wayland with my father, right in the wagon seat with him, all the way. By the time they arrived at the end of their journey, it was plain to see that Kitteneye had enjoyed his daily drink of whiskey. The inspector could not understand when and how.

All mountain folks loved to "put one over on the law." My father loved to tell how they had stopped at this old woman's house to get a drink of water. The inspector and the other passengers on the mail wagon had plain water, but the dipperful she had given my father contained good old corn liquor. The inspector went back to Washington without even knowing the truth.

It is hard for the outside folks to understand this disregard we have for law enforcement. It is not that we are not law-abiding people. My father would have been willing to give his life to protect the mail from robbery. Once he was almost drowned in his effort to save the mail, when his wagon and mules were caught in a flash flood. But he thought it wasn't any of the government's business if he drank whiskey while on the job. To him it was no more than taking an aspirin.

There were many teachers who came from up north to

help Mrs. Lloyd with her school. They all rode the mail wagon from the end of the railroad at Wayland to Pippa Passes.

My father with his quick insight to human nature quickly sized them up. Some of the ladies would be frightened to death at the thought of the ride along this strange road with a person whom they did not know. After all the false stories they had read about us, they did not know what to expect. He would always calm their fears by saying, "Now look a'here. Ye don't know me and I don't know ye, but I have seven girls of my own, and ye are just as safe with me as I hope they would be with ye paw."

Then there were the ones who sat as far away from him in the wagon seat as they could, as if they did not want to be close to him. He would tell them, "I know me and my mules don't smell so good. I work hard and I sweat and get dirty. But it's honest dirt and I'm not ashamed of it. I always say, it's no shame to get dirty, but it is a shame to stay dirty."

It was a long ride. About dinnertime he would stop his mules and feed them and eat his own lunch. He always tried to make this stop at the school house. If school was going on, that much the better. He had a nice visit with the teacher and also the use of their outhouse. He loved to see the look on the faces of his "brought on" riders when he told them they were welcome to use these hillbilly restrooms. Sometimes when he stopped he would give the reigns to his lady passengers and say, "Now hold these mules tight. Don't let them run away." Afterward, he would tell about it, "Those poor souls, scared to death, a'feared them mules would bolt. It would have took fire stuck to their tails to make them move once they stopped to rest."

I think he enjoyed it best when he would have several men teachers to bring as passengers. He would tell them a lot of tall tales: killings, robberies, murders, and ghost stories; so untrue that it was a wonder anyone would have believed him.

Afterwards he would say, "Ye can try to tell these people the truth about us mountainfolks and they won't believe a word of what ye tell 'em. They have already formed their opinion of us, before they leave home. Ye can tell them a passel of lies and they will eat it up like a gang of chickens eatin' corn."

Some came to help at the school and some had reasons of their own for coming to the mountains, like a young woman, who gave her name as Miss Johnson, although it was plain to see when she got off the train that it should have been Mrs. Johnson.

The twelve mile ride in that jolty wagon probably hastened the birth of her baby. It was born two months early, the night she arrived at the school. Mrs. Lloyd knew how some of the mothers on Caney would feel about having an unwed mother teaching their daughters. She told Miss Johnson she'd have to send for her folks to come and get her.

A few days later a man arrived, who said he was her father. True, he had the same bright red hair that the baby had, but he was not over three or four years older than the young woman. If she had said he was her brother, folks might have believed her.

I was not old enough to understand what some old folks meant when they said they feared the little baby would be got rid of before the Johnsons got home.

There was a little boy, who I will call Tiny Tim, who would be waiting by the side of the road every day. My father would always stop, and Tim would say, "Would you give me a chaw of baccer, Kitteneye? Give me and brother both a chaw."

"I han't got a chaw in the world," he would answer.

"I know that joke. Ye named ye left pocket 'the world,' but ye allus got some in t'other pocket fer me."

My father always gave little Tim some tobacco. Once a teacher from the north, who was riding in the mail wagon, disapprovingly said, "You shouldn't give tobacco to a small child."

My father answered, "Tiny Tim has just a few more months to live. Can't ye see he is dyin' of consumption? He has few enough pleasures in this world. His paw and maw both died less than a year ago. I laid them both out fer burial. No, I don't think a little baccer is goin' to hurt him."

My father had nothing but contempt for anyone who was conceited. He loved to "poke fun" at folks who "put on airs." The conductor of the train that met the mail wagon at the Wayland depot each day was such a man.

He was very large and my father's being so small made his imitation more funny than ever. It always drew a great laugh from the crowd of people hanging around the depot and Wayland Post Office.

Kitteneye would wait until the train turned and started back on its return trip. Then he would step up to his wagon, push his old ragged hat back on his head, pull out his watch in an exact imitation of how the train conductor had done, and then in a loud voice he would say, "All aboard, all aboard." Then in his own voice he would finish, "All that can't get a board take a slab."

A GOOD FRIEND of mine, an outsider from Oregon, once asked me, "Why do you like to live in a place where 25 percent of the children born die when they are infants?"

I began to wonder about that. It did not seem to me to be true. I counted all the births and infant deaths in my entire family—brothers, sisters, uncles, aunts, and my husband's family—and I only got an 8 percent average. I thought, well maybe we Slones are just healthy or extra lucky. Then I made a list of all the folks on Caney; even up each hollow and branch. This only came out to a 10 percent average.

Next time I saw my friend, I told him of my own survey, but he still held to his beliefs. Statistics at Washington, D.C., showed that we lost 25 percent of our children. I don't know where they got their records, because many of the women had their children at home by themselves; there was no official record. We were our own undertakers, so there were no official records of deaths until the last twenty-five or thirty years.

Most all the old folks had to use a family Bible record or an old school record for proof of their birth, so as to obtain their "old age pension check." This statistic may be true of all Eastern Kentucky as a whole, but I know it was not true of Caney.

Many people who visit us for the first time are surprised to find us so happy and carefree. They have formed a mental picture of us as sad and bitter people, confused with a life of hard work, and without pride or hope.

My father and his neighbors enjoyed life very much. They did not think of themselves as being poor and deprived. To them hard work was not a drudgery, but something to enjoy and share, a way to meet and work in friendly competition.

They got the same enjoyment competing with each other in hoeing corn, that folks get in playing baseball, swimming, or tennis.

It was not only in their work that mountain people competed. They ran foot races, pitched horseshoes, broad jumped, and had a form of wrestling, which they called "scufflin'."

My father was very strong for one so small. There was only one man he could not win out with in a scufflin' match: Jim Perkins, the father of our congressman.

Once when they were having a friendly tussle, Mr. Perkins threw my father in a way that burst a "risin'" (boil). It was on a part of his body that caused him to sit sideways in a chair. The pain was so much, my father forgot the other man was a friend. He almost scalped him by biting a large chunk of hair and skin. Mr. Perkins wore the scar for life, but it was all in fun. The next time they met, they scuffled again. My father could throw Jim, but he never could hold him on the ground. He said it was because the other fellow had a hump on his back. Maybe this was so or my father might have used this as an excuse to save his pride.

Election day was another highlight in our everyday lives. As far as the folks on Caney were concerned, the selection of who became our school trustee was most important. On election day there would be a lot of horse swapping. Some of the women would bring baskets full of gingerbread made with molasses and lots of eggs and spices. The candidates would pay for the bread and "treat" the voters.

My mother died before women were allowed to vote, but she always got very involved in each election. Once she was celebrating the results of an election by ringing her dinner bell. A neighbor, who was very disappointed in the election returns, shot the bell rope. My father climbed up the pole and tied the rope back, while the man was still firing his gun.

Someone once remarked to my father that he was unlucky because his seven daughters could not vote. He answered, "No, but I'm raisin' seven of the strongest democrats ye ever seed."

In the year 1928, one of Kitteneye's sons-in-law was murdered. He was the only witness to the crime. After the trial he quit his job as chairmaker for Mrs. Lloyd and moved to Dwarf. He wanted to avoid any trouble with the criminal's family.

He bought a small farm and built a house. He started a chair shop of his own and tried to sell chairs to his neighbors. These were the years of the Great Depression; no one had money to buy anything.

My sister Vada and her husband had moved to Virginia. My brother-in-law had bought a farm and worked in the mines. But the mines began laying off men. The ones who did get work, only got a few days each week. My brother-in-law could not meet the payments on his farm, and when he lost his home, my father wrote and asked them to come live with him. So they sold their livestock, loaded all their furniture in a truck, and started toward Dwarf.

The kids were riding in the back of the truck, very weary and tired, happy that they would soon be with Grandpa. They were almost there. As they were coming across the mountain at Sassafras, another truck began trailing behind them. The driver of the other truck was a black man, the first negro these children had ever seen. He looked very strange to them. They tried to get their father and mother's attention by shouting to them. The black man became angry. He hit their truck, causing it to go over the hill and into the river below. He drove off without even looking to see what he had done.

The driver of the wrecked truck was killed. All the rest were hurt. They were taken to a hospital in Hazard. One boy lost his hand, another his leg. My father asked the doctors for the child's leg, so he could bury it. He said it was his own flesh and blood and he did not want it treated as garbage.

I was staying at the Caney school when I heard of the accident. I went to Mrs. Lloyd and told her I was going home.

She said, "Are you asking for my permission, or are you telling me you are going?"

"I have to go," I answered. "These are my folks and they need me."

"You will lose a whole year's work."

"I know, but I want to go. Can I come back next year?"

"Sure, come back, your place will be waiting for you. Who will take you?"

"No one," I answered, "I will walk." It's twenty-one miles from Pippa Passes to Dwarf, and another mile to where my father lived on Bear Branch. I walked the whole way.

It was a long time before my brother-in-law was able to work. The hospital bill was large, and there was a depression going on. We all had to eat. My father decided the only way to get any money was to make moonshine whiskey.

Some bootleggers from Harlan had been trying to get some of the old-timers, who knew how to make the old-fashioned corn whiskey, to provide them with some. My father knew how to sprout the corn, grind it, and make real corn whiskey. Almost everyone had forgotten the old way, and used meal. I don't think my father did very much; I think he just taught the others.

In my yard grows a "bubby bush." I do not know the real name of this shrub. It has a dark purple flower, with a very pleasant smell. My stepmother's great-great grandmother is supposed to have brought the first one with her when she moved to Kentucky from North Carolina, many, many years ago. It is very hard to get one of these to live when transplanted. Maybe our climate is not suitable for it.

I had tried many times to bring one from my stepmother's yard, in her old home place, but each time it would die.

In the spring of 1946, my father brought me another sprout of the bubby bush. He helped me to set it out. He did not believe in any of the old superstitions, that so many of our mountainfolk do, but when he planted this flower, he said to me: "If this lives, I will die. If it dies, I will live." The bubby bush has lived for thirty-two years, and it blooms every year. My father only lived six more weeks.

INDEX

Astrology, planting by signs, 11, 17

Barrelmaking, 7
Beds, 41, 97-98

Caudill, Hazy, 106
Childbirth, 4-6, Granny Frolic, 73-74
Chimney building, 40
Christmas, 73; C.C.C.C., 111-112
Circuit preacher, 115-116
Cline, Miss, 126
Cloth and yarn, homemade, 37, 44, 50
Clothing, 44, 50-52
Cole and Crain lumber company, 92-94
Cooking, 4, 46; fireplace, 113-114
Corn, 56, 114; milling, 108-109; planting, 61-62; uses, food, 65, 67, 113-114; games and toys, 53, 109
Crops, 60-61, 63-71; planting, 45, 60-62, by signs, 11, 17; see also Corn

Devil, 96-97
Dinner bells, 73, 76

Eating customs, 34, 40
Education, 49
Election day, 138

Families: size, 74; unity, 48, 83-84
Fences, split-rail, 9, 46
Fireplace, 2; cooking, 113-114
Fodder, 62-63
Food, 4, 34, 40, 60, 63-71, 113-

114; preservation, 45, 63-71; dried fruit, 8-9
Fugate, Bad Amos, 83-84
Fugate, Flora Belle Slone, 49, 58, 83-84
Fugate, Sam, 83-84, 90, 119
Funerals and burials, 57-59, 116

Geddis, Mrs., 130-131
Ghost stories, 95, 99-100
Gravehouses, 58-59

Halland, Emery, 89
Hillbilly, 127
Hogs, 54, 71; butchering, 3, 42
Home remedies, 2, 12-13, 16-17, 70
Huff, Charley, 50
Huff, G. C., 93
Hughes, Jane, 35

Infant mortality, 136

Johnson, Miss, 134
Johnson, Bish, 109
Johnson, Hayes, 92, 94

Law, attitudes toward, 75-76, 132
Livestock, 54, 55, 71
Lloyd, Mrs. Alice, 108, 110, 112, 125-126, 129, 134, 139
Lofts, 97-98
Log cabin building, 9, 39-40, 89-90
Lumber mill, 90-91, 92-94

Mail delivery, 30-32, 130-135
Marriage, 46-47
Measuring, 10
Mill day, 108-109

Molasses stir-offs, 43-44
Moonshine, 41, 74-76, 139-140
Moorehouse, Mr., 127
Morals, 47, 81
Mosley family, 85
Moving, 88-91

Negroes, attitudes toward, 110-
    111
Neighbors, 40-41, 58, 117-118
Nicknames, 25-29
Noise makers, 2

Owens, Cindy, 16-31
Owens, Milton, 77
Owens, Vince, 18, 35

Parks, Mrs. 124-125
Patton, Dick, 81-83
Peddling, 78-80
Perkins, Jim 137
Plant lore, 12-13; edible plants,
    115-116; wild greens, 70-71;
    see also Home remedies
Planting. See Crops

Quilts, 41-42, 50, 52, 57

Religion, 45, 76, 115-116
Reynolds, Sarah, 50, 57

Sapping, 115
Shoes, 50-51
Short, Henry C., 92
Slone family, 13-14, 25-26
Slone, Alice, 13
Slone, Arminda, 58
Slone, Barbara, 120-123
Slone, Billie, 13, 23-24
Slone, Cleveland, 35-36, 48
Slone, Devada, 94, 104, 106, 110,
    138-139

Slone, Edna Earl, 56, 105, 110,
    119
Slone, ElCaney, 1-6, 50
Slone, Elizabeth, 56
Slone, Frankie, 1-6, 15-24, 33-34,
    110-111
Slone, Hi, 13
Slone, Isom Adkins, 13
Slone, Isom B. (Kitteneye); birth,
    6; marriage, 36; death, 140
Slone, Jezzie Ann, 88
Slone, Jim "Summer," 1, 8, 9, 13,
    15, 17
Slone, Joanar, 82
Slone, John (Summer), 77
Slone, John L., 36
Slone, Katy Reynolds, 13
Slone, Lorenda, 106-107, 109-
    111, 122
Slone, Lou Frances, 57, 64, 109-
    111
Slone, Preacher Billie, 50, 57
Slone, Sally Casebolt, 13
Slone, Sarah Alverta, 92, 104-107
Slone, Sarah Jane Owens, 20, 35;
    death, 55
Slone, Shady Hall, 1, 13
Slone, Square, 58
Slone, Vince, 91, 119
Songs and rhymes, 100-103
Stumbo, Verne
Superstitions, 96, 140

Taylor, Dora Bell, 57
Telling time, 11-12
Thomas family, 85-86
Thriftiness, 52-54
Tied lace, 22
Toys and games, 53, 109
Traveling, 23, 86; by mail wagon,
    131, 133-134; overnight, 31
Traveling salesmen, 77-78

Visiting, 81-82; overnight, 99

Wallpaper, 51
Walking, 116-118
Watson, Martha, 50
Weather lore, 12, 15

Wheeler, Mrs., 123-124
Wishes, 3
Witches, 96
Wood lore, 10
Work, 44, 60, 137
Workings, 39-41